SOCIAL SERVICES IN BRITISH INDUSTRY

INTERNATIONAL LIBRARY OF SOCIOLOGY
AND SOCIAL RECONSTRUCTION

Founded by Karl Mannheim

Editor: W. J. H. Sprott

A catalogue of books available in the INTERNATIONAL LIBRARY OF
SOCIOLOGY AND SOCIAL RECONSTRUCTION and new books in
preparation for the Library will be found at the end of this volume

Social
Services in British
Industry

by

A. F. YOUNG, M.A., J.P.

Author of *Industrial Injuries Insurance*, and Co-Author of
British Social Work in the 19th Century

*Reader in Social Administration, University
of Southampton*

LONDON
ROUTLEDGE & KEGAN PAUL
NEW YORK: HUMANITIES PRESS

First published 1968
by Routledge & Kegan Paul Limited
Broadway House, 68–74 Carter Lane
London, E.C.4

Printed in Great Britain
by C. Tinling & Co. Ltd
Liverpool, London and Prescot

SBN 7100 6157 9

Contents

PART II
SOCIAL SERVICES IN PLACES OF WORK

CHAPTER 4
HOURS, SAFETY, HEALTH, AND WELFARE IN INDUSTRY

CHAPTER 5
WAGES COUNCILS

CHAPTER 6
ARBITRATION

CHAPTER 7
LOSING ONE'S JOB

CHAPTER 8
INCOME MAINTENANCE FOR THOSE NOT WORKING

vi

PART III
THE THEWS AND SINEWS

CHAPTER 9
THE TRADE UNIONS AND
EMPLOYERS' ORGANISATIONS

CHAPTER 10
THE PROFESSIONS

CHAPTER 11
EVALUATION. WHAT CRITERIA?

APPENDIX

Acknowledgements

The material for this book has been acquired through a lifetime of study and discussion, and it would be impossible to name all to whom I am indebted. But my thanks are given to the many trade union officials, social workers, colleagues and those not officially associated with industry or the social services who have provided me with much valuable information.

Though the responsibility for what has been written is essentially mine, the knowledge and experience of what happens in practice, and the thinking which has moulded the way in which it has been presented, are the result of what so many others have contributed. Where the actual compiling of the text is concerned, I am particularly grateful to Mr A. V. Ahier for his comments on Part I, and to Messrs W. H. Marwick and A. J. Rees for reading the typescript and for their valuable suggestions. I am indebted to Miss D. Marshallsay, as always, for her expert help in compiling the bibliography and index, to Mrs I. Bason and her staff for their willing and cheerful assistance in the typing of the manuscript, and finally to Miss O. Simpson for her most valuable help in correcting the proofs.

Introduction

The title *Social Services in British Industry* might seem a contradiction in terms. Industry is concerned with productive processes and the provision and exchange of goods and services which mankind has developed to meet his economic needs. The social services are mostly provided where the individual has been unable, for one reason or another, to realise his full potential, or even achieve sufficient development to make a reasonable life possible. We think of industry in terms of organisation—involving capital, labour, raw materials and finished products. The social services, on the other hand, are thought of in terms of poverty, ill-health, degradation and squalor. Thus the concepts would appear poles apart—different worlds.

Experience has shown how closely connected these worlds are. Most people in a modern urban community rely on industry for the means by which their pattern of life is made possible. In this process they may have become ill, been maimed, dismissed, poorly paid, subjected to pressures that have rendered decent living impossible. In short, they have been put at risk in a variety of ways that no other experience could parallel.

Looked at in another way, industry, in the broadest sense, is the life-blood of a nation, on which all depend, not only for their present livelihood, but their future hopes of betterment. It would be an invalid argument if one were to claim that humanity is at all times more important than productivity. Dignity and happiness are of little moment if the over-riding need is to produce. (Experience during the wars proved this.) But in the long run the human factor must be considered, both because in essence industry depends on it, and must therefore have a force of well-trained workers who feel responsible for its success, and because industry has come to appreciate that workers are not merely living organisms with hands to produce, but people with needs and aspirations.

So social services have had their part to play in industry, as they have in the community at large. But what is a social service?

Definitions have probably three functions. They indicate what the words mean, they try to say something valuable about the concept itself, and above all, they are a means of communicating to others an understanding of what is being discussed. As with most important ideas and institutions, no short, snappy phrase could in any way describe what social services are, and no two writers would agree on a form of words to encompass them. Moreover, the general concept of social services, as they apply to poverty, crime, sickness or disablement, seems curiously inappropriate in the realm of industry.

What is being attempted here is a consideration of services which are associated with working people (including staff and manual workers) and intended to deal specifically with the problems found in industry. They are not exclusively focused on industry. For example, disablement services are frequently available to those who are not gainfully employed as well as to those who are.

Furthermore these services are available throughout the country, and for this reason such individual plant provision as industrial health departments, occupational sickness and superannuation schemes, and numerous miscellaneous services, sporadically provided under the heading of 'fringe benefits', have not been dealt with on their own, though they have been discussed in the relevant chapters. What is universal is almost, by definition, compulsory, and the services considered are, like national insurance contributions, either compulsorily applied to all, or, like the arbitration courts, compulsorily available to all. Further, when a service is nationally orientated, it is usually thought of as being organised and controlled by the community, through one or other of the government agencies, or by some arrangement that has the blessing of an Act of Parliament. Most social services are financed through government means, though this is not necessarily so in the industrial social services, where responsibility for financing schemes has occasionally been placed on the firms themselves (industrial training) or partly so (redundancy payments).

So far, the scope of the analysis has been sufficient to define a 'service', but the crucial question is, what is a 'social service'? Where does it differ from any other service? The answer must surely lie in the motivation. A garage, selling petrol, provides a service, and a very important one. Though the motive for provision is complex, it can ultimately be traced to a desire to make profit for the garage-owner. The Youth Employment Bureau provides a service, but this would be generally recognised as a 'social service', because its motive is not profit but rather the furtherance of a recognised and universally accepted social need. National Insurance against unemployment and sickness is also a 'social service', also without the profit motive, and likewise meeting a universally recognised need. These two examples highlight the great dilemma in any simple definition of 'social service', since the meaning of 'need' can differ so widely. In the one case it is the need of the young for vocational guidance, training and advice about employment; in the other a need for a financial palliative against poverty, should unemployment or sickness strike. The older social services, outside industry, were almost universally directed at the alleviation of poverty, and the British Poor Law is a striking example of this drive.

In industry, the oldest social services were not primarily concerned with poverty, but with the special problems industry itself created. The Factory Acts were a set of rules intended to protect the workers, though they incidentally protected the employers too. Mrs Webb argued persuasively when she wrote, 'In a competitive society there is a case for common rules'. Her reasoning ran as follows: Labour is a commodity and a cost in industry, like any other commodity. But, whereas the employer is bound to pay the total cost of his machines, raw materials, and fixed capital, and has therefore an incentive to conserve them, and keep them efficiently working as long as he can, this is not so with labour, which has been brought to working age by the community to whom it returns when no longer capable of producing. This is not to say the employer has not borne some of the costs, though he does so only to the extent of his rates and taxes and other compulsory dues. Where labour is scarce, the incentive to hoard and cherish it is the greater, but where it is plentiful it can easily be replaced, especially if unskilled, and the burden is thrown off.

In a competitive system an employer is as much a prisoner as anyone else. He has to sell his goods in a competitive market, and to do so the price must be right. To lower his price, he must save here and pare there, and where better than in expenses like safety measures, health facilities, or hours of work? The less scrupulous employer will most certainly do this, and the good employer, faced with the fierce stress of competition, will sooner or later be forced to do likewise. Without legally enforceable common rules to keep his rivals in line with himself, the temptation to lower his humane standards is hard for the good employer to resist.

This results in accidents, sometimes rendering the employee unfit for work and placing the burden of his maintenance—and that of his dependants—upon the community. Other workers, worn out by hardship, retire early and the community again has to pay. In this way the community is forced to subsidise industry.

It might be argued that such matters are best left to the collective bargaining powers of employers and trade unions, but experience has shown that this is not enough. Agreements may be reached, but without someone to police them and to interpret them they are hard to enforce, and the fact is that those who need them most— the young, the elderly, the unskilled—are the very ones likely to be overlooked, or to refrain from claiming their rights—or even to be unaware of them.

The legal enforcement of common rules for working hours and conditions is the only way to protect workers. It also, as mentioned above, protects the good employers from unfair competition, and the community from the accumulated load of sickness and dependency. The arguments Mrs Webb propounded in 1901 are not without their relevance at the other end of the 20th century. For though her experience was of a different age when organisation was less strong than it subsequently became, the dangers inherent in industry, and the ruthlessness of the so-called 'economic forces' have not diminished with growing sophistication. Social services have therefore remained in industry to protect all, the strong as well as the weak, against over-work and bad conditions.

The emphasis so far placed on the need, apparent in all sections of industry, for some form of protection, should not blind us to the fact that many social services in industry were originally intended as a life-jacket for the weak and helpless. The wages councils, and certainly the early national insurances, were so motivated. But latterly, social services in industry have been directed to meet the problem of change: and where fresh ones have appeared, they have been at the point of change, either to ease the passage through the trauma of disturbance, or to prepare individuals for the next stage. Thus the Redundancy Payments Act, and the modern earnings-related national insurance, are examples of the social services ready at the moment of movement, whether permanent, as in redundancy, or temporary, as perhaps in sickness, to help the worker to accept what has come without loss of dignity or decline into poverty. The youth employment service, the industrial training boards, the placement services of the employment exchanges, the government training centres, with their training in new skills and the industrial rehabilitation of disabled persons are examples of services provided at the point of transference from one state to another. These are intended not only to help the individual to lead a fuller life, but even more to ensure a steady and enlarged supply of skilled and responsible workers to further the industrial productivity of the country. By the same token, the various arbitration courts and the Contracts of Employment Act, though not intended to prevent change, were devised to make the process more orderly, less haphazard (therefore less painful) than before.

A definition of social services in industry defies summary, but the motivation has two clear facets. Some of the services aim at protecting the more helpless—the young, the women, the disabled, the mentally afflicted—and at succouring the poor. But their main concern is with the total human factor in business, particularly during periods of potential abrasion, where good material can so easily be lost, and the community at large made the poorer.

What follows is an attempt to analyse the main social services whose focus is industry, and to examine some of the special problems that each has thrown up. Beginning with the agencies affecting the young, the disabled, or those changing their jobs, and the means that are available to train and place individuals, we pass, in Part II, to those services operating within industry itself, and to the way in which obligations have been imposed, with their accompanying systems of policing or inspection; or to such provisions as the arbitration courts, which for the most part are places of voluntary recourse; and then to the financial arrangements for income maintenance during periods of non-earning. Part III, though not strictly concerned with social services, seemed an inevitable concomitant, as without the good-will of the trade unions, the employers' organisations, and the professionals, no social service could last a moment in the industry of modern Britain.

Conclusions are notoriously misleading, and there can be none in such a study as this, but as everyone approaches the social services in his own way, and with his own criteria, it seemed prudent to indicate some of the thinking out of which policy grows. This book is in essence a study of social policy. It cannot avoid economic and financial considerations, nor psychological ones, but these are not its main focus. Fundamentally social policies in a democratic society arise out of the social policy of the time, and in making an evaluation it becomes a matter for each individual to clarify his mind on basic objectives. It was to help towards this end that the last chapter was written.

Changes of a massive kind are constantly being considered. The Donovan Report on the Trade Unions and Employers' Organisations, and the Government's draft of a new plan for the Social Insurances are being published. The work of the Wages Councils has been curbed by the Prices and Incomes legislation. Proposals for Labour Courts are being discussed. In other words Britain is a dynamic society, and change is the watchword. So a book like this can only picture the situation at a given moment of time (*circa* mid-1967). It glances backwards to see how and why the position was reached, and discusses the issues and their alternative solutions to help in forecasting the future, but that is all it can do.

PART I

ENTRANCE TO INDUSTRY

I

ADULTS

Early Development of Labour Exchanges

NO-ONE KNOWS how many posts are filled each year, or has examined the variety of ways in which a person seeking a job is fitted into a vacancy. Millions of transactions must take place, ranging from a man taking his son into the business, through the various private agencies and the advertisement columns of the newspapers, to the State-run employment exchange of the Ministry of Labour.[1] Since the latter is provided by the community, available freely to all, with offices in every part of the United Kingdom, it can properly be considered a social service and worthy of inclusion in this study.

The employment exchange was an invention of the 20th century, starting in a minor way in 1905, when the Unemployed Workmen Act enabled 19 offices to be set up in the London area. By 1909, the idea had been sufficiently accepted for a new Act, the Labour Exchanges Act, to establish a system of exchanges under the Board of Trade. They could be set up in any part of the country, and were to be the neutral meeting ground for employers seeking labour, and workers looking for jobs; the assumption being that the needs of employers and the rights of the workers should receive equal consideration.

During 1916, the man-power problems of the war had assumed such proportions that a separate Ministry of Labour had to be created to take over the functions of the labour department of the Board of Trade, including the labour exchanges. Man-power, in a major war, has not been the easiest problem to solve, and Ince said of the new Ministry that it 'was born in a crisis and for some

---

[1] The name was changed in May 1968 to Ministry of Employment and Productivity.

years proceeded from one crisis to another'. For no sooner had
the war come to an end, and the short lived post-war boom
collapsed, than Britain fell into a major economic crisis, in which
men returning from the war to find civilian jobs found themselves
jostling at the exchange against other men who had fallen out of
employment through the slump. The exchanges were called upon
to cope with an unemployment problem the like of which they had
never visualised, a situation that was to remain with them for the
whole of the inter-war period. Not that every exchange was
equally pressed. Unemployment tended to concentrate in special
areas of the country, particularly those traditionally associated with
'heavy' industry, like Tyneside and South Wales. The government
went so far as to single out these areas for therapeutic treatment,
calling them 'depressed' areas, and later 'special' ones, and
subsequently, when they wanted to strike a hopeful note, 'development' areas.

From the point of view of the unemployed in the vulnerable
areas, the exchanges were not places where workers found jobs
and employers sought operatives; they became the offices where
one 'signed on' twice a week as evidence that one was 'genuinely
seeking work'. Without this, unemployment benefit could not be
paid. For unemployment insurance, since its introduction in 1912,
had been administratively tied to the labour exchanges. When the
scope of unemployment insurance was extended in 1920, to bring
in a further eight million contributors, followed by the greatest
slump in memory, the exchanges became a centre for labour
attendance that had been neither expected nor foretold. The
depression continued, reaching even worse depths from 1929 to
1933, and they continued to cope with the flood of men and
women, upon many of whom long-term unemployment was imposing inevitable demoralisation. 'Signing on' was the prelude to
money payment, and large numbers of the population had come to
depend for their daily bread on the weekly payments made at the
exchange. Those who were 'in benefit', that is, the short term unemployed, received their 'insurance' money, with no questions
asked, except the basic ones covering genuine unemployment, and
being 'able and willing to work'. But after six months, 'insurance'
came to an end, and the exchange could only make payment, if
they could make it at all, to those in need; the worker had to prove
this by undergoing a 'Means Test'. Thus the exchange came to be

equated in the minds of a large section of the population with the payment of 'the dole', and quite unfairly, because they had no hand in it—with the 'Means Test'.

The inter-war years were not a happy time for the exchanges. They had been set up and staffed to provide a meeting ground for employers and workers. In areas of high unemployment this function was almost lost (in spite of a few attempts by the central government and the local authorities to inaugurate public works to provide much-needed jobs), and staff found themselves having to deal with a situation for which they had not been prepared. The exchanges were never over-staffed, and the pressure of numbers, who filed past the counter each day, made it virtually impossible for the treatment of the individual to be anything but impersonal. Thus they gained a reputation in many places that was the anti-thesis of what had been intended, and the struggle to re-make the public image has been long and arduous. In the Midlands and round London where employment was good, the exchanges functioned normally, and their work of filling vacancies and placing people in employment was executed with intelligence and efficiency. But even on them fell the shadow of what was happening in the 'depressed' areas, and they had to share some of the odium that conditions were imposing elsewhere.

The Second World War was in one sense a happy miracle for some, as it brought employment for all, even those who had been out of work for years. For them the exchanges became places of hope, instead of offices of desperation. But they had already run into another problem, which to some extent deferred their return to their original purpose. They had been given the task of implementing the Military Training Act 1939, by which young men were obliged to undergo six months' military service on reaching the age of 20. Though it was an 'historic decision' to entrust a civil department with the call-up of men for the Forces, it was hardly likely to improve public relations in a country so unaccustomed to compulsory service in peace-time as Britain. The threat of war was near, and the full impact of the call-up was not felt till the war itself inaugurated a policy of all-out effort, for which the whole nation was prepared to sacrifice itself to the full.

The total mobilisation of man- and woman-power to promote the winning of the war became the responsibility of the Ministry of Labour, and the exchanges, at the local level, were involved in a variety of directive processes. They had to register, by age-groups, the men and women for the armed forces. They directed others into industry, and dealt with the exceptions and hardships that were bound to arise in so wholesale an operation. Sir Godfrey Ince was convinced the staff were the better able to cope with such a mammoth operation because of the experience of dealing with large numbers they had gained in the years of the depression. Be that as it may, the exchanges emerged from the war, and the post-war resettlement, with a reputation in no way tarnished by the upheavals of the 1940s, and in many ways much brighter than it was in the 1930s.

The greatest fear of many people after the second war was a return of the depression that had spoilt the inter-war years. Much post-war legislation, involving national insurance, was aimed at softening the impact should this happen, though all the major parties were united in claiming that their policy included the maintenance of a high and stable level of employment. Planning in the economic fields was inevitable if this hope was to be realised, and the Ministry of Labour was once more chosen as the instrument through which the organisation of the labour market, and a balanced development of industry in the 'special areas' could be achieved. The method was not to be the 'direction' of labour, the unhappy necessity of the war years, but the supply of facts about employment and unemployment, about man-power trends, areas of labour surplus and shortage, and the extent of short-time and overtime working. These were fed through the monthly reports to the government, to help it to measure the present state and future prospects of various industries. Subsequently special central and regional Departments of State[1] were established to sift the data, and develop them for use in planning.

There was also legislation which involved the Ministry of Labour indirectly in the economic development of the country. For instance, the Distribution of Industry Act 1945, and the Local Employment Act 1960, gave the Board of Trade the right to grant certificates to firms wishing to build substantial extensions to their premises, or to set up business in new areas. These certificates were considered in relation to the labour situation, and information was sought from the Ministry of Labour and its regional

---

[1] National Economic Development Council (N.E.D.C.), 1962 and Department of Economic Affairs, 1964, and its Regional Economic Planning Boards.

office. If labour was short, or there was high congestion, the certificate was usually refused. But in 'development districts' where labour might be plentiful, this would be reported, and would be a powerful factor in granting permission. The delineation of 'development districts' was revised from time to time, again with the help of statistics and advice from the Ministry of Labour.

Thus the importance of the employment exchanges expanded from being a small contribution to the solution of the poverty problem, at the beginning of the century (they had received the blessing of the Poor Law Commission in 1909), to an indirect instrument of national policy, aiming at full employment, by the latter half of the century.

Employment and Training Act 1948

Apart from its vital function of supplying regular up-to-date information about labour resources, the exchanges have made a great effort to extend and improve their original service of finding the right job for each person who registered, and of filling an employer's labour needs adequately and quickly. To do this a new Act was required, not only to consolidate the legislation, modifying the work of the exchanges from their beginning under the Labour Exchanges Act of 1909, but also to give the service a new look, and a new slant to the opportunities opening before it. Thus in 1948 the Employment and Training Act, which fathered the youth employment service, became the legal foundation for the post-war employment service under the Ministry of Labour. Every worker, whether in employment or not, was encouraged to register, if he wanted a new job. Every employer, looking for workers, whether professional staff, skilled craftsmen, or unskilled labourers, was asked to seek the help of the exchange. Apart from the war, and the period immediately afterwards, there was no compulsion on any party to register (except the unemployed seeking benefit) though clearly the more the employers and workers used the exchange, the greater the chance of both being satisfied, since it was easier to fill the job with the right person, if the maximum variety of both were available. (It was estimated that each placing cost nearly £4 in 1965 [Parl. Q, 4 February, 1966].) It was a generally accepted principle that if there were two equally suitable applicants, but one was unemployed, preference would be given to the latter. Similarly, if one were local and the other residing further afield, preference would be given to the local man. On the other hand, the ultimate choice was made by the employer, and it was the exchange's practice to submit several suitable candidates, if a vacancy had been notified, just as it was possible, during full employment, to offer the choice of several vacancies to a person looking for a new job. When vacancies occurred in some firms where the product was of the greatest national importance (for example, extending the export trade), a further principle arose, and though no question was entertained of directing labour into these firms, workers with suitable qualifications would be given special information, and persuasion would be used concerning them. In the 1960s this policy gained greater momentum, as a means of promoting economic progress and change. If a vacancy occurred in a firm affected by a trade dispute, an applicant would be told the exact position, and left to make up his own mind whether to apply or not, but he would not be penalised for refusing. If a vacancy were notified, and the wages or conditions were contrary to the law (for example the Wages Council Act p. 101, the Factory Act p. 73), the Ministry would look for suitable applicants if the position were rectified, but not otherwise.

For the employers and workers, the exchanges have maintained a national net-work of information about available workers with special experience and qualifications, and unfilled vacancies that might suit them in Britain, and most European countries as well (leaflet P.L.362). The embargo on non-commonwealth workers being employed in Britain without a Ministry of Labour permit has been in force since 1920, and was extended to certain commonwealth workers in 1962. Relaxation, in either case, will depend on the political situation, though Britain's entrance to the E.E.C., would certainly affect the position of members of the treaty countries.

Registers for specialised occupations

Throughout its history, the Ministry has modified its work, from time to time, by establishing departments concerned with certain occupations or classes of job. Thus at one time, there was a nursing appointments service (see leaflets N.L.06 and 07); (this was discontinued in 1961, though local offices have always been able to call upon nursing officers for employment advice), a technical and scientific register, maintained in London for scientists, professional engineers, architects, and surveyors (also discontinued in 1961), one in London for hotels and catering, and a few local offices have kept a register of part-time posts. Most of the specialised registers have been abandoned, except the one devoted to professional and executive posts with an average number of 20,000, and another for commercial ones. Although the registers themselves are kept at strategic points throughout the Kingdom, their contents are available to any office requiring the information. Their chief concern is with educated men and women not yet established in a career, for ex-officers of H.M. forces newly leaving the service, and ex-members of H.M. overseas civil service. But they are there for the use of anyone, within the experience and qualification limits, who may be seeking a higher post, or for any employer who has professional and managerial posts to fill.

The role of the exchange in the mobility of labour

While the essence of modern industrialism has been the rapid change in techniques, organisation and personnel deployment, the effect on labour has been profound. Few could expect to start and end their working lives in the same occupations, or even the same firms, without major transformations having taken place. This was true of the expert as much as for the unskilled; and it has meant that two aspects of employment policy have had to be developed as never before: training and transfer.

Training. It was the policy of the Ministry up to the 1960s to leave the actual training of workers to industry itself. This involved the training of new workers, or the re-training of their established employees, for the new machines and processes resulting from technological change. The only exceptions to this policy of leaving it to industry occurred during times of national emergency, such as the war, or for certain categories of workers, like the disabled (p. 51), ex-members for H.M. Forces (p. 15), the young (p. 20), the unemployed with special difficulties of resettlement, and those able-bodied adults willing to work in industries regarded at any one time as being of great national importance (for example, mining, building). By the 1960s government policy had changed, because it was seen that unless sufficient skilled people were available there was no solution to the country's economic ills, and the Ministry accepted responsibility for re-training workers in jobs if their skill had become out-dated, or if they might expect to become redundant within six months. Workers without skill could also apply for training, whether employed or not, the object being not so much to improve an individual's prospects as to increase the economic strength of the country. The cost of training had been provided for in the Employment and Training Act 1948, so there was no legal difficulty in setting up government training centres (p. 60), grant-aiding further education colleges, or individual firms who would provide training, extra grants being available to firms in development areas. Maintenance grants with no deductions for insurance or income tax, but with earnings-related supplements, if appropriate, for the trainee gave some incentive to those without employment to undertake training (leaflet P.L.394). Maintenance grants were seldom high enough to attract workers, earning even an average wage, to re-train under government auspices, but employers frequently seconded workers on full pay, or themselves arranged training schemes as part of the general re-tooling of the workshop. By the middle 1960s the sporadic and haphazard nature of all training had come to be recognised, and the need, not only for a regular system, but for a plan to show how many and what kind of recruits were needed, was accepted. The industrial training boards (p. 28) were given the power to generate the means, since they had responsibilities for training the young and re-training the adult, and the G.T.C.s provided a Ministry training ground, particularly for short courses of training, of six or twelve months. Selection of suitable candidates was usually undertaken by a committee, on which both employers and workers were represented.

Before the Ministry of Labour set up instructor schools at Letchworth and Hillingdon, the supply of instructors and supervisors was a constant source of anxiety, as no training could be viable without them. Towards the end of the Second World War in 1944 the Ministry of Labour evolved a scheme of 'training within industry' (T.W.I.) to solve the problem of training, and an annual average of 20,000 men and women have taken short, intensive courses since then. Each course lasted from four to ten days, and aimed to give a clear description of the steps to be taken by anyone who became an instructor in 'job learning', 'job relations', 'safety' and other aspects of industry, not excluding management.

Transfer

Government schemes to help people move and find employment away from home are not new. They were common in the inter-war years as a means of helping to solve the unemployment problem. Schemes for the transfer of young people, for instance, were publicised in areas of high unemployment, to encourage them to move to areas where jobs were relatively plentiful. After the war, further legislation, such as the Employment and Training Act of 1948, the Local Employment Act of 1960 and the Regional Employment Premium 1967, gave the Ministry express powers to aid transfer and to help industrial growth in the 'development districts', the boundaries of which had not been defined by the 1948 Act, and could therefore be modified when necessary.

A gradual change in emphasis could be detected after 1948, and though helping unemployed to find jobs was still part of the policy, and encouraging firms to move into regions where labour was plentiful was a major consideration, a new objective made its appearance. By September 1965 it was categorically stated in the *Ministry of Labour Gazette* that 'transfer grants' were to be made available 'to facilitate technological progress, and help people to change jobs'. Thus mobility of labour, whether unemployed or not, became a declared part of government policy. There were three types of scheme available to workers under a maximum income (£1,500 a year in 1965), though the grants were only payable if the employer was unwilling, or unable to make the payments himself. They were:—

(a) *Resettlement Transfer Scheme* (leaflets E.D.L.123 and 124). If a worker was already unemployed, or likely to be so within half a year, he could approach the Ministry for grant-aid to take up a post beyond travelling distance from his own home. The Ministry would need to be satisfied that the job was suitable, that alternative local employment was unlikely to be available, and that there was some hope of the new post being permanent; though the worker had no obligation to remain in the job if he found it not to his taste. Once having satisfied themselves on these points, the Ministry could provide travel grants, firstly to get him to the new employment, and then to bring him home, on a limited number of visits. For workers with a home to finance, grants towards lodgings expenses were also available. A settling-in period of up to six months was thought to be reasonable. After that, he would have to make up his mind, and decide whether he would remain permanently or not.

For those who opted to remain, further grant-aid became available, especially for those with a home and dependants (though the single worker might qualify for certain aid). The approved removal expenses of both his family and his furniture would be met, and a lump sum given for incidental expenses. Nor was this all. If he were still liable to pay rent, rates or mortgage on his old house, the Ministry would pay some or all of this in a 'Continuing Liability Allowance'. The expenses connected with selling a house and buying another were not overlooked, and a proportion of the legal expenses attracted grant-aid.

(b) *Key Workers' Scheme.* If an employer, with a Board of Trade Certificate to set up an establishment in a development district, wished to send key workers to train the local labour, he could apply to the Ministry for the various fares and lodgings grants for these specialised workers. The jobs might be permanent, with all that meant in help towards removal expenses, or temporary for an indefinite period.

(c) *Nucleus Labour Force Scheme.* In certain cases where a firm proposed to set up in business in a development district, local labour would be selected, and sent to the parent firm for training. In these cases too, the Ministry could pay lodgings and travel allowances.

Grant-aid towards the cost of making labour more mobile was met out of taxation, there being no special fund, or employer contribution. The allowances were not likely to meet all expenses, and the worker himself had to pay the difference out of his wages. At the same time, if the scheme were widely used, it would be a substantial contribution to industry.

Between 1960 and 1965 the schemes were not heavily drawn upon. For instance, in the Resettlement Transfer Scheme an average of only 2,367 lodging grants a year were given, with merely 811 removal grants. The Key Workers Scheme was little used, as only 58 lodging and 168 household removal grants were allowed, on average, in each of the five years. The 'nucleus labour force' lodging payment was hardly ever made, the average being only 26 a year. Since the grants were hedged round with regulations, it is likely that, for the most part, labour moved about the country at its own or the employers' expense; and it could not be claimed that the Ministry of Labour had any effect on the mobility of labour through these particular grants. But the fact that they have been operating for several years has given the Ministry experience of their administration, and has set in motion a social service which may ultimately have profound effects both on individuals and on the economic situation.

Special categories of workers

From time to time the exchanges have been concerned with sections of the population for whom there were special difficulties. In the course of time a policy has been evolved, and in certain cases a special service. Examples of categories for whom a policy has developed, though no specialised service has come into being, have included: old people, ex-prisoners, and coloured workers. For the disabled (p. 51) and ex-members of H.M. forces a special service has come into being.

The Aged and their problems of whether or not to go on working after the age at which the pension may be paid, has been dealt with elsewhere (p. 163). Should they decide to continue working, though nothing spectacular has been devised to help them, it has become the declared policy of the Ministry that the employment officials should lose no opportunity of trying to fit them into suitable vacancies. Where employment is good, their efforts have not been unsuccessful, but in other places, or where the worker has special needs, results have not been so happy.

Ex-Prisoners have presented quite different problems, even more difficult to solve for an employment agency than those of the elderly. When a person has been to prison, his prospects of getting a job have become complex, while his need to regain his status in the community by finding work is very great. By the 1960s, the process of rehabilitating the criminal was better understood by the prison authorities than hitherto. Part of the process was seen to begin within the prison, but much of it had to be undertaken on his release. For this purpose, a well-trained 'after-care' service was established, concerned with every aspect of a man's life on leaving the institution. The one important aim was to help him to obtain and keep a suitable job. The 'after-care' officers have naturally done what they could, but the main brunt of putting an ex-prisoner into a job suitable to his capabilities, where he might rehabilitate himself, has fallen on the employment exchange. In those areas where the Prison and Borstals department of the Home Office have set up hostels for pre-release prisoners (mainly long-term ones) to gain experience of ordinary industrial life, the officials of the employment exchange have been intimately and continuously concerned with the problem. Their duty embraced the finding of suitable posts, and ensuring that normal rates of pay and conditions of employment were honoured. Pre-release schemes have had their value, but as prisoners have remained within the purview of the prison, and within a regulated atmosphere (albeit much relaxed from prison itself) the problems that would manifest themselves after release were not present.

Not all ex-prisoners have come within the after-care scheme, though all long-term ones, and young ones, have done so. There was therefore no guarantee that if an ex-prisoner presented himself at the exchange seeking a job he had behind him an 'after-care' officer, who would be helping him to sort out his personal problems; adjustment to employment being a highly important factor. The Ministry has long taken the view that all who have been released from custody should be given a fair start. In pursuance of their policy they have arranged to interview every prisoner prior to his release, if he wanted it, and give him a letter of introduction to his local office; they in turn would be notified of his previous experience and training (including that gained in the prison itself). At the exchange he would be interviewed in one of the private interviewing rooms, and re-assured that the fact of his being an ex-prisoner would not be revealed without his consent. This has raised the knotty problem of how much an employer should be told. Many have argued that it is morally wrong to keep the employer in ignorance. They maintain that he would make allowances, and take a special interest if he knew the truth. On the other hand, most ex-prisoners have been anxious to bury the past, to be accepted as normal ordinary people, and have not wanted a special watch kept on them. The Ministry has therefore been obliged to compromise. They have made it a rule that no information, except that relating to the job, would be divulged without consent. Yet a proper responsibility to the employer must be maintained, and if the nature of the vacancy would suggest that the employer ought to know about his record, the consent of the ex-prisoner has been urgently sought. If he refused, in the last resort the vacancy would be withdrawn.

Ex Members of H.M. Forces. The resettlement in civilian life of ex members of H.M. Forces has presented another complicated picture, partly because of the different periods of service under-taken in a peace-time defence force, and partly because of the different conditions between military and civilian life. To help the Ministries of Labour and Defence in 1950 an advisory council was established (including representatives from both Ministries, the Ministry of Education, the L.E.A.s, and from employers and trade unions), to report and advise on 'the relationship between employ-ment in the services and civilian life'. By 1957, due to a change in the defence programme and the premature retirement of many service personnel, further advisory committees, both central and local, were set up to deal with the emergency, though most were disbanded again in 1960.

The problems have been of two types. On the one hand crafts-men, who learnt their trades in the forces, might find themselves without standing in industry, and on the other, men and women without training for civilian work might need opportunities of training, and help to find suitable employment appropriate to their age, experience and ability.

Through the Ministry, the government adopted a two-pronged policy. They undertook negotiations at strategic points to encourage the voluntary acceptance of ex-service personnel into industry; and they made available their own services of grant-aid and training to this particular group (leaflets P.L.407, R.S.6).

On the voluntary side, they consulted the trade unions to see how far trades acquired in the services would be recognised as equivalent to those in civilian life. On the whole, the trade unions agreed to recognise nearly all regulars, with five years experience of a trade, as having the necessary qualification for membership, and work as a tradesman, in the appropriate civilian job. Local government and the nationalised concerns were found to be willing to waive certain entrance examinations if the ex-service members had educational qualifications acquired in the forces. Private industry was also not backward in agreeing to offer concessions, and even to allocate a quota of their vacancies to ex-regulars. The civil service gave priority in some jobs, such as the postal services, to the group.

As for training, ex-members of H.M. forces were one of the categories for whom places might be found in Government Training Centres (see p. 60), and the appropriate Ministry grants to cover tuition, maintenance, travelling expenses, and books were made available, according to the needs of the applicant and the course taken. A special course for ex-regulars only, in agriculture or horticulture, was instituted by the two Departments of State for Agriculture (Scotland, England and Wales); and short courses for those who wished to become foremen or supervisors were held at the Ministry of Labour headquarters in London.

Vocational training for business management, through the technical colleges or private firms, was a further possibility, which the Ministry was prepared to sponsor and grant-aid, while some L.E.A.s gave special consideration to ex-regulars wanting to train as teachers.

Coloured Workers

Experience in the second half of the 20th century underlined the growing difficulty of assimilating coloured workers into British industry. Unrestricted entry from commonwealth countries was regulated by the Commonwealth Immigrants' Act 1962 (leaflet E.D.L.125), when already about two per cent of the British labour force were coloured, and further efforts, in 1966, were made to reduce the flow of immigrants from developing countries, who in the main were non-white. Colour discrimination had, to some extent, been forbidden by the passing of the Race Relations Act 1965, but an insidious growth of anti-colour prejudice flourished nevertheless. In 1967, P.E.P.s Report on Racial Discrimination produced evidence that discrimination against coloured workers was being practised when they looked for jobs, and that it was worse among those possessing higher qualifications seeking better paid posts.

This was something the employment exchanges could not ignore, but how to pursue a positive policy became the problem. They were instructed by the Minister to look out for instances of workers being denied jobs on ground of colour, and all evidence they obtained was notified at once to the regional office, but up to 1968 they had no power to act. They were advised, also, to use every means to give training and find employment for coloured men and women, in the same way as for white. Otherwise there was no particular service laid on that applied only to the coloured, as it was thought at the time that to have done so would only exacerbate an already sorry situation. The 1968 Race Relations Bill was a further attempt to prevent discrimination in which the Ministry was given more specific powers.

The Ministry of Labour has had certain duties towards immigrants, white or not, which have dated back to the First World War, and the Aliens' Order 1920, that followed it. Under this measure, the entry of non-commonwealth immigrants was closely regulated, though some were allowed to work in Britain if a British employer had obtained a 'Ministry of Labour Permit'. It could be given for a limited (renewable) period, but only if no other suitable British worker were available. The 'permit' device was extended to commonwealth citizens in 1962, so the Ministry of Labour had, thereafter, enlarged duties in this sphere.

One other scheme was initiated in 1967, whereby citizens from 'developing countries' (mainly coloured) were welcomed to Britain for specialised training (leaflet P.L.427). The country of origin might be part of the commonwealth or not, so long as the trainees already possessed a certain standard of education, such as a degree, a technological qualification, a teaching certificate, or had been acting as 'supervisors'. The object was to offer practical training in British industry for those with some theoretical knowledge, who wanted to extend their expertise in certain branches. Students wishing to undertake a 'sandwich' course could also be embraced by the scheme.

Finance was supplied by the Ministry of Overseas Development, or the sponsoring country, or a mixture of both. The Ministry of Labour's part was limited to finding employers willing and able to offer the training (normally for six months or longer), and agreeing to employ the trainees on the staff under the same terms as comparable home students. Should accommodation and general welfare supervision be required, this was the province of the British Council.

The service for coloured inhabitants has not, in the main, differed from that offered to all workers, with these few exceptions. Yet the problem of assimilating the coloured into British industry, so that those with greater skill and capacity can make their best contribution, remains to be solved.

Changes in Employment Exchange policy in the late 20th century

In March 1966 a survey in Central London (published by *Personnel Management*), looked into the recruitment of clerical and secretarial staff. It revealed a 'certain prejudice' against the service provided by the employment exchanges. It was a small survey, concerning an occupation for which there has been a phenomenal demand, and it would be unfair to relate these findings to all occupations in the whole of the country. At the same time it would be naive to suggest that the reputation of the Ministry was as good as it should be. Sir Godfrey Ince, formerly Permanent Under-Secretary to the Ministry, admitted that in 1938 the number of men and women placed in employment was over two million, but by 1957, with a larger labour force, and full employment, it had fallen to about one and a half million, and by 1966 was still under two million—proof that the service was being under-used. That the Ministry was fully aware that the employment offices needed a 'new look' became increasingly apparent by 1965, when the emphasis on research began to strengthen. Not that the Ministry has been backward in this respect, but its concern that neutral bodies, like universities, should take a cold clear look at what was being done, was evidence that it wanted both information and ideas from sources other than its own staff.

Changes were envisaged by two pilot schemes begun in 1965–6, the first to introduce vocational guidance, the second to remove the 'dole' image of the employment exchanges. 'Occupational Guidance', said the Minister (*The Times,* 3 February, 1966) would be available for 'young adults who have lost their way, older workers returning to the employment field, such as married women who seek a job when their family responsibilities lessen, and the regular service man at the end of his contract'. By the end of 1967 a number of Occupational Guidance Units had been

established, including one in Northern Ireland. Such a development, involving as it has a change in the training of Ministry of
Labour staff (a special training centre was set up) has brought an
imaginative and creative outlook to many of the exchanges.

The other scheme, though more negative, was nonetheless
constructive. The connection between unemployment insurance
and the exchange, through the requirement to collect benefit after
'signing on', has built up an unfortunate picture in the public
mind, and imposed a strain on the officers, so that their more
important functions have become overshadowed. The experiment
provided for a once weekly signing-on, and the substitution of a
postal draft for cash benefit at the exchange. The result has been a
concentration on the true employment function—the abolition of
the 'dole queue', and a changed public attitude to the exchanges.
(Leaflet P.L.400.)

II

YOUTH EMPLOYMENT SERVICE

Early developments in youth employment bureaux

THE SOCIAL SERVICE that has been established to advise young people about their careers, and to find suitable boys and girls to match suitable jobs has had a long and peculiar history (see Heginbotham, Part I).

Starting with the voluntary and haphazard work of parents and adults, the idea was taken a step further in the late 19th century by the development of State education. For, it was said, one cannot oblige a child to attend school, up to a certain age, without considering what will happen to him thereafter. Thus those teachers who felt the urgency of the problem began, with the knowledge and encouragement of the school authorities, to organise an unofficial advisory service. At first it was patchy and local in its impact, but it supplemented what the more knowledgeable parents were already doing for their own children. The Education Act 1902 gave a fillip to it, through the unification of most State provided schools (including the voluntary ones) under the L.E.A., when not only was the scope of State schooling greatly expanded, but the connection between the problems of educational provision and preparation for a career was appreciated. Another impetus was the plight of necessitous children, for whom, under an Act in 1906, L.E.A.s could provide both free meals and welfare services, including the finding of employment.

By 1909, as a direct result of one of the recommendations of the Royal Commission on the Poor Law (1905 et seq.), and the work for juveniles being done by the schools, labour exchanges were established under the Board of Trade to provide for everybody a rational system of entry into employment. Within such a service, the difficulties of juveniles were quickly perceived, and after conferences between the Boards of Trade and Education, general approval was given to the creation, in the major exchanges, of special departments to deal with juniors; and where appropriate, of juvenile advisory committees, whose chairmen were appointed by the Board of Trade.

Thus, even before the passing of the Education (Choice of Employment) Act 1910, there were in existence advisory committees for the employment of young people, some focused on the L.E.A., and others on the labour exchange. The 1910 Act was designed to strengthen the hands of the L.E.A.s for higher education, that is, the County Councils and County Boroughs, by empowering them to set up Youth Employment Bureaux to advise young people up to 17 years (raised to 18 years by the Fisher Education Act 1918), on the choice of suitable employment. At first, it was believed that the educational function, of giving advice, should be the prerogative of the bureau, but the actual placing in employment should be a labour exchange concern, and that the two should work together in the same building if possible. Such a split in function was doomed to failure, and though the First World War had to be fought before official policy was changed, changed it was, by slow degrees, after the publication in 1918 of the Report by the Ministry of Reconstruction on 'Juvenile Employment during the War and After'. This report advocated a unified local scheme for the advising and placing of young workers, though whether under the L.E.A., or the Ministry of Labour (created in 1916) was not stated. 'The method that works best is best' seemed to be their motto.

By 1919, of all the major local areas in England and Wales (Scottish Local Authorities were not permitted to establish schemes), 87 L.E.A.s had developed a Youth Employment Service or were in the process of doing so, 40 had achieved a juvenile section in the labour exchange or were about to do so, and in 22 areas no schemes of any kind had been projected. It took some time for the new official policy to bear fruit, and for several years the L.E.A. bureaux concentrated on their advisory function, leaving the labour exchanges to exercise their industrial role, with all the friction that was inherent in such a situation. To this, the Unemployment Insurance Act 1923 presented a new factor, as it permitted the L.E.A.s to operate an insurance scheme for juveniles, and the Ministry of Labour to reimburse them for their trouble. Most L.E.A.s (with bureaux) took advantage of the development, which meant they were officially exercising a function not wholly advisory or educational.

Meanwhile the difficulties of operating a Youth Employment Service through wholly distinct authorities were leading the local officials to work out compromise solutions, to which the government gave approval as they were formulated. Even in 1927, when the Ministry of Labour set up a National Advisory Council for Juvenile Employment, with strong L.E.A. representation, it was made abundantly clear that no uniformity would be imposed locally; and that subject to certain basic requirements, such as the right of the Ministry to inspect L.E.A. bureaux, the bureaux would be free to exercise their advisory and placing service in their own way, with the help and co-operation of the labour exchanges; but that in areas where no L.E.A. bureau functioned, the Ministry would develop its own juvenile employment department.

The pattern of the new service was now visible. For though it entailed a dual system in the localities, some presided over by a labour exchange, others by a youth employment bureau (a few by none at all), and an almost inextricable web of communication between them, it was a pattern that, with few modifications, was to persist for many years.

The Ince Report 1945

It has often been suggested that the modern Y.E.S. obtained its charter through the recommendations of the Report. This would be grossly to underestimate the developments that took place from 1910 onwards. What the Report did was to suggest an extension of the service, so that all children in State schools would have similar opportunities, and to outline a scheme containing all that was best in the existing ones. Inevitably it meant an end to local freedom, and to the establishment of national standards of provision that would be applicable everywhere. But it did not propose a wiping of the slate and replacement by an entirely new scheme. Sir Godfrey Ince and his colleagues were prepared to work with the existing pattern, to accept its illogicalities and opportunities for friction and inefficiency, but to use something that had been hammered out, on the anvil of experience, for the good of the greatest number of young people. The best way to illustrate how this would be done is to quote the summary of the proposals:—

1. L.E.A.s should be given a date by which they would decide, once and for all, whether they would exercise the power to run a Y.E.S. If the choice were in favour, the power should be exercised over the whole L.E.A. area—and not in parts, as had happened in certain county areas.
2. Scottish L.E.A.s should be given a similar choice.
3. The service should be administered at the national level by the Ministry of Education, the Department of Education for Scotland, and the Ministry of Labour, through a Central Executive Committee, as a joint service. But its spokesman in Parliament would be the Minister of Labour, and the cost would be met by the Ministry of Labour's vote. The Central Executive would ensure an adequate and satisfactory service, approve the local schemes, and inspect them. A National Juvenile Employment Council should be appointed to advise the government.
4. Locally, no change in the administration was recommended, but if and when County Colleges were established, there should be space allocated on the premises for the Y.E.O.
5. Finally, local schemes should be conducted according to national policy, and national standards, and the practice of allowing the L.A. to decide these matters should end.

One of the most valuable aspects of the Ince report was that it was widely read and much discussed, and though it contained nothing that the best agencies for youth employment were not already practising, it summarised in one official document those items in the service which had come to be regarded as desirable. As one youth employment officer has said, 'Its main justification was that it emphasised the importance of child study, and the study of occupations; it recognised the needs of boys and girls with special bents; it endorsed the proposal for a central juvenile employment executive; and it brought the L.E.A.s face to face with the need to decide once and for all whether to exercise their powers or not' (Heginbotham p. 132).

Legislation was not long delayed for, in 1948 the Employment and Training Act (section 10) provided the legal power to set about establishing an employment advisory service for all young people under eighteen who attended school. Thus by the deadline

(12 January, 1949), 43 County Councils and 73 County Boroughs in England and Wales and three Town Councils and ten County Councils in Scotland had submitted schemes for their own service. Those who did not left the work to the Ministry of Labour who carried on as before under national control. In 1965 the question of giving another chance to the non-opting authorities was considered by the N.Y.F.C. working party (under Lady Albemarle), but in the absence of sufficient trained staff to man any new bureaux that might be set up, no recommendation was made.

Methods used by the service

An analysis of the service provided by the Y.E.B. (leaflet P.L.354) has shown it to consist of eight aspects: Contact with school. Knowledge of opportunities available. Contact with potential school leavers. Training. Placing. Review of progress. Disabled children. Unemployment insurance.

Contact with school. All schools, whether State supported or not, have been obliged to give the local Y.E.O. a school report for all their pupils leaving school at the statutory school-leaving age. Such reports have provided the essential knowledge upon which officers have built their advisory and placing work. For children leaving above the minimum age, a school report might be given; in most cases it was available if asked for, though if it were refused the Y.E.O. had no power to demand it. The timing of the actual contact between the children and the Y.E.O.s has been the subject of considerable discussion, both in the service and in the schools. A general consensus has been reached that no useful purpose is served by leaving it until later, so in some cases it has been as early as two years before the statutory leaving age, though in others it has been later.

Knowledge of opportunities available. The Y.E.O.s' thorough working knowledge of local industries and occupations, and of opportunities for 'progressive' employment for young people beyond the local boundaries, has been one of their most valuable assets. In this they have been aided by a network of agencies, particularly other bureaux, and Ministry of Labour offices, who have regularly circulated throughout the United Kingdom information about vacancies, growing industries, new opportunities, and training schemes. Moreover, the volume of 'careers' pamphlets, film strips, handbooks of prospects in particular firms and industries, has grown to a formidable size, so that no officer can plead ignorance through lack of knowledge of where to find the information. Paper knowledge of this kind is enough to make the officer feel himself equipped to interest the young in possible careers, and every efficient officer has taken the opportunity to make his advice living and real, by visiting factories and other places of employment. This he has supplemented by service on apprenticeship and other advisory committees. He has got the feel of the job, its advantages and snags, has made contact with the employer, and when, later, a young person has to be placed, the whole process has been lubricated by a personal relationship.

Contact with the potential school leaver. The first meeting, a general one, like a talk or film show, has been designed to introduce young people to the idea of a career, the realities of going to work, and the opportunities available. At one time this was thought to be sufficient. But later, a closer involvement of potential employers has been developed, including the 'careers convention', where displays of pamphlets, handbooks, films, recordings, and other propaganda material have helped everyone to understand each other better. Young people and their parents have found these events a useful means of resolving their problems, and clarifying their minds. A different approach has been the 'work experience' scheme, limited to those above statutory school leaving age, where the potential school-leaver has been given leave of absence from school, to work in a factory or shop for a short period. There have been misgivings in some quarters, especially the trade unions, about this method and it has had only limited popularity.

The next stage has been private and personal, where the child can, if he wishes, seek an interview with the officer, whether at school, at the bureau, or both. The Y.E.O. has used these interviews to the full, as they have given him the opportunity to make his own assessment of the child. Most Y.E.O.s use the N.I.I.P. seven-point assessment:

1. Physical characteristics.
2. Attainments.
3. General intelligence.

4. Specialised aptitudes.
5. Interests.
6. Temperament and disposition.
7. Personal circumstances.

(Items 6 and 7 have been banned from the school report by the 1948 Act.)

Some have argued that the personal interview should be compulsory, as no true assessment, with or without scientific vocational testing equipment, is possible without it. (In 1967, the University of Reading inaugurated a one year diploma in vocational guidance.) But the voluntary principle has prevailed, as in all other parts of the advisory service, and both children and their parents have been free to accept or reject it. In the event, a large proportion of children under 18 have sought advice and been placed in work by the officers.

It has been the aim of the Y.E.O. to encourage parental participation at every stage of the process, not unduly to influence what a child's choice should be, but for both parents and child to be made aware of the opportunities, whether of training, further education, local jobs already available, or jobs in other parts of the country. Choice of a career, one would think, would be too vital for a child to decide on his own, without the support and knowledge of his family. Whether the facts measure up to these ideas, no-one knows. The Y.E.O.s themselves have reported a growing attendance of parents at the public functions and the private interviews. But how far parental advice has been given, or accepted, has not been revealed. A few small studies of the situation have been made, of which the one in 1955–6 by P. M. Mann and S. Mitchell, might be quoted. It was a study of parental attitudes in Stockbridge, Yorkshire, and concerned 177 boy and 188 girl school-leavers. It was found that in this small town of about 10,000 population, dominated by a large firm, the parents, when asked, expressed no preference for or against particular jobs in more than half the cases, though the percentage was significantly lower concerning fathers' preferences for their sons (no preference 52 per cent, but for daughters 63 per cent). Where parents did say what they thought, they seemed, on average, to prefer a craft for their sons, and an office job for their daughters. When the young people themselves were asked who, if anyone, helped them to make up their minds about what to do in their first job, the overwhelming majority of both sexes said it was their parents, or their siblings. So the home was apparently more potent in its influence than the parents were prepared to admit to the research team. The other important sources were the teachers and the Y.E.O.s. The ratio of home influence to school (including Y.E.O.) influence was 8:3 for boys and 10:3 for girls. If this result were typical, and it might well be, the policy of the Y.E.S., of including the parents, would seem well-founded.

A further question that has often been discussed is whether the organised contact between the Y.E.O. and school-leavers from grammar schools should be developed as far as it has been in other secondary schools. It is a problem that resolves itself where L.E.A.s adopt the comprehensive principle. But where grammar and independent schools have persisted, they have shown some reluctance to take advantage of the full Y.E.O. service, claiming that as most of their school-leavers have proceeded to universities, further training, or better paid jobs associated with 'white collars', they deserved a more specialised service than that of the Y.E.O. In consequence, 'careers teachers', who have been appointed in most types of school, have tended to be more specialised in this category. Such an isolationist attitude has not received the general approval of L.E.A.s, or of the Ministry of Labour, which, as long ago as 1952, authorised the appointment of careers' advisory officers attached to the Y.E.S. for grammar and independent schools. Further, in the face of the growing opportunities to take G.C.E. at 'O' level in all secondary schools, the chances of these children entering higher education and the professions have never been greater, and the reason for the grammar schools to maintain a separate service has consequently declined. Many L.E.A.s, having adopted the comprehensive school system, have changed the name of the Y.E.O. to 'careers' advisory officer', to emphasise his ability and willingness to advise on the whole spectrum of careers, and the totality of children needing advice on them.

Training. When both child and officer have reached a reasonably clear agreement about the kind of occupation that appears most appropriate, future developments might follow a number of courses. They could lead directly into a job, or into some specialised training. It has been convenient to differentiate between 'training', and 'placement', but the two are by no means separate, as training often takes place on the job, involving payment for what the trainee has produced; and being placed in a post has not meant that training would be ruled out. Indeed few people have been able to start in new employment without some training (one of the reasons why changing posts has been so expensive to the employer). Whichever way the child might go, the Y.E.O. has remained the linking factor.

Industrial Training Act 1964

The best known source of training for young school-leavers has been craft apprenticeship, and one function of the Y.E.O. has been to present suitable youngsters with the opportunities for training in the various trades, and to find vacancies for them. This has not prevented employers recruiting their own apprentices, though most of them with good training to offer have tended to work through the bureaux.

The Industrial Training Act 1964 has had considerable effect on this situation, but has not altered the fundamental duty of the Y.E.O. to provide information, and to place if possible. On the other hand the Act has not covered all trades and industries, so the supply of vacancies in certain trades has continued to be an individual matter, with which the officer has to deal.

The traditional method of acquiring skill while working on the job, though it has changed with the industrial needs of the times, has maintained a constant pattern for centuries. Of all the aspects of apprenticeship, four have remained fixed. The first has been the age at entry and completion. Apprenticeship has been an activity of the young, to be completed at 'coming of age', that is, 21 years. Compulsory school attendance and the higher school-leaving age have been embarrassments to trades where the training period has been prolonged, and means have had to be found of curtailing it, so that apprenticeship would be over at 21 years. Extending the upper age of completion has been acceptable to no-one.

The second element was in the learning process itself. This involved watching a craftsman at his daily work, being instructed by him, and gradually beginning to work at the craft under supervision. In the course of time, modifications to this on-the-job tuition made their appearance in a few firms. Some would select special craftsmen for training duties, and pay them for the training they gave. Others would set aside rooms in the factory for training purposes, where highly skilled trainers gave young people a concentrated course of theory and practice. Other firms co-operated with local further education colleges, where both theory and practical experience might supplement what was being done at the factory; and between 1960–68, the Ministry of Labour offered first year courses in their G.T.C.s for apprentices. But the general provision was haphazard and unplanned. The best was very good, the worst was not, and there were many areas where insufficient was done.

The craft itself was the third aspect of this pattern. Obviously industrial and technological change have resulted in the rise of new crafts, the decline of old ones, and changes in all. But it has always been necessary, for the very safety of the craftsman—as with professional men (see page 206)—for the boundary between one craft and another to be clearly defined, and a youth learning one craft should not learn a second one at the same time. The effect of keeping crafts in watertight compartments, though very desirable in reserving a field for each 'qualified' man, has been endless demarcation disputes, and the regrettable insistence that a youth, once having embarked on a craft, has been unable to change to another, if he found the first not to his liking.

Fourthly, qualification to perform a trade did not lie in the proved competence of the person, but in the fact of his having completed the stipulated period of the apprenticeship. It could happen, therefore, that a badly trained, inept, carpenter of 21 years could command the same status and the same rate of pay as the most exquisite craftsman, provided both had undergone a recognised apprenticeship of the approved number of years.

Added to these constant factors were others not quite so constant, but which, like the rest, were both the strength and weakness of the system. The most important was that apprenticeship has been a matter for each employer to undertake if he thought fit. Thus an employer would review his need for skilled craftsmen, weigh up the expenses or benefit of training his own men, decide how far the expense of an apprentice in his early years was balanced by the cheap labour he gave in his later ones, and then make up his mind whether it paid him better to take on apprentices, or simply to advertise for skilled men who had been trained by someone else. Some employers hoped to improve their progressive 'image' by keeping their apprenticeship section to the fore, others thought this a needless extravagance. Nor was training limited to apprenticeship, as semi-skilled jobs could involve training too, and in certain cases the trade unions have recognised this by the issue of a trade union card of the appropriate status.

Though group apprenticeship schemes have appeared (for instance the Enfield and District Manufacturers' Association; the West London group of the Engineering Industries Association), the individualist approach to training has been the most common, with all its advantages and defects. In the end the defects became so intractable that the system was in danger of breaking down unless there was a thorough overhaul. For instance, to leave the important function of training for skilled occupations to the individual decisions of thousands of employers could not be expected to produce the right number of skilled workers when they were wanted (for instance, experience has proved that too few were being trained after the Second World War). What was needed was a co-ordinated plan, so that the number of skilled workers in training would be enough to provide for a steady economic growth. Then there was the cost. It was clearly unfair to expect certain individual firms to bear the whole expense of providing for national needs, so some system of grant-aid or cost-pooling that would divide the burden equitably was necessary. The appearance of these two problems gave rise to the Industrial Training Act 1964.

As in many British developments, the changes envisaged by the Act had been discussed and experimented with for years before the final step was taken. In 1942, for instance, the Ministry of Labour initiated discussions with the Joint Consultative Committee (representing the British Employers' Confederation and the Trades Union Congress), which in 1945 submitted a report 'The Recruitment and Training of Juveniles for Industry', advocating the establishment, in each main industry, of a national joint apprenticeship and training council, composed of employers' and workers' representatives, with local counterparts to work with the Y.E.O.s. Since the planning of apprenticeship vacancies could not neglect the standards of training to be given, these quickly came to the fore as one of the main objectives in the new schemes. Each industry was urged to establish agreed standards of competence, and where appropriate, to ensure that qualified supervisors became responsible for the training. If possible, firms were encouraged to co-operate with L.E.A.s, so that all available resources of training would be tapped. Further, each of the main industries was to establish standards of employment for their young workers in order to avoid the exploitation that had occurred all too often in the past, and to guarantee that an adequate training was being given. To implement this, all apprentices, without exception, were to be given written indentures, signed by the youth, his parent, the employer, and the local apprenticeship committee.

The recommendations of the report were accepted by the government, and had they been universally honoured by individual firms there would have been no need for further action. About 100 industries had set up schemes ten years after the report. But when Y.E.O.s made local surveys, they found many employers had never heard of them, and others did not approve. Some, on the other hand, were doing excellent work, employing apprentice masters, using day release of young workers to attend the local technical college, and even having their own fully-fledged work schools.

In 1958 a further committee of the National Joint Advisory Council presented a report (the Carr Report) on 'Training for Skill', to the Ministry of Labour. By this time the need to increase the number of training vacancies had gathered momentum, through the 'bulge' in the number of school leavers about to enter the labour market by reason of the high birth rates of the immediate post-war years, and the fact that National Service was to end in 1962. Compulsory military training had, on the whole, been a disincentive to employers, who saw their trained workers disappear at 21 into the Forces, perhaps never to return. The end of National Service seemed the moment for a change. The Carr Committee recommended a National Apprenticeship Council, to follow up the committee's proposals, and to disseminate information about training to industry in general. But apart from pious hopes that apprenticeship would be better, and wider in scope, no fundamental proposals for change were suggested.

It took a Government White Paper in 1962, closely followed by the Industrial Training Act in 1964, to make suggestions that would alter the whole complexion of apprenticeship in Britain, or at any rate in those industries to which the Ministry of Labour thought the Act ought to apply.

The main provision contained in the new legislation was the appointment of a Training Board for each of the designated industries, to be responsible for all apprenticeship training; the private firms to be used as the instrument; or the setting up of a Board training school, according to circumstances. The whole would be paid for by a levy on each firm in the industry, with the addition of a small government grant. Thus training became a national process, no longer left to the whim of separate employers. No firm could evade its responsibility in training, as all were obliged to contribute to the pool.

The details were left to the decision of each industry, but the provisions of the Act became the blue-print of the scheme. It was the duty of the Minister of Labour to eastablish each board, but he could not do so without first consulting such employers' organisations, trade unions, and nationalised industries as were relevant. Once having decided, each board was appointed by the Minister and was composed of a chairman, a vice-chairman, and an equal number of representatives of employers' and workers' organisations. The Home Secretary and the Minister of Education were consulted on all appointments, and could themselves send non-voting representatives to the meetings on certain occasions. It was quickly realised that unless the boards invited representatives of the L.E.A.s responsible for technical colleges, there could easily be chaos. If each devised a syllabus of training and examinations without the co-operation of the other, both would be the losers. Fortunately, the examining body of the City and Guilds of London Institute already possessed an advisory committee, on which industry and education were represented. But the first time the need for this close co-operation was recognised officially was in the operation of the Industrial Training Act.

The expressed aim of each board was to provide industrial training to suitable persons over school-leaving age. How many were to be trained for each skill was at first difficult to estimate, and in 1965 the Ministry of Labour set up a Manpower Research Unit to review the future needs in each trade. The standards of 'suitability' in the applicants were decided by the board, whose duty it was to set up a training scheme, or approve one already established in a private firm, or a nationalised industry. This meant that responsibility for the standard of training was put squarely on the shoulders of the board, on whom lay the duty of inspection. There was nothing to prevent one board offering training to members of another industry; in fact the establishment of 'generic' training for the whole or part of the training for several crafts, came to be the policy of the boards.

The financial provisions of the Act were crucial, but in practice not the most difficult part to implement. The maintenance of the trainee could be met by the board, through the Ministry of Labour training grants (leaflet P.L.394; see pp. 10 and 39), by wages from the employer, or by the parents or by a mixture of all these sources. Those employers who were already running training schemes, or who started them as a result of the Act, were allowed to charge the cost to the pool. The pool itself was made up of a levy from the firms in the industry, on a formula decided by each board. The formula was often a percentage (about half per cent to three per cent) of the firm's wages and salaries bill. In addition the government had the right to grant-aid the boards (a maximum of £50 million in aggregate was given in the Act, but the Ministry was empowered to increase this by statutory instrument).

Appeal Tribunals. Disputes were likely to arise from a change as fundamental as this, and the Act set up a system of Appeal Tribunals to hear objections against decisions on the assessment for the levy. The system was an interesting one, being, from the first, semi-judicial in character. It became the duty of the Lord Chancellor to appoint a President of Tribunals and a panel of Deputies. Each was a barrister or solicitor of at least seven years' standing and was appointed to hold office for five years, though eligible for reappointment. It was the President who decided on the number of tribunals, and on their place and date of meeting. The tribunals themselves consisted of a chairman (the president or one of his deputies) and two other members, one selected from a panel of employers' representatives, and the other from a trade union panel. These panels were appointed by the Minister. The hearings were normally in camera, though they were open to the public if the appellant wished it. Both sides could be legally represented. A parallel arrangement for Appeal Tribunals in Scotland came into being in the same year (1965).[1]

To assist the Minister of Labour in fulfilling his training responsi-

[1] Besides the difference in the constitution of these tribunals from the ones used for the N.A.B. and the M.P.N.I., (for example, the creation of a President, and the automatic approval of legal representation), the way this was used for subsequent legislation, e.g. Redundancy Act, p. 140, and Terms and Conditions of Employment Act, p. 129, etc., is of great interest.

bility, a Central Training Council was appointed to advise him on any matter relating to industrial or commercial training. The council was fairly large, being made up of 33 members: a chairman, six from each of the employers' and workers' sides, two from nationalised industries, up to six chairmen of Training Boards, and twelve others, half of whom were appointed after consultation with the Ministry of Education and the Home Office. The size of the body did not inhibit its activities, and memoranda and reports soon began to flow from its office, dealing with such matters as the number of boards, the importance of training for safety, the question of off-the-job training, and others.

As for finance, the boards arranged their levies according to the idiosyncracies of the industry, frequently allowing the smallest (and presumably poorest) firms to escape altogether. Letters of protest appeared (for example, in *The Times*, 20 February, 1965), suggesting that Parliament had acted improperly in putting no limit on the boards' power to collect and administer these new 'taxes' on industry, but, on the whole, industry seemed compliant in accepting the training plans.

A far more serious matter was to recruit and train sufficient trainers and supervisors of a calibre suitable for the new standards. It was clear that the old habit of putting an apprentice in the care of a good craftsman ('sitting next to Nellie') was no longer good enough, since what a man could do with his own hands in no way reflected his power to teach others. As an interim measure, Technical Colleges and Colleges of Advanced Technology were approached by the Minister of Labour to organise short-term courses for trainers, and the Ministry itself initiated short 'instructor' courses at Letchworth and Hillingdon: but deeper, longer courses were the real answer to this problem.[1]

The Central Training Council issued a memorandum on staff training to help management appreciate the general principles involved, and also inaugurated research into training practices.

Issues

What each Board had to decide was: What is involved in skill?

[1] Training Within Industry (T.W.I.) was a further method of instruction that had been in use since 1940 (p. 10) and from 1966 onwards, the Ministry sent their own men on to the shop floor of a plant to help to train the instructors (see Leaflet P.L. 292).

What shall be the pattern of the training for skill? How long shall it take? Shall there be a recognised test of competence?

What is skill? The intention of craft apprenticeship had always been, that a body of theoretical and practical knowledge could be learned and practised by the person who had given his time and concentration to the processes. This was not to say that the boundary lines were not subject to modification, or that new craft skills had not been evolved with technological change. What it did mean was that it was no longer enough for a boy to learn one skill by the time he was twenty-one, and earn a comfortable living from it for the rest of his life. Workers preparing for the 21st century have to contemplate changing their occupation several times in their working life, and being re-trained for new skills. The point was illustrated by Dr A. King, U.N.E.S.C.O.'s Director for Scientific Affairs (quoted in *The Times*, 4 May, 1965). He believed that not only workshop craftsmen, but scientists and others of the educated élite would need retraining during their careers. For example at the French Atomic Energy Establishment at Sacley, the diploma awarded in reactor engineering was timed to last for five years only; thereafter further courses and examinations had to be passed to validate the qualification. The same issue was raised by the Central Committee of Study Groups (an organisation of managers, trade unionists, and others) in their 1965 report on the 'training of young people in industry'. They urged the need for people to transfer easily from one occupation to another, at all levels of skill, and the need for facilities to make this possible. Experience among the industrialised countries of the commonwealth has pointed in a similar direction.

The seriousness of the problem has provoked one of the most fundamental criticisms of the Act. For in *The Economist* (22 May, 1965) it was suggested that instead of creating about 30 Training Boards on an industrial basis (most of them using a different industrial demarcation from that of the Department of Economic Affairs), it would have been better to organise training on a regional basis. This might have brought the L.E.A.s into closer co-operation with industry, and might also have avoided the problem of duplicating certain training, like that of clerks and secretaries (though in practice the Central Training Council has itself taken responsibility for devising training schemes for certain clerks and secretaries). So long as training has been by industry, the problem of the common occupation has had to be solved, either by a joint board (as in iron and steel, and engineering, for training foundrymen), or by frankly recognising that parallel training schemes, with an individual industrial slant, have had to be provided by each firm. Moreover, there has been a real danger that the industrial levy might, in the end, build a new set of rigidities into the British economy.

The pattern of training. One way of meeting the demands of change was envisaged by the White Paper in 1962 (Cmnd. 1892), which emphasised that a first priority was the need to establish a full-time training school (at a technical college, or specialised centre) where all those hoping to train in a skill might spend their first year. 'Experience has shown', declared the White Paper, 'that if young people, on leaving school, were given a systematic course of training, in the basic principles of their trade, their progress thereafter to full skill would be more rapid, and their adaptability within their trade much greater, than if they started out on a narrow range of production work.' Though thinking at this stage had been confined to the best methods of obtaining one skill, the idea of a preliminary year, common to all wishing to become skilled workers, but leaving the training for specialised skills until a more advanced stage, has had wide acceptance.

One interesting experiment, first tried out by the Engineering Industry Training Board, was the division into 'modules' of training and experience. The various modules could be arranged according to the skill that needed to be learnt by the various kinds of craftsmen. It provided a flexible supply of programmes that could be tailored to the needs of the individual, and the new skills that industry was constantly demanding.

Another method, favoured in certain fields, notably the building trades, has involved each apprentice learning two or possibly three trades, thereby giving him both inside and outside work opportunities, for example, bricklayer-plasterer-tiler. The multiplication of crafts in one person would give flexibility in a static situation, and if properly taught would provide the adaptability needed to meet changes. But one could envisage great problems arising if another generation were to abolish all bricks, plaster and tiles, and substitute plastics or other new materials.

That the boards have been fully alive to the dangers and the possibilities was quickly made evident. The Engineering Industry Training Board, for instance, aimed from the beginning, at placing each apprentice recruit, for his first year, in a place separate from general manufacture. There he would receive a basic training from instructors, practical men, used to the snags of everyday work in the factory, but with some instruction in the art of teaching. No scheme has been approved by any board unless it included provision for 'Day Release' for the trainees.

The concept of 'Day Release' was greatly misunderstood in the middle years of the century. It was not made compulsory, though some employers may have thought it was; nor was it in all cases easily implemented, since the absence of convenient technical colleges, and the inadequate facilities in some of them, have made nonsense of a scheme which would otherwise have had a good deal to commend it. Further, the variability in the quality of the on-the-job training made the programming of a viable course for the young students (in whose selection the college had played no part) a very difficult task indeed. It has consequently been difficult to point to tangible results from the Day Release courses. For instance, when Professor Williams made a survey in the Home Counties and East Anglia of the number of students who passed the Intermediate City and Guilds examination, it was found that only five to ten per cent of the apprentices who started day release classes were successful. It was phenomenal for anyone to reach a higher standard. Education is notoriously poor at showing tangible results, and it would be grossly misleading to write off the day release schemes as inadequate because of their negligible results in examinations; this is particularly so in the case of the City and Guilds Intermediate which is theoretical, and possibly unsuited to the needs of many students. The City and Guilds Institute appreciated this, and later inaugurated a Craftsman's Certificate, based mainly on a practical examination. Further experimentation along these lines has been accelerated by the boards, who have been concerned about the standards of competence a trained craftsman should exhibit. Day release has of course had other advantages in helping a youngster to secure a more even passage from school to industry, in assisting him to adjust to manhood, and in reducing the hours and strain of industrial life. In the absence of more concentrated industrial education, the idea of a day-a-week away from the factory, yet paid on a time rate, has had much to commend it for young workers. So much, in fact, that in 1966 the government empowered technical colleges to charge the cost of day release schemes to industry.

Length of the training. It has been generally taken for granted that the acquisition of a skill, and of the coveted trade union card, should be undertaken before the age of 21. For a time this dogma remained unbreached, but what the Central Training Council did challenge from the beginning was the total length of the apprenticeship. The five years common to most apprenticeships was thought too long for most occupations, and boards have looked critically and freshly at this point. In consequence the whole programme of training (in many cases this has meant the first concrete programme they have ever had) has been carefully reconsidered in the light of the time factor. Changes so fundamental have naturally caused concern to the traditional element among craftsmen, and some compromise has had to be considered. One of the first to suggest a solution was the Construction Industry Training Board, who drew a line between the 'length of the training', as a matter for the board to decide, and the 'length of the apprenticeship', to be negotiated between employers' organisations and trade unions. But the board realised that were the gap between 'training' and 'apprenticeship' to become very wide, an unrealistic and undesirable situation would arise, in which 'apprenticeship' would be the sufferer.

The test. The need for an assessment of competence at the end of the training has been recognised by all, and has found its way into the Act. We saw earlier that ordinary written examinations, like the traditional ones of the City and Guilds, might not be the answer to this tricky question, and in practice it has been for each board to decide its own measures. In this they have been helped by experience in other countries, notably in America, where trade testing on a big scale for military recruiting purposes was introduced early in the century. Similarly, commonwealth countries have had well developed proficiency tests for many years. In Britain a few industries have used them, as have our defence services, especially in engineering. In the face of such widespread experience, it is surprising that testing did not become common practice in British apprenticeship long ago, especially as between 30 per cent and 40 per cent of boys leaving school in 1960–65, for example, were indentured, and had nothing to show for their training to potential employers, or the standards they had reached, apart from their indenture papers and the years they had spent as apprentices.

Training boards have been primarily concerned with the training of craftsmen, but since it was their function to organise training at all levels and all ages they were interested in the training of semi-skilled workers as well. From the beginning this was recognised; as Mr J. C. Coleman (*Southern Evening Echo*, 16 December, 1965) said: 'If a firm's own known or anticipated needs were for large numbers of semi-skilled workers, then that firm would be encouraged to train a preponderance of such workers'. Thus for the first time in the history of Britain, vocational training for industry has been put on a national basis, with a coherent plan for the orderly provision of all types of skill.

Training Allowance Scheme

Reference has already been made (p. 33) to the maintenance of young trainees. But since 1947 the Ministry of Labour has developed a special service of grant-aid for young persons whose interests and aptitudes could not be satisfied near home (leaflet P.L.366). The scheme has involved the selection of the young boy or girl with 'more than average capacity to train for a skilled occupation in industry' (the final decision being made at the regional office of the Ministry of Labour), and his placement in a suitable firm for training. His lodgings have to be approved, and his maintenance grants must be enough to cover their cost, along with pocket-money and travelling expenses for a reasonable number of visits home (usually about three times a year). Parents are required to contribute where possible, while the local offices, helped by members of the advisory committees, are expected to concern themselves with his welfare. Thus a fairly comprehensive scheme has been established.

Up to 1957, all apprenticeship vacancies were offered first to local applicants, and if possible filled by them. This had advantages in saving money, and building up a local supply of skilled workers.

But it was a severe handicap to young people in non-industrial areas, for whom only the unfilled vacancies were available.

The year 1957 was a period of contraction in apprenticeship vacancies and expansion in the number of teenagers available, so the policy became increasingly unpopular, and it was decided that firms with apprenticeships to offer should be allowed to choose from all applicants, whether they lived locally, or at a distance, provided the names were submitted through the Y.E.S. This left the firm free to choose the recruit it wanted, and the youngster from a distance was not automatically left out in the cold.

By March 1961, the Allowances Scheme had been extended still further, and was now available to young people under 18 who wished to leave home for 'progressive employment', which usually meant employment offering prospects of in-training, permanence and promotion.

Meanwhile, another complication in the training field brought an extension of the Ministry scheme of grant-aid, in this case to the firms themselves. The Industrial Training Act had confined grant-aid to firms undertaking apprenticeship, leaving academic courses to the L.E.A.s and the Ministry of Education. The new factor was the development of 'sandwich' courses composed of periods of study in an educational institution (University, College of Advanced Technology, Technical College, etc.) and of field-work study in the factory. For though the student might be covered by a maintenance grant from his sponsoring firm, and the educational institution would receive grant-aid from the Treasury, the firm might not be recompensed in any way for its part in the training, except by a contract of service from the student, if such were asked for. By 1965 the government had recognised the anomaly, and being anxious to relieve the shortage of technicians and technologists, instituted a system of grant-aid to firms for the periods of study on the job, which were integral in the 'sandwich' courses. Such grants were paid through the Industrial Training Board if one were in existence, or direct from the Ministry of Labour.

Placing. The fifth and crucial responsibility of the Y.E.O. has been his duty to find the right job. It had been the central doctrine of the Ince Report in 1945 that unless a youngster were found 'progressive employment' early in his career, his prospects later would be seriously compromised, and his whole personal development damaged. Therefore the first priority of the new service, said Ince, was to fit the right child to the right job. If, through some mischance, he was in a job that might be harmful to his health or his character, or one unlikely to lead to a career suitable to his ability and aptitude, then he should be diverted from it if at all possible. These criteria have influenced the thinking of all concerned with the employment of youth since the Second World War, and could fairly be described as the 'Commandments' of the Youth Employment Service. There have been times when youngsters have been placed in 'dead-end' jobs while waiting for an apprenticeship, or for an opening in the firm of their choice, but officers have been anxious to avoid such situations if possible. The dangers of non-progressive employment were illustrated all too well in the inter-war years, when school-leavers were sometimes inveigled into jobs, given no training, and actually dismissed at sixteen or eighteen when their insurance stamps became a disincentive for the employer to keep them longer (cf. Jewkes and Winterbottom). Many factors in the post-war era have served to reduce this practice, of which not least has been the vigilance of the Y.E.O.s. For instance some young people, ignoring their advisers, are still tempted by relatively high wages or the comparative glamour of certain semi-white-collar jobs like that of shop-assistants, to fall into the trap. Yet the shortage of young workers, and the growing sense of responsibility among employers, have done much to improve matters.

The Ince Report suggested a third criterion about the placement of young workers that has not been so widely appreciated. This was 'that the limited supply of juveniles be distributed in accordance with national need'. The dangers of 'directing' young people into employment were too apparent to need any argument, yet the economic development of the country has demanded that labour should be available where it was most needed. The dilemma will probably never be resolved, and each Y.E.O. has been left to deal with it in his own way. He has been able to bring the opportunities and vacancies in the under-manned industries to the notice of his clients, leaving them to choose. The higher wages in areas of labour shortage and the Ministry transfer schemes to posts of 'progressive employment' may have been an incentive to some, though going away from home would always be regarded as a big step for a young person to take.

The placing of young people in jobs has not been limited to first jobs. The changeability of youth, the intrusion of adverse influences, the possibility that the youth and the job have not been well matched, have had to be taken into account; and many young people, having become unsettled in their first post, have returned for further help. Placement in subsequent jobs has demanded as much skill and understanding as in the first, but the officer has been able to build up a fuller picture of the personality and work potential of his client, and has therefore perhaps been able to give him more meaningful advice and help than he could at the beginning.

The filling of a job has always been a two-sided responsibility, and the service would be completely unworkable if it did not recognise its duty to the employer who has asked for applicants. Every efficient officer would agree that his function has been just as much to find the most suitable candidates to present to the employer as to put a youngster into a job. The employer himself has had to make the final decision, but the Y.E.O. has picked out the most suitable of his boys or girls to offer. The service would not last long if he made too many mistakes in preliminary selection.

Review of Progress. To have launched a boy or girl on a career has never been enough. A follow-through of some kind has been considered an essential part of the service, partly because a youngster might be unhappy in his job, and unaware of the reason; or might be unsettled and ready to hand in his notice; or there might be social reasons why he needed help and advice from a neutral person. The majority of the young people placed by the bureaux have not needed after-care, but experience has shown that some have done so. Thus by various methods, such as a 'follow-up' letter several months after appointment, asking the young worker to call if he needs help; the 'open evening' to which all young employees have been invited, and where skilled officers have made themselves available, on a social basis, if loneliness or need for adult companionship have been evident; or on an advice-basis, if the youngster has wanted to discuss his job and his prospects; as well as by other methods, the officers have tried to keep in touch. Most Y.E.O.s have extended their 'follow-up' service to all youngsters in employment under 18, whether they have been placed by the service or not. So long as the insurance cards were deposited at the Bureau, they have all been known to the office.

Following-up has not been limited to concern for the welfare of the young, but has included appraisals and assessments of the value of the service itself. Vocational guidance has needed constant testing, and in the long run the only feasible test has been the successful matching of the job and the youngster.

Disabled Children. A further aspect of the Y.E.O.'s work has been his effort to improve the employment prospects of young people who are disabled. Before 1948, the Special Schools and the L.E.A.s attended to this, but the establishment of a national network of youth employment agencies enabled the function to move to the bureaux.

It was not intended that the Disabled Persons Employment Scheme (p. 53) should be duplicated in the Y.E.B., nor was it possible to disentangle the young handicapped from the ordinary run of young applicants to the bureaux. So, by the early 1960's, the Ministry had agreed to meet the difficulty by approving the appointment of specialist officers in some of the large L.E.A.s to take care of the industrial needs of disabled youth, while at the same time underlining the continuous need for the fullest co-operation with the D.R.O. at the exchange. Meanwhile, as a result of the Piercy Report (1956) on 'Disablement', disabled boys and girls as young as 15 could attend the Industrial Rehabilitation Units for the assessment of their capabilities. The other disablement services which were part of the Ministry scheme were open to the young, as well as to the adult disabled.

The problem of young people unable to enter employment on equal terms might be relatively small for each area, but together they form a sizeable group. When about 20,000 disabled youngsters have had to be catered for each year, it was not a matter that could be laid aside with impunity, even if humanitarian impulses would allow it. In consequence, the service has given rise to a certain amount of controversy. The Y.E.O.s have in all cases given of their best to the disabled, as to normal young people, and have offered their assessment, training, placement, and follow-up help as much to the one as to the other (leaflet P.L.379). Where specialist officers were available, everyone benefited, but they were few in number, and to discover a supply of adequately trained men and women to fill the appointments was not easy. Many, for example the

Albemarle Committee (1965), wanted to see more officers recruited for the purpose, and perhaps joint appointments between contiguous areas where appropriate, but the real stumbling block was lack of personnel. Others, notably the Thomas Committee (1961) criticised the provisions for assessing the potentialities of disabled young people, especially those of the I.R.U. service. They were quite ready to believe that the I.R.U.s were efficient in helping disabled adults to return to the habit of regular work after an accident, and that the facilities for assessing them were good. But they were not persuaded that an I.R.U. could function equally well for adults and for the young at one and the same time.

In their view the problem of youth was quite different. There was no work experience in the background to use as a yardstick, it was a case of making the first and only evaluation so far available for the youth, and worst of all, the atmosphere would be unlikely to make a disabled boy or girl feel at home. In contrast, some voluntary agencies such as the Spastics Society and the Royal Institute for the Blind, were setting up their own assessment centres for the young, where people experienced in particular forms of handicap would be available for the work. It was observed that a large number of handicapped children were unable to go to any assessment centre at all, either because there was none near enough, or the parents were reluctant to let them go from home. A better alternative, it was argued, was the local assessment centre, in which medical, social, industrial, and other interests could combine to make an evaluation of the youth's employment potential.

In 1960, the Ministry of Labour made a survey for the Thomas Working Party of the employment experience of a sample of disabled young people. They investigated 3,000 cases in 83 areas to find out whether there had been a 'reasonably satisfactory start in employment' (that is, 'reasonably satisfactory' to the school-leaver, the employer and the Y.E.O.). Their conclusion was that in all but four per cent of the boys and girls, the start had been 'reasonably satisfactory', and of the four per cent, a quarter were unemployable, a similar number in unsuitable jobs, and the rest might have worked in sheltered workshops, if there had been any available, or if they had been willing. As for the 96 per cent, 19 in every 20 were in ordinary work in a factory or a shop. The Thomas Committee were a little critical of these findings, and suggested that too many disabled youngsters were in comparatively unrewarding routine jobs, because it was work they could do without further training. Further training had been denied them, because they had not received a good enough education, in the first place, to obtain entrance into a training course. Whether many handicapped young people have been given the chance to work up to their potential, and if not, why not, would seem a fruitful topic for further investigation.

Unemployment Insurance and supplementary allowances. Since it has been the policy of the country that able-bodied unemployed should collect their Social Security benefit (along with any supplementation) at the office where available jobs were registered, it was logical that youngsters under 18, seeking benefit, should be obliged to register as 'able and willing' to work at the Y.E.B., and thus be on the spot, if suitable jobs happened to materialise. In the inter-war years, when unemployment was rife, and many young people were obliged to collect benefit, the policy of 'signing on' tended to associate the bureaux, in their minds, with the payment of benefit. Though this did not earn for the bureaux the title of 'dole offices', as it did for employment exchanges, there have been many who would gladly see the function removed from the Y.E.S. altogether (p. 19). The service should be regarded, in their opinion, as one for careers advice, where youngsters would go in hope and anticipation, not as a compulsory reporting centre without which no cash benefit could be obtained. Others have seen the advantages of the compulsory visits, claiming that young people needed the discipline, when they were out of work; that the best way for them to find gainful employment was through this means; and above all that the most satisfactory method of keeping track of young people, and ensuring their achievement of 'progressive employment' was by keeping regular contact with them.

Administration

The responsibility for the administration of employment advice bureaux was established under the Employment and Training Act 1948. At that time, following the advice of the Ince Report, local authorities were asked to decide whether they wished to set up their own bureaux, or to allow the Ministry of Labour to exercise the function. This was the first time Scotland had been given the power to establish a service, and both there, and in England and Wales, a majority of the local authorities opted to accept responsibility. Even so, the central control remained in the hands of the Ministry of Labour, as it was they who were empowered to recognise local authority schemes, if they were of the accepted standard. Not that this meant national uniformity. The Ministry was prepared to tolerate experiments, and deviations from their 'model', provided the basic necessities were honoured—necessities like staff, premises, and the scope and objectives of the service itself.

It was the Ministry who represented the service in Parliament, grant-aided the local authorities up to 75 per cent of expenditure, and in the last resort had the power to withhold grants, or even to withdraw recognition of a particular scheme. At the Ministry a new executive, the Central Youth Employment Executive, was established to perform the employment-of-young-people function under the Act. Composed of senior staff from the Ministry of Labour, the Ministry of Education, and the Scottish Education Department, it was hailed, in 1948, as unique in bringing three departments of state together in one enterprise. The Central Executive has exercised a continuing watch over the youth employment departments of the Ministry, and of the Y.E.O.s, through its inspectors. These have worked closely, in the localities, with the Ministry of Education inspectors, and have attempted to make a formal inspection of each office about once every seven years. Though the grossly inadequate number of inspectors has made the contact less substantial than it might have been, the Y.E.B. policy has provided a counter-balance. For instance, they have all maintained continuous relations with the regional and local offices of the Ministry of Labour, a contact all the more valuable because the youth section at regional headquarters has appointed officers, in the senior grade, with experience and skill in youth employment matters, and the Ministry has equipped itself to supply advice on modern trends in vocational guidance.

National Youth Employment Council. Another central body, established by the Act, was the National Council, appointed by the Minister of Labour for three years at a time, consisting of up to three dozen members such as teachers, employers, trade unions

and some 'independent persons' who represent the relevant
interests. Its function has been mainly advisory, but it has published reports which have shown it to be a lively, active organisation, able to give useful and informed advice to the Minister. It has
been assisted by advisory committees for Scotland and for Wales,
which have kept the special problems of these areas in the eye of
the national council. For instance, Day Release schemes in Scotland had not been everywhere available before 1948, and the
difficulties experienced by both employers and young people in
establishing these schemes were analysed by the Scottish Committee. Wales had similar problems, especially that of a shortage of
further education colleges for young workers to attend. Sparsely
populated districts offered a challenge in both areas.

Local administration. As for local arrangements, the Act laid down
that if a L.E.A. wished to operate, it would be obliged to do so for
all school-leavers up to 18 years, and for those still at school
beyond the age of 18, within the whole of its area. Provision was
made for consultation and joint action with other areas, and for the
establishment of one or more Youth Employment Sub-Committtees
of the Education Committee, to whom the L.E.A. could delegate
part of the functioning of the scheme. These sub-committees have
tended to contain equal numbers of employers and trade union
representatives, who together have comprised not fewer than a
third of the total. To these were added L.E.A. representatives,
teachers and a few 'independent' members. The constitution has
therefore been a reflection of that at the national level, but has been
flexible enough to perpetuate a membership that was satisfactory
before 1948; and to meet the needs of scattered county communi-
ties, where local interest and support were felt to be more
important than strict adherence to a model scheme. Since the
Committees have usually contained more co-opted members than
elected members of the Council, they have remained advisory, the
executive function being exercised through the Education
Committee of the local authority.

Special problems in youth employment

Several of these have been analysed as they arose in the foregoing
paragraphs; such questions as the extension of the service to all

grammar schools, the place of the 'Careers Teacher' vis-à-vis the
Y.E.O., problems of training in skill and the difficulties of
disabled children, but two problems of some difficulty remain to
be considered.

Unemployment among the young. Since the last war it has been the
declared policy of all political parties to maintain a high level of
employment, and the fact that unemployment has kept at a
phenomenally low level might be considered evidence of the
general success. This has not prevented the emergence of a higher
than average incidence of unemployment in certain areas, and at
certain times; and a service dedicated to the matching of the right
young person to the right job could not be blind to the special
dangers of the lack of gainful employment to the young. That
there has been no widespread repetition of the tragic circumstances
of the 1920s and '30s, has not been entirely due to the economic
prosperity of the country. The low birth-rate of the pre-war
period meant a relative scarcity of young people coming on to the
labour market, and a consequent buoyant demand for those who
arrived. Added to this came the raising of the school-leaving age
from 14 to 15 in 1947, which removed the potential school-leavers
of a whole year from the labour supply (about 150,000 young
people). In 1970, if the leaving age is raised to 16, a further
batch will be removed. Meanwhile, since about 1950, there has
been a tendency, encouraged by the authorities, for children to
stay on at school for a period after compulsory leaving age. The
incentive to remain has been partly the improved facilities in all
secondary schools, and partly the development of G.C.E.
examinations in secondary modern schools. The introduction of
the Certificate of Secondary Education in England and Wales, and
in Scotland, that of the 'O' grade of the Scottish Leaving Certificate, has provided an added inducement to stay longer at school.

These factors have profoundly affected the employment chances
of young people. Moreover, the growing realisation that the
youth of a nation was an asset not to be lightly squandered has
encouraged a feeling that the potentialities of youth must be
carefully husbanded. If pockets of unemployment should arise, it
should be possible to clear them quickly. One such occasion was
in 1962, when the under-use of young people was reported from
several centres, notably the South East of Scotland, the North

East of England, and Merseyside. The National Youth Employment Council made a survey of L.E.A. activity at this time, and found several schemes being tried. The most successful seemed to be the effort to fit youngsters into various further education courses. On the other hand, the provision of special courses for them, or the opening of youth clubs during the day for their use appeared to have little success. Later, an attempt was made to transfer youngsters to areas of good employment, or to fit them into local industries. An example of the former was the 'holidays with a purpose' scheme, pioneered by the Church of England, to bring boys from the North East to London for a holiday, to see if they would like a job there. Through the Y.E.S. many were fixed up with suitable jobs in this way. Another example was the joint enterprise of two youth employment departments, Tyneside and Birmingham, whereby the former selected recruits for jobs in Birmingham, and the latter settled them in both jobs and lodgings. These boys were given three months' preliminary training in a technical college before entering the factory, and thereafter were guaranteed at least twelve months' 'day release'. Joint enterprise between Y.E.B.s has been envisaged as a useful development of the service since it was written into the Act in 1948, but consistent and constructive use of the provision needs more imaginative handling.

It would be idle to think that all long-term unemployment amongst the young can be eliminated, as personal factors necessarily affect a youngster's prospects. This was illustrated by the National Youth Employment Council's survey, made in 1963, into the experience of 11 bureaux in various parts of the United Kingdom. Of the 368 young people who had been unemployed for six months or more, nearly half were handicapped or educationally sub-normal. When a tally was taken a year later, though employment prospects had improved greatly, 30 per cent of the original number were still unemployed, mainly through physical or mental handicap, or both.

Shortage of staff for youth employment offices. It has been generally recognised that a service demanding so much skill in human understanding, and so much knowledge of the possibilities open to both employers and the young, would demand a well developed body of trained personnel. The problem of finding men and women suitable for such an exacting task has been great, and most

49

offices have suffered from a chronic staff shortage. Were the maximum age of the young people catered for raised higher than 18, as recommended by the Albemarle Committee (1965), the problem would only be the more acute. The full-time training courses at Lamorbey Park, Sidcup, Kent and Manchester College of Commerce, though providing a good training, have not always been full, and shorter courses such as the four weeks' one at Birkbeck College, London, have been tried. Similarly, the Ministry of Labour has developed in-service courses, which have been extended by the setting up of the Ministry training unit to cope with the needs of experienced officers (for advanced training) as well as new recruits. In spite of this the required numbers have not been forthcoming. Recruitment for training would seem the point of failure.

By 1966 the average case load per officer was down to 500 for the first time in the history of the service—but this was a national average, with considerable variations both above and below. As 500 was generally regarded as the maximum number of youngsters for whom an officer should be responsible, and as many factors meant the load should be smaller for some officers, the problem of staff shortage has remained acute.

III

ENTRANCE TO INDUSTRY FOR THE DISABLED

THE PROVISION OF special employment facilities for the disabled was brought about by the Second World War. For in spite of the King's Roll (p. 62), and the growing interest in the medical rehabilitation of the handicapped between the wars, it took the war-time need for a fully mobilised labour force, and the humane reactions to war casualties to create a service, which has justifiably become the envy of the world.

The milestones, that marked the progress of the scheme, were the reports of the Tomlinson (1943) and Piercy (1956) Committees, and the Disabled Persons (Employment) Acts of 1944 and 1958. Though, in this context, it is to the Tomlinson report we owe the most, it is in no way to denigrate the various Acts bringing into being the National Health Service, since they built up a system of home and hospital care for all kinds of mental and physical disablement without which other schemes would have been impotent. Nor must the value of the Social Security provisions (p. 225) be omitted, as they have guaranteed a minimum income for the disabled, as for other people.

Tomlinson Committee 1943

The Tomlinson report did two important things. It defined for the first time what was meant by 'disablement', and it sketched a scheme for the adaptation of existing services, particularly those of the Ministry of Labour, to provide new employment arrangements for the disabled.

The definition, that was subsequently incorporated into the 1944 Act, stated that a disabled person was one who 'on account of

E

injury or disease of a character which is likely to last for more than six months (subsequently increased to twelve months), or on account of congenital deformity, is substantially handicapped in obtaining or keeping employment of a kind generally suited to his age, previous experience and qualifications'. Thus the emphasis was on a person's eligibility for employment, and not on why he became disabled, or how badly, as in the Industrial Injury Acts of 1946 and later. On the other hand, if a person had a disability, but it in no way conflicted with his power to obtain, and keep, a post suitable to his age and ability, then he would not be regarded as disabled for the purposes of the scheme. For instance, a man had a congenital handicap, whereby one leg was considerably shorter than the other; when walking he limped badly, and anyone might have thought he was a typical example of a 'disabled' person. He had a job as a press operator, which he had obtained quite easily, and had kept for many years, with complete satisfaction to his employer and himself, and no physical deterioration. He was therefore not included as a 'disabled' person, because the 'getting and keeping of suitable work' had been no problem.

Like most developments in British life, most of the provisions in the plan outlined in the Tomlinson Report had been tried out earlier. In 1941, for instance, at one of the most critical moments of the war, when labour was so short that even the prisons and the mental hospitals were combed, to discover what labour resources might be available, the Ministry of Labour initiated an interim scheme for the training and resettlement of disabled persons. As the scheme expanded, its possibilities became clearer, and the Tomlinson Committee was appointed to think out how a permanent scheme could be evolved.

Its first concern was to decide the principles on which disabled persons should be placed in jobs. Should the job be tailored to suit the handicap, or should the person be so selected, trained, provided with aids, and generally toned-up, that he would fit into a normal job, and compete on an equal footing with his non-handicapped neighbours? Most charitable provision had previously worked on the assumption that a handicapped person would require sheltered employment, perhaps even a workshop reserved for sufferers from a particular disability. The Tomlinson Committee thought otherwise. It stressed the deep need, felt by all disabled persons, to be treated as normal. It began, therefore, with the assumption that a man should return to his old employment, if at all possible. Were this not feasible, then in collaboration with the doctors, he should consider what type of job would suit him best, and how he should be rehabilitated and re-trained to use himself to the maximum. It was not good enough simply to place him in a job. He should be employed in work that demanded from him the greatest skill of which he was capable. It was quite out of date, said the committee, to think that ordinary jobs could be filled only by completely fit workers. Many posts in industry and elsewhere were adequately filled by people with a handicap. When a disabled person was so employed, the stress should be on his ability to compete equally in productivity with anyone else. It has often been thought that the use of the disabled in industry would be viable only so long as employment was good. This would be to misunderstand the underlying philosophy of the scheme, and to neglect the main aim, which was to match employment and worker effectively, so that if he were disabled, he would be no worse off in bad times than anyone else.

The plan that emerged was of four parts, and the 1944 Disabled Persons (Employment) Act gave effect to them: Ascertainment; Industrial preparation; Training; Employment.

Disabled Persons (Employment) Act 1944

It would be impossible to organise a service to place the disabled in jobs without knowing who they might be. So the Ministry of Labour set up a Register of Disabled Persons (leaflet D.P.L.1), on which the disabled might apply to be entered if they wished. There would be no obligation to be included, and many disabled persons—no-one knows the number—have not applied, and would not wish to appear on the list. Of those who have applied, only those capable of work, and satisfying the criteria mentioned earlier, have been accepted. Separate registers for the blind and the deaf, or nearly so in each category, have been established. The numbers reached their peak in 1950, when just over 900,000 were registered; after that, for various reasons, the numbers declined, and an average of two-thirds of a million would be a fair summary of the registered disabled in Britain at any one time. Registration has not been for all time; the length has varied according to the severity of the disablement, and might be anything from one year to ten. Thereafter, another application has had to be made. The decision whether or not to accept any application has not always been straightforward, and the local officer of the Ministry might have to submit the case to adjudication, as, though he has power to accept, where the case clearly satisfies the conditions, he has not had power to reject. To meet this eventuality local Disablement Advisory Committees were established, from which panels were selected to help the officer in those cases which presented a problem. Each panel contained one or more medical representatives and they, with the lay members, decided whether to issue or re-issue a certificate of registration.

The origins of a person's application to be registered could be various. A severely handicapped person might make his own decision to apply, or, having attended a special school, he might be advised by them to ask for registration. Many doctors, medical social workers, and other hospital staff have been responsible for bringing the register to the notice of the patients. In some cases the employer has urged his disabled workers to put forward their names, so that when it has come to the count, the firm would have its full quota (p. 62) of disabled on the payroll. In such cases, if the worker could prove disablement, and the employer substantiated his claim to have had difficulty in finding and keeping a job, his name would be entered. If, thereafter, the certificate was not renewed, he would, if he were still in the same employment, continue to count in his employer's quota, even though his name was no longer on the register.

When Ferguson, Macphail and McVean enquired into the employment problems of disabled youth in Glasgow, they found the origin of registration had a significant effect on the employment of the young. For instance, if it were at the suggestion of the special school, a high proportion seemed to find their way into skilled and semi-skilled jobs. Should it be the hospital staff who urged registration, most of the cases investigated were unemployed, as their disablement was severe, and the limited type of work they could do was not available in Glasgow. But young people registered at the instigation of their employers, were probably already settled in jobs, and unlikely to become unemployed.

The Disablement Resettlement Officer (D.R.O.). The linch-pin of the Ministry of Labour employment service for the disabled has been the establishment of a special officer, the D.R.O., to keep the Register, place a non-employed disabled person in suitable training if necessary, and ultimately help him find a job. His function, in some respects, has resembled that of the Y.E.O., in his efforts to match the person to the job, ensure progressive employment, and deal with any problems in a 'follow-up' service. A certain amount of controversy has arisen over the training and status of the D.R.O. It has been claimed that such an officer ought to have training at least as long as that of a Y.E.O., and because of the social and personal consequences of disablement, he should know something of the theory and practice of social casework. The Ministry has maintained, and has been supported in this by the Piercy Committee (Cmd. 9883, p. 94), that the job of a D.R.O. has been primarily to place a disabled person in suitable employment. To turn him into a social worker, with a special grade in the service would in their opinion be both unnecessary and undesirable. The D.R.O. has remained, therefore, part of the complement of the Ministry of Labour, drafted into the work for a period, usually of five years, and out of it again into another department. The Piercy Committee recommended that an officer's suitability and inclination for the work should be considered before being selected, and that he should have more than the three or four days of preliminary training which has previously been customary. Some attempt has been made to implement these suggestions. But the training afforded to the D.R.O. has in no way resembled in length or depth the preparation given in the training centres for the Y.E.O. On the other hand, his previous experience of the department, and of its placing service, have been invaluable, and the establishment of a specialist grade might block his road to promotion, and therefore create a barrier for those who would otherwise be attracted to the work.

The service has expected the D.R.O. to mobilise all the help he could obtain to promote the placing of a handicapped person in suitable work. He would constantly seek the co-operation of employers, and make himself familiar with the local occupations, where his clients might find work suitable to their capacities. The officer would be in close collaboration with hospitals, to help focus patients' minds on the idea of what jobs they could do, and to give them hope that even severe handicap would not necessarily mean the end of everything. Thus, after medical treatment the patient would be able to obtain a report for the D.R.O. on his condition, and an assessment of his medical possibilities for employment. Many hospitals have adopted the 'case conference' method, with doctors, medical social workers, and the D.R.O., to assess the case from all angles (leaflet P.L.412). If there should still be difficulty, the D.R.O. would be able to call in the Regional Medical Service of the Ministry of Health, or the Department of Health for Scotland. In addition, a regular system of medical interviewing committees, based on hospitals, has been established in various parts of the country; and in a few areas, regional medical advisers have been appointed to give advice on medical problems connected with rehabilitation and resettlement. With these and any other local resources, such as family casework agencies, S.S.A.F.A., and organisations for the disabled, including the local authority welfare department, the D.R.O. should not lack informed advice; and it has been for him to decide how far he could use it.

Advisory Committees. The 1944 Act set up a National Advisory Council on the Employment of the Disabled, to help the Ministry of Labour on the manifold problems arising from the new service. They have been particularly active on industrial rehabilitation, vocational training, sheltered work-shops, and the employment of the blind. At each of the major local employment exchanges a disablement advisory committee was appointed, representing workers and employers in equal numbers, and a few independent members, with an independent chairman. The local committees have had both an advisory and an executive function. Advisory, in the sense that problems of disablement arising locally might be reported to the Minister, with recommendations on how to meet them; and executive on certain specific matters. These have included decisions on admissions to the Disabled Persons Register, and questions about whether or not an employer should accept his 'quota' obligations, and if not, under what circumstances he could claim exemption. To help them, committees have often appointed panels of experienced people, such as medical practitioners, and representatives of employers and workers. Local advisory committees have tended to be a feature of modern statutory social services, but because of their executive functions the disablement committees have been more significant than most.

Industrial Rehabilitation (Leaflet R.H.L.1(E)). To prepare those who have had a disabling accident for full-time work in modern industry is no small task, but to build up the confidence of handicapped persons who have never done a normal job is even more difficult. The problem is not only whether a person is medically ready, or skilled enough, but whether he can bring himself to face all that working in a full-time job means. It was recognised from the beginning of the scheme that medical rehabilitation would have to start on the first day of treatment, and that industrial rehabilitation should follow rapidly. Thus medical and industrial preparation for employment have been inextricably mixed, and one of the regrets of the Piercy Committee was that the Industrial Rehabilitation Units (I.R.U.) had not been built on hospital sites.

The building of I.R.U.s was part of the Tomlinson scheme incorporated in the 1944 Act, though the I.R.U. at Egham, Surrey, was established even before the Act as the first and only fully residential centre. Its purpose was primarily to induce physical well-being with good food, fresh air, pleasant and comfortable surroundings, physical training, medical treatment, and a limited amount of useful indoor occupation. But it soon became clear that the problems of disablement went deeper than this; that the loss of physical robustness was probably the least of a disabled man's problems. All too often he had lost confidence in his ability to do any work at all, was deeply apprehensive about the future—particularly if he was unfit to return to his own job, and had neither the skill nor the understanding for any other. He was often beset by all kinds of psychological and social problems about himself, his family, his friends, and his role and status in his own community.

In consequence, the I.R.U.s began to change in character. The purely residential centre was not repeated, but new I.R.U.s were placed conveniently close to industrial areas, where the men and women, who needed them, could travel home at night. In this way the domestic problems, inevitable after a period of illness and perhaps separation, could sort themselves out at the same time as others were being tackled at the unit, and the person could find his level in his own community at the earliest moment, without an additional period of absence in a residential centre. The theory of the completely non-residential I.R.U. was not without its drawbacks. Some of the disabled had no home, while others lived too far away to commute daily, so the residential centre at Egham remained. Other units, like those at Leicester and Edinburgh, built their own hostels, and Coventry used a local authority hostel. By 1968, 17 I.R.U.s of all types had been established.

A second change was to use employment as a means of rehabilitation. One way of exercising a weakened limb would be to go into a gymnasium and use one of the machines designed for the purpose, but a better way would be to use a machine producing a useful article of commerce. The psychological satisfaction of the latter was soon seen to have incomparable value. More important still, by using his effort for productive purposes, a disabled man was accustoming himself to the atmosphere and tempo of industrial life, getting used to its stresses and disciplines, and regaining his old confidence in the handling of machines and tools.

A third development was in the type of staff employed at the I.R.U. The doctor remained part of the team, but leadership moved into lay hands. These two, helped by social workers, vocational officers, and a group of occupational supervisors, though in no sense giving industrial training, were able to impart simple instruction, and to assess a man's potentialities. Another, and very important aspect of the I.R.U. was to test, under practical conditions, a man's aptitudes and potential skills in various crafts, and his ability to stand up to the pressures of a working day. In this general appraisal, the D.R.O. has naturally played a major role as, without his knowledge of the actual openings, a man would have little chance of getting a job when his industrial rehabilitation was over.

Disabled men, women or young people (15 and over) registered as disabled were not automatically recommended for a course at the I.R.U. About 70 per cent applied at the suggestion of their medical advisers, others at the instigation of the D.R.O., because for long periods they were unable to find work, and have tended to lose confidence in themselves. Young disabled people may have been recommended by the Y.E.O. as part of the process of deciding what sphere of employment they would most satisfactorily fill (p. 43).

The period of training has been eight to twelve weeks, and for each trainee a course has been planned to offer the maximum advantage both in the work-shops and out of them. The work-shops have necessarily become the centre of the unit, and a variety of occupations has been made available, for example, machine-operating, bench engineering, wood-work, assembly and other light work, commercial and clerical, gardening, heavy work like concreting; every person had some choice. The units have usually been mixed, in the sense that all disabled were grouped together, men and women, adult and young. But a small minority, like Roffey Park for those with psychiatric handicaps, and Queen Elizabeth Homes of Recovery for the newly blind have segregated those with certain disabilities in special units.

The Ministry began some specialised experimental work in 1963, by establishing Industrial Therapy Organisations (I.T.O.) for long-term mental patients at Epsom and Hanwell. At these centres, opportunities for industrial rehabilitation in work-shops were offered to patients graduating from psychiatric hospitals and hoping to find their feet in normal employment. Entrance to them was normally, though not inevitably, via the hospital.

The problem of psychiatric maladjustment has always been difficult for the I.R.U.s, and several Ministry reports have pleaded for more orthopaedic, and other physical injury cases to be admitted, to secure a better balance between mental and physical disabilities. But many of those with physical handicap were found to be suffering from mental disability too.

The financial security of the trainee and his family (leaflet P.L.393) became the responsibility of the Ministry of Labour, who offered maintenance allowances on the same basis as if he were undergoing a recognised training (p. 10). As these allowances have always exceeded those of the National Insurance benefit, there has been a certain incentive to accept training if recommended; an incentive that was increased by the wage-related allowances of the 1966 Act (p. 161).

Since the I.R.U.s started, an average of about 7,000 trainees a year have completed courses. It is estimated that about one in six have left before the end, mainly for medical reasons, and that 70 per cent went straight into jobs, or training, from the centre. A check at the end of six months showed that two-thirds of these were still there. It has not been the policy of the Ministry to recommend 'unemployables' for I.R.U. training; at the same time, one has to recognise that only difficult cases have gone to the units. Whether a failure rate of approximately 40 per cent would be regarded as a serious criticism of the I.R.U.s depends on an estimate of what would have happened if there had been no scheme. On balance the contribution of the I.R.U.s to the health and productivity of the disabled would seem well worth the money and effort put into them.

Rehabilitation in industry. A few industrial firms have provided special rehabilitation work-shops for their own workers who have been disabled, holding that a man could best recover tone and skill in surroundings to which he was accustomed. The special work-shop set up by the Austin Motor Company in 1943 was probably the first of its kind in the world, and two years later Vauxhall Motors started a similar scheme. Other firms and some nationalised industries did the same. The outstanding features about the scheme were that the worker was productive for the firm and was paid. His status was therefore quite different from that of the I.R.U. trainee. The cost of these schemes would probably put them beyond the reach of any but the largest firms, and their success has depended upon close co-operation between all concerned—the medical team, social workers, the hospital and the firm. Where practicable, they have been a valuable element in the total provision for rehabilitation.

Government Training Centres

The Ministry of Labour training schemes have been available to various classes of workers, but up to the 1960s, and the change in government policy towards training, more than half those trained in government training centres were disabled. So this might appear the appropriate place to discuss the training service provided by them (leaflets P.L.406 and 408).

Government training centres were a creation of the First World War, being designed in 1917 primarily for the training of ex-servicemen unable to return to their former occupations. By 1919 they had become the responsibility of the Ministry of Labour, and remained active for a few years helping to re-train repatriated members of the armed forces for civilian life. They were not completely abolished in the inter-war years, so that when the Second World War demanded skilled workers, the organisation quickly sprang into life again. The G.T.C.s continued until after the war was over, and the next re-training of ex-servicemen for post-war civilian life had been achieved. Nor have they ever again sunk into the torpor they experienced in the 1930s; they have remained to be expanded or contracted according to the needs of economic policy, or the changes in the philosophy of governments. The centres were well equipped, and staffed by qualified supervisors, giving intensive courses of training for a variety of occupations. Building, hairdressing, radio and television servicing, tailoring, watch repairing were among the trades taught, and any visitor would be impressed by the standard of skill reached by the trainees. The work-shops operated on a basis as near to ordinary industry as possible, and in certain cases the trainee would continue his training for an agreed period, with selected employers, after the initial course, the Ministry paying a fee to the firm for the service. Most courses lasted six months, but could be extended, especially where the skills could not be acquired in less than a year. What was surprising was the high degree of competence that could be acquired in a relatively short time through intensive training; and what was saddening was the failure in many cases to recognise men and women trained in this way, as fully-fledged tradesmen, though in fairness it should be said that many ex-trainees, after several years' experience, have been able to work their way up to craftsmen's status, and others, by special agreement (e.g., A.E.U. Dilution of Labour Agreements) have been accepted on completion of training. It was a universal principle that no-one should be selected for training, either in a government centre, or in other establishments recognised by the Ministry, unless there was a reasonable prospect of employment in the occupation for which he was trained. In practice, a high proportion of those trained were so placed immediately, or within a short time of completion.

Though the vocational training of adult able-bodied workers has been almost entirely in the G.T.C.s, the disabled have been offered wider opportunities, and have been trained at Ministry expense, at local technical or commercial colleges, or in appropriate cases, have gone to a university. If local facilities were not available, or the person suffered a handicap for which specialised provision had to be made, the Ministry had power to place him in a residential establishment.[1] It is estimated that in the 1950s about 5,000 men and women, both able-bodied and disabled, were in

[1] For example, St. Loyes College Exeter, Queen Elizabeth's College Leatherhead, Finchale Abbey Durham, Portland College Mansfield, Lingfield Epileptic Colony.

training at any one time, but in the 1960s the average annual intake had been multiplied many times (to over 100,000), the vast majority being able-bodied. A small number of disabled (for example, a few adult blind at Letchworth) were placed, at the expense of the Ministry, with private employers, to be trained in a skill, under ordinary industrial conditions, and side by side with ordinary able-bodied trainees.

The training of the blind for open employment was for years the concern of the education authorities, local and national, but from 1948 it was put on the same footing as for other disabled persons (leaflet D.P.L.8), and though the administration of sheltered workshops for the blind was to remain a local authority responsibility, training passed to the Ministry of Labour.

Maintenance grants, whether for the able-bodied or not, were made available to all who took advantage of Ministry of Labour courses. Under certain conditions they were wage-related (leaflet P.L.394) (p. 161), and covered the needs of the trainee and his family, his travelling expenses, and any special expenses, such as tools.

The quota. The majority of disabled adults and young people, whether the accident or disease was contracted at the place of employment or not, were able to return to their old jobs, and after a few months of adjustment, achieved their former standards of skill and output. For a few this was not possible, especially for those born severely handicapped, where normal employment has never been obtained, or where the disability was such that return to previous work would be injudicious.

It was for these that the Disabled Persons (Employment) Act 1944 (amended on some minor points in 1958) put obligations on employers to accept a proportion of disabled on their payroll. The 'Quota', (leaflet D.P.L.2) as it came to be called, was nothing new for employers, as it had been developed in principle as early as 1919, with the establishment of the King's National Roll. A completely voluntary scheme, it was inaugurated by employers concerned about the fate of ex-service men and women disabled in the 1914–18 war. Those who joined the Roll covenanted to accept disabled ex-servicemen in ordinary employment, up to at least five per cent of their payroll. The Roll did not recognise civilian disabled, or disabled ex-service personnel from any other war; but as a voluntary gesture of goodwill it was undoubtedly effective. From the beginning it was under Royal patronage, and the firms accepted by the King's Roll were assured of preference in the allocation of government contracts. It is difficult to tell whether or not this was the reason, but it continued through the major part of the 20th century, even after it had been superseded by the 1944 'Quota', and when disabled personnel of the First World War, still able to work, had dwindled to very few.

The success of the King's Roll emboldened the legislators in 1944 to incorporate a 'Quota' in the new Disabled Persons (Employment) Bill, and to make it compulsory on employers. They excluded the very small employer from the mandate, as he would not have the variety of jobs, or the same room for re-shuffling, as the larger firm, but firms employing more than twenty were thought capable of fitting a small proportion of handicapped workers into their normal establishment. It was not intended that management should employ a disabled person unfitted for the work, but that, with the help of all concerned, a suitable disabled person could be matched to an appropriate job.

The quota percentage was at first fixed at two per cent, and raised to three per cent in 1946. This was smaller than that of the King's Roll, though being compulsory it was deemed large enough to avoid being a burden on industry. Compulsion did not mean it was a statutory duty to employ a quota of disabled people, but every employer employing less than the minimum had to notify the Ministry of Labour, and was expected to fill his quota before taking on any other staff, unless he obtained an exemption permit from the Ministry. Thus, at any one time, a number of firms would not be employing their full complement, since for one reason or another they had not been able to fit the available disabled to the vacant posts; but every employer was under pressure from the Ministry to fulfil his obligations generously. An inquiry undertaken in July 1965 revealed that of 66,361 firms, who should have employed at least three per cent of their employees from the Disabled Register, 31,038 were employing fewer than the minimum. At about the same time 47,223 disabled persons were unemployed. Ministry success in making firms fill their quota has varied from time to time, but no firms have been penalised for omission. It was the view of the Piercy Committee in 1956 that the main value of the quota lay in its educational importance, because it demonstrated the wide range of occupations that could be successfully under-taken by the disabled.

In a limited number of cases the Ministry has been willing to lend special aids to workers who would otherwise be unable to take or keep a job in ordinary industry—for example, a special seat, or an attachment to work a machine. But such aids would normally be provided by the employer, or even the worker him-self, and the D.R.O. has been obliged to follow up the loan to see that the aid has been used, and to have it repaired or replaced if necessary. Workers confined to their own homes have borrowed tools and machines on the same basis.

Designated Employment (leaflet D.P.L.2)

The suggestion that certain occupations should be reserved for the disabled has often been canvassed as a means of fitting them into industry. But it was the view of both the Tomlinson and Piercy Committees, and of most thinking people, that to do so would be severely to restrict the prospects of all. If the aim were to make a disabled person feel as normal as possible, there would always be danger in artificial segregation. If the reserved jobs were too numerous or too high-grade, the willing co-operation of both sides of industry would be hard to obtain. But if such jobs were limited to low-grade employments, it might create the impression that the disabled were only fit for menial tasks. The 1944 Act did allow for the creation of designated classes of employment, but the power has been used sparingly, and two occupations only have been agreed to, those of passenger electric lift attendant, and car park attendant. Since 1946 these have been reserved (with a few excep-tions), for handicapped workers, it being understood that employ-ment in them would not be included in an employer's quota.

Sheltered workshops. In spite of the general theory that disabled people should be employed as normal workers in ordinary industry, people have had to recognise that a few would be too unfit for this, and that they would have to content themselves with the status of parasites on society, or work in 'sheltered' employment. For many years voluntary organisations have refused to accept the idea that human beings should be permanently relegated to the social dust-heap, and have established places where the blind and crippled could do some useful work, even if it were subsidised. In certain cases the local authorities set up independent work-shops, or grant-aided those already provided by charitable bodies. Such sources of work, for handicapped people, were sporadic and varied in quality. But they at least provided the impetus for a national scheme which would recognise the human right of disabled men and women to take their place as workers in society, as well as the need of society for what they could produce.

The Scheme of grants. Shortly after the First World War, the Ministry of Labour was giving grants to voluntary bodies, such as the Lord Roberts Memorial Workshops for sheltered employment for the badly disabled. Grant-aid was continued in principle by the 1944 Act, which allowed the Ministry to make up trading losses, and finance the capital expenditure of undertakings employing disabled people under normal industrial conditions, provided the products had a substantial economic value.[1]

Meanwhile local authorities had been active in providing sheltered work-shops, especially for the blind (leaflets D.P.L.8, 11, 12), for whom they had responsibility under the Blind Persons Act. This responsibility was exercised, either directly by the local authority, or indirectly through grant-aid to voluntary organisations. The 1944 Act empowered the Ministry to give financial assistance to local authorities which had established work-shops for the blind, and the 1958 Act brought them under the general supervision of the Ministry of Labour, though administration remained with the local council. The National Assistance Act 1948, besides making the welfare of the blind a statutory duty of the larger local authorities, also laid upon them the responsibility for the welfare of all disabled persons within their area. This permissive power became an obligation in 1961, and several county and borough councils have interpreted welfare as the provision of sheltered workshops for both blind and sighted disabled citizens. Some of them have used the workshops for the blind for all suitable disabled workers needing special provision, but others have preferred to segregate those suffering from different forms of handicap (blind, tuberculous, etc.) in separate establishments. Since 1958, provided the work-shops have been approved by the

[1] In 1961, 30 undertakings were grant-aided in this way, and 67 work-shops for the blind.

Ministry, the local authorities have received grants for them (for deficiency payments, or towards capital expenditure incurred for either training or employment purposes), and have become eligible, as 'priority suppliers', for government contracts. Not that this has conferred any favours about price, but it has meant contracts being offered to them at a price the purchasing departments considered 'fair', or sub-contract work from the trade.

One of the problems of the sheltered work-shops, particularly for the blind, has been the practice of 'augmenting' wages, to bring the income of disabled workers to a reasonable level. The Piercy Committtee in 1956 was concerned about the effect of this. For if workers knew their wages would be made up to a minimum in any case, there was little incentive to increase production to a level commensurate with the wage. While the committee recognised that by the very nature of the situation no-one would work in a sheltered work-shop if he could compete in the open market, they thought it right to point out that the work done in these work-shops was employment, in the true sense of the word, and that the goods produced were sold in the open market. It was wrong to confuse 'employment' of this kind with 'diversionary occupation', the function of the welfare department of the local authority. The Piercy Committee recommended, therefore, that the work done in sheltered work-shops should contain an incentive element in the system of payment, and that 'augmentation' of wages should be withdrawn, as far as possible.

On the other hand, one has to remember, a sheltered work-shop has a dual purpose. It has provided permanent employment for those unfitted for normal industry, or has constituted a half-way house for injured or diseased workers, who at first have not been able to enter open industry, but who later have managed to work up to the speed or skill of an ordinary job. The young handicapped have needed special consideration, because their confidence in their ability to work in open industry has been sadly lacking, and their capacity to acquire the necessary manual dexterity for modern industry has occasionally been slower than normal. The Thomas Committee made a strong plea to admit them to sheltered work-shops as a start, even if it meant supplementing their wages; suggesting that once they became used to an everyday job, they should move on. It was pointed out, for instance, that some spastics were not able to take full advantage of the training offered by the Ministry of Labour, but that if they were given training at a slower pace in a sheltered workshop (for example, Sherrards), their confidence in themselves would improve, and they would later be able to move to more advanced training, and perhaps subsequently to open employment.[1]

Remploy (leaflet D.P.L.12)

By the middle of the 20th century the value of sheltered workshops had been proved, so it is not surprising they should find their place in the national scheme for the employment of the disabled. The first Remploy factory was set up in 1946, under the authority of the Disabled Persons' Employment Corporation (known as Remploy Ltd.). This was a public corporation, under the Ministry of Labour (1944 Act) and was required to apply its income (including profits if any) for the promotion of its aim, the provision of sheltered employment for the disabled. It was a commercial concern, not a charitable undertaking, and though it expected to employ only the severely disabled, its goods would necessarily compete on the open market, and its costs would, as far as possible, be met out of its sales. Losses, if any, would be met from public funds.

The employees, though recruited mainly from those who could not 'hold their own on level terms under competitive conditions', included a small percentage (the Act allowed up to 15 per cent) of able-bodied or less severely disabled people to fill key posts such as those of craftsmen or skilled workers who would be able to give training to the rest, or to provide a core of staff without whom it would have been difficult to make the factory commercially viable. Each worker, whether disabled or not, worked a standard week, with scales of wages not inferior to those for similar work in open industry, and with provision for periodical increases.

A large proportion of the products was disposed of, through the normal channels, including government departments, nationalised industries and other public bodies, at competitive prices. At first Remploy tended to follow the practice of local authority and voluntarily sponsored workshops for the disabled, and produced

---

[1] By 1961 some 49 workers with cerebral palsy had entered jobs in this way, and had kept them for four years.

goods requiring a high degree of skill. Later, it saw the advantage of mass production by machine processes capable of being divided into a linked series of simple operations, quickly learnt by otherwise unskilled workers. In this, it was much helped by a 'sponsoring scheme', where private firms provided the plant, equipment, materials and know-how, agreeing to take the finished product at an arranged price, and Remploy provided the factory space, labour and skilled management.

The success of Remploy, financial and social, depended on management. What was needed was all the managerial skill of normal industry, plus an understanding of handicapped people, combining the right mixture of sympathy and firmness.

The Piercy Committee received evidence that was critical of the operation of Remploy. It was suggested that jobs had been given to some workers who were not suitable, either because they were not disabled enough, and could have found work in open industry, or because they were so severely unfit that they could not make a fair contribution to production. In consequence, the Committee recommended that Remploy should review its practice, to see whether a better assessment of aptitude and capacity could be made before a person was offered a job. It was this proposal that resulted in the development of I.R.U.s as assessment agencies.

Further difficulties faced by Remploy were the relatively high average age of the operatives, (in 1956 nearly half were 50 years of age or more), absenteeism due to sickness (sometimes a third were away ill), and a high labour turnover (more than 10 per cent leaving each year), some having found jobs in ordinary industry. In consequence the annual deficit has been fairly high (on average about £2 millions).

The essential issue to be faced has been the real purpose of Remploy. Was it a government owned factory, whose costs were covered by its sales? Some Remploys were in this position, and this led many to argue that if it could happen in one factory it ought to be possible in all, and that given good management, and an effective sales policy, every Remploy could be self-supporting. But others argued that this was a social service, offering to the disabled and their families psychological as well as material advantages, and allowing the community at large to reap some benefit from citizens whose condition might otherwise have rendered them completely dependent. If Remploys (like any other 'sheltered' work-shops) became half-way houses for the severely disabled to find their way back to open employment, the protagonists continued, then all to the good, even if it meant the factory losing its most efficient and effective workers.

How to reconcile these different points of view has been Remploy's dilemma; and since it was public money that met the deficit, requiring parliamentary sanction through the Ministry of Labour vote, the dilemma has been argued first in one way and then in the other, throughout the history of the service. How far a compromise has been struck, it would be unwise to speculate. But it has been to everybody's credit that the social service aspect has never been abandoned, though every Remploy has been increasingly conscious of the need to meet its own costs if at all possible.[1]

Home-workers. Home-working schemes (not to be confused with the occupational schemes of the welfare services) would seem, at first sight, to be an obvious way of providing employment for the disabled. Several local authorities and voluntary organisations have organised such schemes, particularly for the blind, and have augmented earnings, receiving in return grant-aid from the Ministry of Labour of up to 75 per cent of approved expenditure. Remploy have had the right to do likewise, and several have developed local schemes. The difficulties of keeping these schemes in being have been immense, partly through the scarcity of suitable work for people so severely disabled that they have not been able to leave home, partly through the difficulties connected with standards of output, distribution of materials, and collection of the finished article. Moreover, work in the home could not be supervised, and workers might be working long hours to produce what was required. In any case, home-work has usually meant 'hand-work', such as the making of toys, lamp-shades, baskets, or the assembling of components. Without adequate machinery and the equipment of a factory, there has always been the danger of 'sweating' in such enterprises. Opinion has therefore moved away from encouraging more work at home, towards providing adequate transport to bring all but the completely immobile together into a factory.

[1] By March 1965 there were 88 Remploy factories, with a turnover of £7 million, employing about 7,000 disabled workers.

Grants to set up in business. A further measure for which the Disabled Persons (Employment) Act 1944 made provision was the grant of a lump sum to those disabled persons who, though too unfit to be employed by others, might, with the help of relatives, start their own business. In the first few years the idea had a limited usefulness, but setting up in business, particularly small business, proved a risky venture in most cases and few succeeded. It was decided, therefore, that the scheme should be severely restricted, and that only in exceptional circumstances, where other means of resettlement had been found impracticable, should assistance be given. Where it was used, careful supervision and follow-up was exercised, to ensure that the recipient had expert advice and guidance whenever he needed it.

The rehabilitation and resettlement of the disabled is a major undertaking, involving resources of money, goodwill, skilled medical and social care, and a profound sense of responsibility by the community. The services developed in the United Kingdom (Northern Ireland has had its own legislation, but the services have not materially differed from the rest of Britain) have gone a long way to ensure that a disabled person, whether young or older, shall have the opportunity to gain enough confidence and training to undertake a job, and be helped to find employment suitable to himself. All the same, the rate of unemployment has, throughout, been significantly higher than for the working population as a whole.[1] Whether the rate could be reduced is something the Ministry might well consider as a subject for further research.

---

[1] January 1966 of 659,000 on the Disabled Persons' Register, 48,000 (or 7·3 per cent) were unemployed (including 7,000 severely disabled and suitable only for sheltered employment).

PART II

SOCIAL SERVICES IN PLACES OF WORK

IV

HOURS, SAFETY, HEALTH AND WELFARE IN INDUSTRY

THE EARLIEST SOCIAL service to be applied to factories and other places of work, such as mines and quarries, came into being in a haphazard, piecemeal way. At the beginning of the 19th century, when the first Factory Acts were passed, no-one would have thought they were witnessing the birth of a social service, and many have failed to recognise it as such down to the present day. Yet here we have a system of obligations and responsibilities, aimed at avoiding or reducing the dangers to work-people— dangers that have arisen out of their occupation, whether through the risk of accident or of damage to health; aimed also at promoting the 'welfare' of workers in certain clearly defined spheres.

The legislation itself followed the failure of employers and others to appreciate the sufferings of many workers, especially those of women and young people, and was an attempt to redress a situation in which the individual was weak, and required the protection and humanity of the community when in need. Modern historians, while accepting the accounts of the horrors and abuses of the industrial system as true, have tried to put things into per-spective by reminding us about the general standards of the times. Long hours of work, with little regard to health or hygiene, were the norm. Cruelty and pain were generally accepted, if they were kept within bounds. A rigid class system was approved both by those who were 'high-born' and those who expected to be subordinate all their lives. In view of such generally accepted standards, abuse must have been excessive and widespread to give rise to the gathering volume of protest, such as can be read in the official writings of the day, like minutes of evidence to Royal Commissions, and which led to the formation of societies seeking reform, and ultimately to legislation itself.

While factory law began as a 'negative' service, in the sense that it set out to stop certain things being done, it could not long remain so, and 'promoting' became just as important as 'preventing'. For instance, a factory owner was obliged to see that his workers were not maimed by unsafe machinery. To do this, he had to put guards on the parts that were unsafe. From this it was but a short step to the recommendation that certain guards were better than others, and that ineffective guards would not be tolerated. Or again, the earlier Factory Acts were concerned with dangerous appliances, or dangerous conditions of work, but this could not long remain a policy of avoidance, since healthy or safe machinery, materials, and places of work have been shown to depend as much on their safe usage as on their own intrinsic safety. So the promoting of 'safety' as an attitude of mind, or a method of working, has come to be an accepted aim of the social service itself. Thus has the more positive, even educational aspect of factory law come to play a part as large as the correctional side.

When tracing the growth of the factories' and mines' legislation, historians have customarily pointed to the 1802 Act as being the earliest, since it was concerned with the ventilation and cleanliness of textile mills, in an attempt to improve the lot of child apprentices. But the really important foundation stone of modern practice was the Factory Act of 1833 which, though it did not deal with the fencing of machinery, or the safety of the work-place, went some way towards regulating hours for women and children, and introduced the Factory Inspector, to ensure that the law was not a dead letter. It was the appointment of the inspector that was the turning point. For he not only checked abuses, he was able to advise the 'occupier' on measures that would lead to greater health and safety, and to supply the government with facts to make up the blue prints of subsequent legislation. After 1833, a vast array of statutes, regulations, orders in council, and other legal measures have appeared, and will most probably continue to appear, as new inventions disclose new dangers, and the public conscience about health, safety and welfare at work becomes sharpened and refined. Yet the shape of the social service has shown little change since 1833, when the appointment of the earliest officials first took place.

If one asks what the service is about, it is clear that it covers four main areas of industrial life: hours of work, safety, health, and welfare; these four aspects have been dominated in the later 20th century by several major Factories' and other Acts of Parliament[1] and much contributory legislation.[2] There has been no blanket Act covering every aspect of the problem, and gaps in the service have remained unplugged for many years. Thus it was as late as 1963 before legislation provided much needed protection for clerks and other workers in offices, and it was to the same Act we owe the legal pronouncement on 'securing' the health, safety and welfare of the appropriate persons, rather than the 'prevention' of untoward happenings; although this more positive concept had been common practice for many years.

Hours of work

Statutory regulation of working hours may have appeared super-fluous since the Second World War, as trade union power in these matters has asserted itself, and for the majority of workers national agreements about weekly hours of work, and days of leisure, have been negotiated. Such a view would neglect the minority, who have not been covered, and most important of all, would omit the children, adolescents and women, whom the experience of two centuries has shown to be most in need of protection, not least from themselves.

In reviewing the development of British policy towards hours of labour, three aspects strike one as surprising. Firstly, it took so long to bring in any legal regulation of hours at all. Secondly, when an Act was passed, it nearly always referred to one industry only. Thirdly, with few exceptions, adult males have been excluded altogether from any legal control of working hours.

The historian has provided ample evidence of the prolonged struggle to achieve a limitation of hours. In spite of the traditional habit of outdoor workers, who worked from dawn to dusk, and even longer in the home industries of the 18th and 19th centuries,

---

[1] The Factories Act, 1961; Mines and Quarries Act, 1954; Shops Act, 1950; Agriculture Act, 1956; Offices, Shops and Railway Premises Act, 1963. By 1968 a major review of the legislation was in hand.

[2] For example, Employment of Women, Young Persons and Children Acts, 1920, 1936; Children and Young Persons Act, 1933, 1963; Education Act, 1944; Young Persons (Employment) Act, 1938, as well as Public Health Acts, Merchant Shipping and Civil Aviation Acts. The Acts have generally applied to the whole of Britain, though in most cases, Northern Ireland has introduced its own parallel legislation.

it was soon realised, by those who experienced it, that work in a factory was a very different matter. The confinement of indoor work, the tyranny of the machine, and the need to keep up production, both to satisfy the overmen, who were expected to produce a certain amount each day, and the need to earn enough for the worker himself to live on, resulted in physical and emotional stress that was highly exhausting. There seemed only two answers—a rapid turn-over of labour or a limitation of hours. Against the social background, and the fact that labour was plentiful, it was a rapid turnover through wastage of labour by reason of illness and death that was accepted as the natural order of events.

Hutchins and Harrison have described the first piece of legislation in 1802, limiting the hours of apprentices in cotton mills to 12 a day, as 'merely an extension of the Elizabethan Poor Law relating to parish apprentices', and this perhaps illustrates, in an age of laissez-faire, the reformers' difficulties in achieving some legal control of working hours as a change necessary in itself. The difficulties continued, and progress throughout the 19th century was erratic. Thus in 1833, youngsters up to 18 years of age in textile factories were limited to a maximum ten-hour day, and in 1848 women's hours were similarly controlled. Gradually, other industries were obliged to limit the hours for women and children to ten, and then to nine. The 48-hour week was not secured for all adolescents between sixteen and eighteen (only 44 for under 16s) and all women working in factories until the 1937 Factories Act. In 1961 the possibility of the five-day week was recognised, and daily hours for these workers was limited to ten[1]. Night work for these categories was abolished, by the stipulation that work should not begin before 7 a.m., or continue after 8 p.m. (6 p.m. for children under 16). In special circumstances an employer was allowed to seek exemption from these limitations so that, for example, shift work for women could be organised.[2] The span of work attracted official attention, and women and children were normally obliged to take at least half an hour's rest after four and a half hours' work, though if a ten minute break was organised, the span could be five hours. Similarly, overtime was severely

[1] Factories Act, 1961. Short Guide by Ministry of Labour.

[2] Exemptions covering about 90,000 women, and 10,000 juveniles over 16 have been granted annually (cf. *Ministry of Labour Gazette*).

limited, to six hours a week (nil for under sixteens), or 100 hours in a year, during not more than 25 weeks in the year, and the daily working hours with overtime were restricted too.

Sunday work in factories for this class of worker has been forbidden (except for those observing the Jewish Sabbath), and all women and young persons in the factories of England and Wales have been assured of six days holiday each, including Christmas Day, Good Friday, and the four Bank Holidays, while workers in Scotland have also had six days, three of which must be taken between March and October. Apart from this, and the statutory holidays awarded to workers under wages councils (p. 101), legal holidays for the British worker have not yet been secured.

The outline of the main provisions of the Factories Acts as they relate to hours of work has illustrated to some extent the point that they usually dealt with one group of workers, or one industry, at a time; it might be juveniles, or women, or textile mills, or the hosiery trade, or even all manufacturing industries; excluding the rest, and leaving many gaps. Women, for instance, were banned from working underground in the mines, in 1842, but they could still work above-ground, and were not then subject to the Factory Acts. Their position was finally controlled by the Mines and Quarries Acts, though it was not until 1954 that they reached the protection given to other women under the earlier Factories Acts.

Another forgotten group were the shop assistants, whose hours and conditions of work, right down to the 20th century, were appalling. In 1886 there had been an attempt to limit adolescents to 74 hours a week, but it was not enforced, and therefore seldom obeyed. There were no recognised meal times, and assistants had to snatch something to eat while keeping an eye on their counters. The first effective respite came in 1912 with the legal half-holiday, and the Early Closing Acts of the First World War produced a further curtailment of their hours of duty. At that time the closing of the shop was not synonymous with stopping work; as clearing up, stock-taking, and preparing goods for the next day were to be done after closing time on an ordinary day, and sometimes during the half holiday too. Shop assistants had to wait until 1934 before a Shops Act gave them adequate protection, following the recommendations of a Select Committee in 1931, and until the Shops' Act 1950, for further improvements. There was one vital difference between the regulation of hours in shops and those in factories.

In shops it was the hours of young people only that were controlled—women were excluded.

Otherwise the provisions of the Shops Acts were similar to the
Factories Acts, including a maximum 48-hour week (44 for those
under 16), limited overtime for those between 16 and 18, with not
more than 50 hours in any one year. An interesting modification of
the 48-hour week has been the 96-hour fortnight, allowed in certain trades such as garages or catering, to cover the special needs of
businesses in holiday resorts. The system of averaging has been
strictly controlled, and where it has been used, overtime has been
illegal. As for closing times, local authorities have been permitted
to decide on the actual time, which must ordinarily not be later
than 8 p.m. Mondays to Fridays and 9 p.m. on Saturdays, with
1 p.m. on the day of the half-holiday. The Shops (Early Closing
Days) Act 1965, amended the power of the local authority, by
permitting traders themselves to decide on the day they would
observe for early closing. Traders were thus enabled to introduce
the five-day week without having to close on another afternoon
fixed by the council.

Sunday trading has been illegal in England and Wales (but not
in Scotland) for many years, and the Shops Acts have simply
continued the prohibition. On the other hand such goods as fruit,
flowers, vegetables, refreshments, and cycle accessories have been
exempt, and traders have been allowed to carry on business to
8 p.m. or even 9.30 for the sale of tobacco and sweets. The Sunday
trading anomalies have been widely deplored, and much play has
been made on the right to buy a fresh peach, but not a tinned one,
and on the temptations for illegal trading that shops have faced.

Even the normal week-day closing hours have had many
exemptions, particularly over the sale of tobacco and sweets, and
the whole question of trading hours in Britain has long been a
subject of controversy. The intention was partly to protect the
shop assistants (the Half-Day Holiday Act 1912), and partly to
husband resources, and discourage late shopping during wartime
(the Early Closing Acts). But, it has been argued, much greater
flexibility is needed. Evidence from Europe and the United States
has been used to stress the greater profitability to shop-keepers,
and the greater convenience to shoppers, if shops keep open most
of the 24 hours, closing, say, between midnight and 6 a.m. Shop
assistants would still be protected, it is alleged, basically by legal

regulation of hours (allowing for a shift system), and also by voluntary negotiation.[1] In 1965 an inter-departmental document (Retail Trading Hours) reported that retail trading was a key sector of the economy, where, if faster economic growth and higher living standards were to be achieved, a more efficient use of resources was essential. Further, if it were to provide the maximum service to the community, the greatest flexibility, subject to the necessary safeguards, in retail arrangements should be the aim. The Committee's proposal of a 7 p.m. closing hour (9 p.m. on a Saturday) has not been widely acclaimed as meeting the case of the critics. On the other hand, it cannot be often enough emphasised that without a well enforced legal limit to working hours for assistants, the abolition of a legal closing time would open the door to the most serious abuses. Moreover the owner-operated shop would have no protection at all, and individuals might be tempted to work excessive hours.

The employment of school children has been another problem to be separately dealt with. Before the Education Acts, and the institution of a minimum school leaving age, the gainful employment of children was not a problem of regular attendance at school, as it is now, but of the possible abuse of child labour. The earliest legislation to improve the conditions of work and hours of labour was therefore concerned with this aspect of the matter. The introduction of compulsory school attendance presented a new factor, since it was now necessary not only to protect the health and normal development of the growing child, but to safeguard his scholastic career. As the years of compulsory attendance lengthened, the problem deepened. For, it was said, many boys of 12 years or so were quite able to undertake light employment during the hours they were not at school. They enjoyed earning money, and it was far better for them to be gainfully employed than lounging about the streets, getting into mischief. Against this, the educationists argued that the danger of exploitation was ever-present. Once you tolerate school-child labour, who knows what hours of work, what threat to health, what interference in the normal development of a child, his studies and his chances of social intercourse, might occur? It was better, in their opinion, for

[1] U.S.D.A.W., with a membership of 350,000, is strong enough, it is said, fully to protect the shop-assistants.

all to be barred from the temptation of gainful employment during their school career, than to jeopardise the prospects of the minority who might suffer. There was plenty of experience, as late as the early 20th century, of children falling asleep over their desks at school, of health undermined, and studies affected).

A compromise has been reached (mainly in the Children and Young Persons Acts 1933 and 1963, the Education Act 1944, and to some extent in the Young Persons Employment Acts 1936 and 1938) with an overall embargo on the employment of children within two years of school-leaving age, and with L.E.A.s having the right to make bye-laws raising the age of an embargo on employment within their own areas. Some have raised it to the minimum school-leaving age. Others have limited school-child labour to boys only, and have stated the kind of employment they might accept, for example, that of messengers. All have been concerned about the number of hours a child could work. On school days this could never be more than two, and could not begin earlier than 6 a.m. or finish later than 8 p.m. On Saturdays there was no limitation except those laid down by individual L.E.A.s. Inevitably, exceptions to the general rule have been allowed. For instance, a child working for his parents on the land could start at ten years, the assumption being that a parent would protect the welfare of his own child. Similarly, a child under 13 could be employed on a stage show, provided his education was not interrupted, and the facts were registered with the L.E.A., who must give approval. Factories themselves have been forbidden to employ children under school-leaving age, which, in practice, has meant after the end of the spring or summer term after they have reached the minimum age for leaving. Establishments not registered under the Factories Acts have not always been limited in this way.

The above has illustrated the piecemeal growth of a hetero-geneous array of prohibitions on the amount of time certain categories of workers might spend at work. The one group that in almost all circumstances has been omitted has been the men, including young men of 18 and over. It should not be thought that no efforts were made during the heyday of factory reform in the 19th and early 20th centuries to bring the adult male worker within the ambit of legal regulation. But in spite of the efforts of Cobbett and other parliamentarians to introduce Bills, nothing was achieved. It was said to be an infringement of the basic freedom of a man to work as long as he wished. When he no longer wanted to work such long hours, he would stop. In practice, this is what ultimately happened, as by strengthening his trade union, and bringing hours of work into the domain of collective bargaining, men have succeeded in drastically reducing the length of the working day. But much time elapsed, and in the meantime the hours of adult male labour could be very long. They would have been still longer, but for the legislation controlling the hours worked by women and children. For in those areas, especially the mills of Lancashire and Yorkshire, where girls and women were extensively employed, it was uneconomic to keep the mill open for men alone, and the ten-hour day for women meant, in most cases, a ten-hour day for men too. This gave rise to the famous remark by an Oldham Spinners' secretary, that the men's industrial battle for shorter hours was fought from behind the women's petticoats.

Though the majority of men had no legal regulation of hours, several pieces of legislation were passed for exceptional trades, particularly those where over-work might mean danger to the workers themselves, or to the public. A good example of the latter were the lorry drivers, who might be the cause of road accidents if they drove too long and became too tired. Thus Acts were passed making it an offence to drive for more than five and a half hours at a stretch, or longer than 11 hours in any 24. This applied to all drivers of public service vehicles, heavy or light locomotives or goods vehicles (Road Traffic Acts 1960 to 1967).

The earliest legislation was designed to protect workers in the most dangerous occupation of all, the coal mine. Underground working was limited in 1908, and by 1954 had been reduced to seven hours a day. The only other example of the legal control of men's hours has been by the wages councils (p. 101). In this case, the object was not to reduce the hours of work, since overtime was unlimited, but to safeguard the hourly rates of pay. Thus the intention was quite different from the statutory control of women's hours, though the effect was not so different. It has been estimated that about 12 per cent[1] of all working men in the country

[1] Out of a total male working population in England and Wales of about 17 millions, miners represent about half a million, drivers and others about half a million and men under wages councils another million, a total of about two million adult males whose hours are controlled in some way.

have been affected by the limitation of hours regulations.

Hours of work have been a favourite topic for research for many years, particularly since World War I. Surveys[1] have been made, showing that long hours have tended to increase the time lost through sickness, by both men and women, or that productivity has actually increased when hours have been shorter. On the other hand productivity has been affected by the method of operation. Where a man worked on his own, shorter hours meant higher output, up to a point, and then the reverse process set in. Where a number of individuals worked together, each setting his own pace, this fact was disastrous to group output. In consequence there was a tendency to take the pace-setting out of the hands of the individual and transfer it to the machine. The moving belt, made famous in the 1920s by Henry Ford in the U.S.A., was the prototype. Thus shorter hours could mean lower productivity, unless the pace of the machine were speeded up, when it meant a greater danger of accidents.

In any operation demanding the active participation of workers, productivity depends on a nice balance between hours of work and the human capacity to stand the strain without spoiling work or causing accidents. But when the need for human intervention declines, and the 'press-button' factory becomes a reality, the actual time worked by each operative becomes less important than the fallibility or otherwise of the machine.

Productivity cannot and should not be the only consideration. The health, welfare, and progressively improving standards of living for those involved are of vital importance too. Shorter hours, with greater opportunities of leisure and freedom from the strain of modern industry, have become a goal in themselves. What started as an attempt to protect the weak, and those in very dangerous jobs, has become an objective of the 'better life'.

Safety

As we have seen, there has always been a close connection between long hours of work and danger to the worker, but the campaign for greater safety has had to be fought on a wider front than that, since by the very nature of industrial life people are put at risk.

[1] For example H. M. Vernon 'Hours of work and their Influence on Health and Efficiency'. British Association for Labour Legislation 1943.

The extent of the risk has been all too tragically illustrated by the steady rise in the number of accidents during the latter part of the 20th century.[1] For in spite of all that has been done, and the small consolation in the fact that fatal accidents have declined, the persistence of serious accidents is a source of much uneasiness in the Ministry of Labour, which is responsible for the factory service, and in the trade unions with their consciousness of the danger to life and limb to their members. It gives rise to much concern in many industries and to many individuals, but apparently not enough to the 25 million gainfully employed persons (employers and workers), without whose constant vigilance and care safety cannot be assured.

The gradual build-up of safety provisions has been achieved by more than a century and a half of enactments, the details of which have varied, so that anyone concerned with a particular type of work would need to familiarise himself with the appropriate statutory provisions, and the local bye-laws. (For instance the Ministry of Power, through the Mines and Quarries Act 1954, was made the safety authority for about 2,000 mines and quarries; the Ministries of Agriculture for Scotland and the rest of Britain under the Agriculture Acts 1952 and 1956, for farms; the Ministry of Transport under various Acts for the merchant navy, railways and roads. Air safety has been passed to the Air Registration Board under the appropriate Ministry.) Nevertheless, by the latter part of the 20th century two general principles may be discerned. The first is to ensure that the work-place, machines, and conditions of work have been made as safe as possible; the second to promote the idea of safety, as a positive state of mind, sensitive to persuasion, training, or even force.

The Ministry with most experience of safety promotion and its frustrations has been the Ministry of Labour, which was given the major responsibility for the well-being of more than a million building sites, road works, ship-yards, factories, offices, and other premises, by the Factories Acts, and the Offices, Shops and Railways Premises Act 1963. An examination of the Ministry's methods and their results would seem, therefore, the most profitable source for this survey.[2]

---

[1] The number of work accidents in 1938 was 180,103; in 1948, 201,086; in 1958, 167,697; in 1964, 268,648; and in 1966, 296,610.
[2] The Factories Act, 1961. A short guide. H.M.S.O.

It has long been known that the main causes of accidents have been quite simply: workers falling, being struck by an object, or being hurt by handling articles. Many fewer accidents have arisen out of machinery (about one in five), the result, perhaps of the complicated safety regulations surrounding machines. But modern concern has centred round the measures likely to improve the general environment. Thus safety regulations have insisted on the sound construction of floors, steps, stairs, passages, gang-ways, and all means of access to the place of work; on their being kept free from obstruction or substances likely to cause people to slip, and on the provision of hand-rails on stairs, or places where people might fall through, or sideways; and all precautions against falling have had to be taken wherever the working place has been sited more than six feet up. Dangers from polluted air through gas or dust have been a constant source of anxiety, and every occupier has been obliged to foresee them, and guard against explosions or gassing, as well as against the less visible and more insidious dangers of dust inhalation.[1]

Though machines are not a major source of accident, fencing and guarding were obvious precautions, and were among the first rules to be enacted. Everything that moves on a machine that is liable to catch the clothes, or the person of those near it, must be made safe. The same applies to liquids, whether scalding, corrosive, or poisonous; and to hoists, lifts, cranes, chains, ropes and all lifting gear, which have had to be inspected regularly to ensure their constructional soundness and safe working. Protective clothing, shields for the eyes, and anything likely to make for greater safety has had to be provided, though persuading workers to wear them was another matter. Experience has shown that the cleaning of machinery, and the area nearby, is a risky job, and women and young persons are forbidden to undertake it if there is any danger from moving parts on or near the place to be cleaned.

Fire has been a constant source of danger, and with the co-operation of the local authorities, the Ministry has maintained the closest supervision of the precautions taken, and has initiated

---

[1]'Occupational Hygiene', or the control of substances likely to be a health hazard has been the concern of four complementary groups: (a) Factory inspectors; (b) Employers; (c) Some universities, medical schools, and research associations, who carry out tests; (d) The 'Occupational Hygiene Units' at Manchester and Newcastle universities, who have provided a service to firms, mainly on a contractual basis.

prosecutions. Plentiful means of fire fighting is an obvious requirement, as well as a good alarm system, and the means of escape.
All these have to be tested regularly, and where ten or more
people are employed, doors must open outwards.

In spite of these manifold regulations accidents have not
declined, and though the number of work-people at risk has not
declined either, the fact of an enlarging labour force has made the
second part of the policy—the need to promote the idea of safety—
increasingly important. Every year the report of the Chief Factory
Inspector has contained accounts of what seem almost incredible
happenings. For example (Cmnd. 2724. H.M.I. Rept. 1964, p. 22),
'A boy was working on a treadle guillotine with an unguarded
blade. He failed to notice that when he was holding down a metal
sheet for cutting, the tip of his finger was directly under the blade.
He pressed the pedal and cut off the top of his finger. This was the
first time the boy had ever worked the guillotine. The guard for
the blade had been removed by the works foreman for adjustment,
and the boy was actually set to work on this dangerous machine by
the works manager himself.' This is merely one of many examples,
but it illustrates that safety as a positive concept must be present in
all those involved with work, from top management to the newest
recruit.

This concept of safety appears to involve three factors: training
for safety; vigilance in ensuring that every safety precaution is
observed all the time; and research into new and better methods of
safety.

Training has become a statutory obligation in certain cases.
For instance, under Section 21 of the Factories Act 1937,
strengthened by a number of special regulations, it has become an
offence for an occupier to fail to train and supervise a young
person in the use of 'dangerous machinery'. A list of such machines
has been supplied by successive Orders in Council. Further, until
he has received sufficient training, it is illegal for him to work a
machine except under the supervision of a person with a thorough
knowledge and experience of it. The 1963 Offices, Shops, and
Railway Premises Act has gone further, and laid down that no
person of any age may work on a machine declared by the Minister
to be dangerous, without adequate training and supervision.

Training in the safest and best methods of using dangerous
machinery is the first necessity, but only the first. The policy now

is to put safety at the centre of all activity. The Ministry has consequently given its blessing to any schemes of teaching the general principles of safety, whether to foremen, line management, or top management. Such teaching should include the best methods of ensuring that safety becomes a living issue. Many bodies have taken a hand in the process. Birmingham Industrial Training Centre at Acocks Green was established in 1951 to train local foremen and supervisory staff in safety measures. 'T.W.I.' arranged one of its courses around the principles and practice of safety. Other organisations such as the British Safety Council, and the Royal Society for the Prevention of Accidents, have been active in promoting short courses. One vital development in the 1960s was the creation of the Central Training Council, which lost no time in drawing the attention of the industrial training boards to their duty to include training in safety in their programmes.[1] This ought to pay dividends in the future, but it would be idle to think it will be enough. The young are notoriously venturesome and prone to copy the unsafe habits of their elders, as the continuing toll of accidents and fatalities among them has proved.

Other methods to which the Ministry of Labour has been committed have included a properly constituted safety organisation in the factory. Its precepts have been (see 'Industrial Accident Prevention' 1956 Report): (a) Safety is an essential part of good management and good workmanship. (b) Management and workpeople must co-operate to secure freedom from accident. (c) Top management must take the lead in organising safety in the works. (d) There must be a defined and known safety policy in each workplace. (e) The organisation and resources to carry out this policy must exist. (f) The best available knowledge and methods must be used.

In practice, the larger the factory, the more ready it has been to set one up, and the more it needed to do so, since the accident rate has tended to increase with the size of the plant. Safety officers, full or part-time, have been appointed, and safety committees brought into being for the whole factory, or for separate depart-

[1] They itemised four simple principles: (a) To avoid dangers, such as those from a loose hammer head; (b) To keep the work-place tidy, and clear away obstructions that people might trip over; (c) To be of good behaviour, and avoid the 'skylarking', which experience has shown can cause many unnecessary accidents; (d) To preserve a sense of responsibility towards others, for instance, never to switch on electric current without warning. (C.T.C. Memo. 2, 1965.)

ments, but their effectiveness has been uneven. Some have enjoyed the continuing interest and enthusiasm of all ranks; others, having started with a flourish, have lost momentum before many weeks have passed, when the dull apathy of boredom has settled on the meetings, and on the propaganda as well. How to combat apathy is an unsolved problem. It might perhaps help if a careful enquiry were made into the reasons why some schemes succeed and others do not, though it is more likely that interest is greater or less according to the enthusiasm of those at the top. In 1966 Mr P. Archer sponsored a private member's Bill to establish a national occupational and safety council of employers and employees, in order to review and co-ordinate provisions relating to occupational hazards and safety in all types of employment, and to make safety committees obligatory in all work-places. Though the Bill got no further, the government itself announced in the same year (11 July, 1966) that they would continue to encourage industry to set up joint consultative machinery for safety purposes, and that, if the opportunity were not taken, compulsory powers would be included in the next major revision of the Factories Act.

Another factor is the continual search for new and better safety devices. All the government departments responsible for safety at work have been empowered to promote research, both by their own staff, and through research bodies. Machine-makers have concentrated on built-in safety, while work-shop architecture has attracted fertile brains in an effort, for instance, to reduce the dangers of falling or being struck by an object. Psychological factors have not been omitted, and interest has centred on fitting the worker into the right job, and keeping those known to be 'accident prone' away from potential dangers.

Health

Linked closely to the problem of safety in employment, there has been a growing interest in the promotion of health, which in practice has meant the struggle to maintain and improve standards of health in the work-place, and to protect the individual worker from the health hazards involved in the nature of his employment.

The work-place. Over the years, much detail has accumulated on what is to be expected in a good working environment. It was felt that over-crowding would be avoided by allowing a minimum of 400 cubic feet of space for each person in the work-room. The temperature must be reasonable, particularly where the work is sedentary (not less than 60 degrees after the first hour was considered the minimum). Lighting was another important factor. Work cannot be efficient if lighting is poor, and bad lighting has a depressing effect on morale. At the same time workers have needed to be protected from undue glare, either from unshielded lights or from the sun. Sanitary conveniences should be available for each sex, and should be adequately lighted. Special regulations for these are in force where food is manufactured or sold, and include the supply of hot and cold water, soap, towel and other washing facilities. But the provision of these, in or near all toilets, has come to be compulsory in most cases nowadays.

The first report in 1965 of the inspectors' findings under the Offices, Shops and Railway Premises Act 1963 was enlightening, because they commented on conditions discovered in premises that had not previously been regulated.[1] Though only 14 per cent of the premises had been visited, they found cleanliness at its best in food establishments, where they had already been inspected under the Food Hygiene (General) Regulations 1960. On the whole, shops owned by multiple firms were cleaner than those of the small owner. But offices varied from the very clean to the very dirty, and those that were out of sight of the public were the worst. By and large, the temperature and ventilation of offices were better than those of shops, but lighting was always better in the sales areas of shops than in the back premises. Overcrowding seemed to accompany old buildings, where low ceilings often made it difficult to achieve the minimum space for each worker. Toilets and washing facilities were all too often poor. The impression one gains from the report is that where premises have been visible to the public, the standards have been reasonably high, but where they were out of sight, they were nobody's business, or at any rate not until they came under inspection. Which seems to suggest that one cannot leave these matters to the good-will and efficiency of the occupier, and that 'common rules' are necessary if a reasonable working environment is to be attained.

The Individual. Protecting the individual from work hazards

[1] *Ministry of Labour Gazette.* November 1965.

involves a complicated balance between State control and private
benevolence. The State has insisted on certain fundamentals. The
annual medical inspection of young workers, preventive action
against certain diseases, plus the reporting of them as well as of
ordinary accidents if they should occur, and the provision of first-
aid for emergencies are cases in point. But it has left industry to
decide whether to appoint professional personnel (apart from
first-aid workers), build clinics, or supply equipment. Research
into the effect of work conditions on the individual has been the
concern of both sides, though not always in partnership.

State effort—The Appointed Factory Doctor. This part of the service
was started in 1844, when a 'Certifying Surgeon' was given the
duty of stating that any child starting work in a textile factory had
the ordinary strength and appearance of a nine-year-old or more.
But by 1948, when his title became 'Appointed Factory Doctor',
his functions had become more precise. He had to make a medical
check on all boys and girls under 18 when they first entered
employment in a factory, or if they changed jobs, and in any case
once a year. (A similar scheme was established for mines and
quarries, but not for other employments, like shops, offices or
agriculture.) His duties included the medical examination of people
of any age for whose jobs regulations required periodical medical
investigation. Workers poisoned by such substances as lead, or
injured by fumes, or having contracted diseases, the details of
which have been laid down in the Ministry of Labour regulations,
were to be investigated and reported upon. Should death occur
from any of these causes, a report was obligatory.

The Appointed Factory Doctor has had therefore an important,
though limited, role in industrial health. Yet he has been neither
specially trained for the job, nor given the pay and status of a full-
time expert. The A.F.D.s have been recruited from the general
practitioners in each area; partly, it was said, to increase public
interest in industrial health, but also, one suspects, because they
were handy, and could be obtained at little expense. Their
remuneration came from curiously mixed sources, since the
medical examination of young workers was paid for by the
employers on a scale laid down by the Ministry, but investigations
into cases of gassing or prescribed diseases were financed by the
Ministry of Labour itself. Many doctors have taken a great

interest in the work, equipping themselves with specialised knowledge, taking part in surveys, and making important contributions to the health of workers. Others have contributed the least possible time and effort. Such differences were inevitable in a system that left the initiative with the individual doctor of doing only the minimum required of him or of showing enterprise and initiative.

By 1966, a sub-committee of the Ministry of Health Advisory Committee had enquired into the criticisms that were beginning to be heard, and had issued a report on the whole service. They found that the main objection was the lack of expert knowledge by the A.F.D.s, their large number (over 1,500 in 1966), and lack of uniform standards. They also found that there was growing doubt whether the bulk of their work, that is the routine examination of youngsters, had any real value. The establishment of a National Health Service after 1948, together with an improved school medical service, had transformed the situation, and it seemed a gross waste of time, particularly medical time, to persist in these routine checks. Over half a million were made each year, the number of rejections being only about a quarter of one per cent.

The Committee suggested two quite fundamental changes. Instead of the mass medicals for young workers, all school leavers should be armed with a medical certificate from the school doctor certifying whether he would be fit for any job, or only for certain ones. Secondly, the A.F.D.s should be replaced by a much smaller number of full-time or part-time doctors, to be called 'A' doctors, having specialised knowledge, and experience of occupational health problems. The 'A' doctors would examine, and keep under review, all youngsters declared by the school doctors to be fit for selected jobs only, and would take over the supervision of persons in hazardous employment, or where diseases had developed. Their new functions would be to advise employees on occupational health problems. This might be specially helpful to the disabled, the chronic sick, and the older workers. It was the pious hope of the Committee that the new system might be gradually extended to all occupations, and not limited to those under the Factories Acts. Were this to come about, a national unified industrial medical service might become a reality.

Prescribed diseases. For purposes of industrial injuries insurance

(p. 169), certain diseases arising out of industrial processes have been scheduled for special consideration. It was in 1906[1] that workmen's compensation was first applied to industrial diseases, and subsequent legislation (notably the Industrial Injuries Act 1946) extended the coverage. Only certain diseases were included, and since 1948 the test of designation has been whether the cause of the disease could, with reasonable certainty, be traced back to the circumstances of the employment, and not to the ordinary hazards to which anyone might be prone. The case of bronchitis has often been cited to illustrate this principle. It has long been a trade disease among flax workers, a large proportion of whom have suffered from it. But since numerous workers in other industries have endured it too, it has not been scheduled as a 'prescribed' disease. If it were so scheduled, it would attract endless dispute, as no-one would be able to decide whether it was contracted from flax-dust irritation, or from some other source, as many non-flax workers, living in the same town, also suffered from it.

To clarify the position, a schedule of prescribed diseases subject to review from time to time has been drawn. Most of these diseases are specific to a certain occupation, and would be recognised for benefit purposes only if the sufferer was, or had been, a worker in that trade. The main exceptions to the general principle have been pneumoconiosis and byssinosis. Both are generic terms for lung conditions caused by various kinds of dust found in industry, chiefly coal mining and the cotton industry. But since 1954, workers suffering from these distressing lung complaints who could show that they had worked in dusty occupations, other than mining and cotton, or in the other trades mentioned in the schedule, could apply for benefit.

Many efforts have been made by the T.U.C. and others to extend the list of prescribed diseases, efforts which have not been unsuccessful. But the attempt to open the door of injury benefit to all illnesses contracted at work has been resolutely resisted.

The existence of a schedule has been a powerful factor in the drive by the Ministry of Labour, and by industry itself, so to clean up the processes of work that operatives will not be exposed to risk. Measures to prevent injurious dust being breathed in, or harmful chemicals and organisms being used, have become a major preoccupation with the industrial medical service, as well as

[1] A. F. Young, *Industrial Injuries Insurance*, p. 28 et seq.

with management. Many articles, such as matches, which were once made of phosphorus and produced a deterioration of flesh and bone in the workers (called 'phossy jaw'), are now made with alternative materials, and the danger from that disease has receded. The drive to prevent disease has not been limited to the prescribed ones, since anything in the industrial situation likely to be injurious to health has become a matter of research and concern to those responsible for the social service covered by the Factories and similar Acts.

Though compulsory reporting has been limited to diseases on the schedule, many managements have been interested enough to report other disorders too, especially dermatitis, a non-notifiable complaint, but one that has caused almost more loss of working time than any other. The Ministry has asked for voluntary co-operation in notifying any cases that have appeared, and the returns published each year in the reports of the chief inspector have been not only illuminating in themselves, but have illustrated how much can be achieved by voluntary co-operation.

First Aid. The other important statutory requirement has been the provision of first-aid boxes, and of qualified workers to use them. The first step was taken in the Factories Act 1937, which laid down that all factories should have a box containing certain articles, that the box should be available at a known place, and that someone with skill in first-aid should be ready to act. The actual number of the workers in the factory dictated to some extent what was provided, but the general principle was, the larger the staff, and the more dangerous the process, the higher should be the standard. By 1960 the haphazard working of this arrangement led to a new First-Aid in Factories Order, copied subsequently in the Offices, Shops and Railway Premises Act 1963, whose intention was to improve the general standard of all first-aid boxes.

Larger factories and shops (usually employing over 50 workers) had now to have a minimum number of first-aid personnel, trained according to the requirements of the Ministry. In practice this usually meant taking courses regularly, and passing examinations in first-aid. Even smaller businesses were enjoined to ensure that someone was made responsible for the smooth and satisfactory first-aid arrangements, including replenishing the contents of the box.

Voluntary effort. The more dramatic developments in the industrial health services have been promoted by the occupiers themselves. The establishment of a medical department in a factory, with full or part-time doctors and nurses, has occurred in many firms, and has often been regarded as a sign of good management. The actual number of such departments and such staff at any one moment is not known; but in 1965[1] it was thought that about 5,000 factories employed doctors, mostly part-time, and it would probably be safe to guess that each of these factories had a medical room, and a nursing staff. An unspecified number of factories employed nursing staff only. The function of the medical staff varied from firm to firm, but could include: giving general advice to management on industrial hazards; promoting safety precautions; ascertaining the causes of and helping to prevent, industrial disease; examining individual workers to see if they were suitable for certain jobs; or if exposed to occupational risks, whether they were in good health; supervising the therapeutic services, first-aid and medical care in the factory; and developing health education among all personnel.[2]

Where medical departments have been established, they have worked well, because they have helped to ensure that the workers' health has suffered as little as possible through the nature of their work, and that minor accidents, or simple illnesses, have been quickly treated, thus avoiding more serious complications. They have also helped to reduce the pressure on the National Health Service.

Group services are something the Ministry has always approved,[3] and where a number of small factories were built in the same area, they have been encouraged to set up a common industrial health service. The oldest and best known, inaugurated in 1947, is at Slough, and covers over 300 firms, with about 30,000 employees. But several others, notably West Bromwich, Smethwick and District Manufacturers' Occupational Health Service Ltd., Dundee and District, Rochdale, and Central Middlesex, have established group medical centres, sometimes with the aid of grants from the Nuffield Foundation, sometimes solely financed by the member firms. The development of trading estates in

---

[1] C.O.I. Pamphlet 31. 'Labour Relations and Conditions of Work in Britain'.
[2] Industrial Health Services. Committee Report (1950–51 Cmd. 8170 XV).
[3] Ministry of Labour Pamphlet No. 35: Health at Work.

different parts of the country would seem to have offered unparalleled opportunities for group occupational services of this kind. Unfortunately these have seldom materialised.

Meanwhile, pressure has grown to develop specialised industrial accident services in some of the major hospitals in each region. Such a service, besides providing the accommodation and equipment to deal adequately with accidents brought to the hospital, might include a 'flying squad' of mobile, trained personnel to go swiftly to the scene of an accident, and give emergency treatment on the spot. In 1965, the amended ten-year plan for hospitals accepted the idea in principle, and contained a modified scheme of 'accident units'.

Welfare

A statutory minimum of welfare facilities has been relatively slow to appear and it was not until the shops and factories legislation of the 1930s, that it was spelt out in any detail. The main aspects were concerned with washing, drinking, seating, cloakroom and canteen facilities.

Thus wash-rooms with wash basins (number according to pay-roll), running hot and cold water, soap and drying facilities have had to be provided; though requirements varied according to the business, basic standards have tended to rise. It has become an obligation to provide drinking water for all workers, preferably of the jet type, or accompanied by a cleansable or disposable drinking vessel. Seating for workers was always a difficult problem, especially in shops, where customers have expected to see the assistants on their feet. But the law has stiffened; seats have not only to be provided, but workers must be allowed to use them, if it is 'without detriment to their work' (a loop-hole with many possibilities). Where the job has been a sedentary one, as in offices and many factories, proper seating has been customary for years, but it is now stated that the seats must have a back to them, and be available to workers regardless of age or sex.

Accommodation for clothing not worn on the job has been a source of many disputes. It involves an element of safety from possible marauders, opportunities for drying it on a wet day, and protection from dust and other substances involved in the processes. All that has been stipulated is that 'adequate and suitable accommodation' should be provided, with arrangements for drying clothes. The employer has been left to devise the appropriate method.

Factories have frequently provided eating facilities as a 'fringe' benefit. There has been little legislation about them, except in dangerous trades (such as where poisonous substances have been used in the process), where the eating of meals has been forbidden, unless in a separate room. The law on shops has also mentioned meals, and stated that where they are taken on the premises, there must be 'sufficient and suitable' accommodation, which in practice has meant the provision of a separate room.

A few miscellaneous matters have come under the heading of 'welfare'; these include the control of work in underground rooms, the prohibition of work by women and young people in mines or in certain dangerous trades, and the exclusion of pregnant women from factory work in their last four weeks before childbirth. It is perhaps significant that this last prohibition does not extend to all occupations. A word might also be added about 'home-workers', a body of people hard to control, who have been a source of anxiety for many years. All that has been achieved for them is an obligation on the part of occupiers and contractors to keep a list of their names and addresses, and to send it to the local authority and the factory inspector. The council officers have been empowered to visit them, and forbid their work, if their homes are dangerous or injurious to their health, when used as places of employment.

The truck system

It is seldom remembered that factory inspectors were made responsible for the protection of workers against the abuses of 'truck', or that the Truck Acts are still playing some part in the industrial organisation of the country.

'Truck', or payment in kind, is a relic of the feudal system, and was to continue for many years, as a method of paying wages. Intrinsically, there was nothing objectionable in it, provided both employers and workers were agreed about the value of the goods offered by the employer, in terms of the output or hours of work by the employee, and that both agreed that this should be the form of payment. Where it failed was in its abuse by some employers, particularly during the 18th and early 19th centuries. For instance in mining, and several other trades, employers set up their own retail grocery, clothing, and other shops, and paid their workers in vouchers, cashable at the 'tommy' shops. Complaints were made that the goods were inferior, and the prices higher than at non-company shops, and that truck was simply a method of reducing wages. The argument was pressed by workers, and some of the other employers, who had no 'tommy' shops of their own, complained of the unfair competition and wage under-cutting by those who had. Moreover there was a general objection to truck, which interfered with a working man's right to spend his wages in his own way, and to seek other jobs when he wanted. Further, it was said that 'tommy' shops became credit shops, and that workers were held to their jobs through their debts to the employer.

A series of Acts, dating from very early times, had sought to control the use of the truck system; but it was not until 1831 that there was any real change. Under this, and subsequent Acts, it became obligatory for payment of wages to be by coin of the realm, and that no contract was to stipulate where, or how, wages were to be spent. If there were a written contract which included certain commodities in lieu of cash (for example rent, fuel, etc.), their exact value was to be stated. Similarly, if deductions from wages were to be made for faulty workmanship, or misdemeanours, the exact nature of what would lead to a fine was to be stated clearly by a notice prominently displayed in the plant. The Truck Acts abolished the habit of paying wages in public houses, and put their enforcement into the hands of the factory inspectors.

By the middle of the 20th century, an unexpected development occurred over the question of payment in coin of the realm. Wages were usually paid weekly, and such had been the effect of inflation that the amount of legal tender required by big firms to pay wages was very large indeed. As this had its dangers, especially from possible criminal raids, employers sought a change in the law, and the Payment of Wages Act 1960 (applying to Britain only), was passed. This laid down that wages could be paid by cheque, postal order, or direct payment into a worker's account at a bank, if both sides agreed in writing, and provided either side could change back again by giving notice. Each employee was guaranteed a full statement of his gross and net pay, with details of each deduction made.

It has been suggested that the Truck Acts no longer serve any useful purpose, since trade unions are strong enough to prevent abuse. This may well be true in the majority of cases. Yet there has been no campaign for their abolition, except over the one issue of payment by cheque. They would appear therefore to be no hindrance to workers, and may well be a safeguard for a minority, especially women, who are often unorganised, and liable to find themselves in a weak position in their wages contracts.

Personnel of the service

What now remains is to examine the organisation and powers of the servants themselves. In a service as old as industrial protection and welfare, it is not surprising that the name 'inspectors' should have been given to men and women who visited work-places and advised on better methods of achieving safety and promoting health. In a sense they have remained inspectors, poking round to see that no infringement of the law has gone unchallenged, and prosecuting those who have deliberately and dangerously flouted it. But it would be untrue to believe that their function ended there, or indeed that their main purpose was punitive. On the contrary, their concern has been to promote both a healthier and safer working environment for all, and the development of any means likely to improve the health and welfare of the worker himself.

To accomplish this highly exacting work a small bank of fewer than 600 factory inspectors, employed by the Ministry of Labour, has struggled to keep an eye on what was going on in the factories, shops, offices, and other establishments, for which they have been given responsibility by the various Acts. A further group (under 200) was appointed by the Ministry of Power to deal with mines and quarries, while others under the Ministry of Agriculture have been made responsible for farms, and a growing number under local authorities have been concerned with shops and offices. The chief problem here, as in all the social services, has been the difficulty of recruiting sufficient suitable staff, and there has nearly always been a 10 per cent gap between the establishment approved and the number actually in posts.

The inspectors have been composed of 'general purpose' men and women, and 'specialists'. Thus, for watching over the mines there have been specialists in electrical and mechanical engineering, and for the factories, chemical and medical specialists as well as others. Whatever their speciality, or previous qualification, they have had to be trained in the theory and practice of inspection, just as have the 'general purpose' officers. In consequence, the making of an expert staff has been a long and costly process. In the main, apart from the local government appointees, inspectors have worked on a regional basis, or from headquarters. The Ministry of Labour has divided the country for administrative purposes, and placed a number of 'general purpose' inspectors, along with perhaps one each of the specialist staff, in each division. The divisional medical factory inspectors have worked with the local A.F.D.s and the medical staff of the factories, to anticipate anything likely to be injurious to health, and to devise means of preventing it. Their strength has lain in their wide contacts, their own expertise, and their opportunities for research and investigation; and the local medical staff have been helped to see their problems in the light of the most up-to-date knowledge and experience. At headquarters, too, specialist staff, concerned with the country as a whole, have been stationed ready at any time to help and advise their local colleagues.

Assessment of the success or failure of these 'specialist' and 'general' public servants has posed its own problem, since their methods of advice, exhortation and warning, in their daily contact with industrial occupiers and workers, do not respond to ordinary analysis. It might be said that the number of surveys on which they have reported is a sign of their desire to ascertain the facts. In that case, the impressive list published each year by the appropriate departments has been a healthy indication. Another suggested criterion is the annual number of prosecutions, because it is the duty of the inspectors to bring cases of breach of the law before the criminal courts. If they were to prosecute every case they found, the courts of justice would quickly be swamped, and in practice, such action is looked upon as a last resort against the recalcitrant occupier, on whom warnings have had no effect, or where an accident has occurred, as a result of such serious neglect, that the perpetrator could not remain unchallenged. Thus, in any one year the number of firms prosecuted by factory inspectors has represented less than half of one per cent of all the firms lying under the jurisdiction of the Factories Acts, and the average fine for each offence has been about £20. (In 1965 the average penalty where death or bodily injury had been caused was £48.) It has been suggested (A. F. Young, op. cit., p. 173) that prosecutions and fines on this scale might be thought derisory when put against the annual number of serious and fatal accidents. The impression of futility.could be strengthened by the percentage of prosecutions that are successful (over 90 per cent), showing that only those cases that are almost certain to be proved are ever brought to the court. In fact, as a measure of the success or otherwise of inspection, court action has little to recommend it, and we are left without any satisfactory method of giving an objective assessment of the inspectors' work. On the other hand, most people would agree that the strongest evidence of their success has been negative rather than positive, and that without their vigilance, firms would have been more lax than they actually were in carrying out the requirements of the Acts, or the policy of the government. The evidence of the earliest reports, after the passing of the Offices, Shops, and Railway Premises Act 1963 (p. 88), might be thought a significant pointer to the truth of this assertion.

There is one other aspect of the problem of personnel that has wider implications, and has received all too little ventilation. This is the problem of multiplicity. We have referred earlier to the way in which different government departments have been made responsible for the operation of the service in different occupations, with different statutes and regulations. To add to the confusion, local authorities have been given extensive powers too.[1] For instance, as planning authorities, they must have safety requirements in mind when approving plans for building or altering work-places. As sanitary authorities, they have been obliged to see that drinking water is pure, and sanitary conveniences adequate and maintained in working order. As health authorities, they have been concerned with cleanliness, including the regular removal of dirt and refuse, and the application to walls and other surfaces of 'a compact, continuous film capable of being washed', a film to be renewed every seven years, or as often as necessary, to keep the film 'compact and continuous'. Similarly, overcrowding, temperature, ventilation, and the drainage of floors, have been their concern. As fire authorities[2] they have had special

---

[1] Ministry of Labour 'Duties of Local Authorities'. H.M.S.O.

[2] Ministry of Labour 'Fire Fighting in Factories' Booklet 10, Safety, Health and Welfare Series. H.M.S.O.

H

responsibilities to issue certificates to factories to ensure that means of escape are sufficient, and fire precautions adequate. It has been the duty of the factory inspector to see that safety precautions against fire were being observed, and to prosecute in exceptional cases, but it has also been the duty of the fire authority to enter premises for purposes of granting or renewing the certificate, or if there was reason to believe that fire risk was present.

The foregoing might be considered the general duties of a local authority to maintain a healthy and safe environment for us all. But it has meant that Ministries and Councils have had over-lapping functions and areas of responsibility. To add to this, under the Shops Acts 1934–50 and the Offices, Shops, and Railway Premises Act 1963, the duty of inspection, the promoting of safety, health and welfare, and in one case (young shop assistants) the control of hours of work, have been laid directly on local authorities, and not on the central government, in spite of the fact that the work involved has been so similar to that under the Factories Acts. Indeed, the 1963 Act raised such possibilities of confusion, that a share-out of the work had to be made. Local authorities were asked to supervise offices associated with shops the Ministry of Labour was given the inspection of offices connected with factories, local government and railways, while the Ministry of Power concerned itself with offices and shops forming part of mines or quarries. Even so, the greatest increase in work has fallen on the local authorities.

The central point of the criticism is not how well or how badly each responsible agency is carrying out its functions, but that there are so many agencies. It would be hard to conceive a social service so prodigal in the number of its masters, and so extravagant in its demand for qualified personnel to carry out the work. A unified service, pooling its resources, might have produced something that was adequately staffed, by people whose training, quality, status and pay would be ever improving. Instead, it is a patchwork of autonomous authorities, with overlapping functions, and an insatiable and unsatisfied demand for more and more inspectors.

V

WAGES COUNCILS

ARRANGEMENTS FOR NEGOTIATING wage rates and conditions of employment would normally be excluded from a book on social services in industry, but wages councils might be the exception, since they arose out of grim under-payment and exploitation, and were started in response to a humane desire to prevent the 'sweating' of large numbers of apparently defenceless workers. They are, moreover, the one outstanding example in British industry of the statutory negotiation and legal imposition of minimum wages and conditions.

Historical review

Wage regulation was not unknown before the 1909 Act, but it had been abandoned over a century earlier, so that free competition and voluntary negotiation, those twin supports of 19th century philosophy, might rule unimpeded. The extreme results of this freedom offended the susceptibilities of many of those who witnessed the hardships of young and old working for long hours and earning a bare pittance, and set in motion a movement for reform. A House of Lords Select Committee reported on the abuses in 1890. As the years passed without any apparent result, the storm of protest gathered, and resulted in the organisation, in 1906, of an 'anti-sweating league', and the holding of a large exhibition, in the Albert Hall, of articles such as beaded slippers, shirts, and matches made by 'sweated' labour.

One of the aims of the new Liberal Government had been to combat low wages, by legislation if necessary. This was to meet the fiercest opposition, not least from the wage theorists, who had long held that on a free market, a labourer would get as much as he could, and an employer would pay as much as a man was worth to him. If the employer were obliged to pay more, he would either go out of business himself, or substitute other methods; in either case, instead of the worker receiving low wages, he would get no wages at all, and the latter state would be worse than the former. As for the free market, several generations of industrialists had proved its value to themselves, and were not likely to countenance state interference easily.

How to overcome these ingrained feelings (they were more than doctrines) demanded considerable subtlety on the part of the legislators. If the principle of voluntary bargaining was important, nothing should be done that would depart too far from it, in appearance. But if the evil of low wages was to be tackled, and a legal minimum achieved, it seemed wiser to change the system slowly—at any rate at the beginning.

Fortunately experiments in minimum wage legislation had been going on for some years in the State of Victoria, Australia, and these became the prototype for the British system. The Wages Boards in Australia had required the co-operation of workers and employers, with a few neutral members. This seemed to the British a useful method of incorporating both sides, thus preserving the appearance of the voluntary system while giving government supervision and statutory force to the decisions themselves. Then, by guaranteeing a minimum wage for a very few industries, and those the ones known to be seriously under-paying their workers, it was believed that a breach in the free market theory could be tolerated. In the event, the government chose four industries where the wages were known to be low (ready-made tailoring, paper-box making, chain making, and machine-made lace and net finishing), and instituted a legal minimum wage for the workers in them. The first Trade Boards, created in 1909, were successful, because they did not try to do too much, or to upset too many deeply felt theories.

The principle of these early trade boards was a simple one, that is, to set a minimum wage. There was no attempt to interfere with the length of the working week, or to establish a 'subsistence' wage. The weekly wage was geared to what the reasonably successful employer could pay, and though this meant that the marginal employer might suffer, there was no question of the workers suddenly finding their pay-packets bulging. It was a small beginning, but it was to have its effect; in the war that followed, the Whitley committee on Reconstruction (p. 125) was to recommend a continuation of the scheme, and an extension of the principles upon which trade boards should be established. By now, attention had begun to centre on the development of workers' and employers' organisations, and the very absence of effective organisation on either side seemed a good reason to set up a trade board. This principle was accordingly included in the next Trade Boards Act in 1918, and became the dominating influence when inaugurating new trade boards.

In 1922, when the Cave Committee (Cd. 1645) enquired into the working of the boards, a change had come over the industrial scene. The thinking that permeated the war period was beginning to give way to more traditional ideas, and the Committee reminded parliament that trade boards had been set up to combat low wages. To ignore that fact was to forget the original cause of the agitation. In future, they suggested, no trade boards should be created without both criteria being present, viz: low wages, and poor negotiating machinery. Though no legislation followed the report, administrative action, within the Ministry of Labour, ensured that both principles were involved if an industry became subject to a board. The Cave Committee had wanted the boards to fix the rates, so that wages would come up to subsistence level. This recommendation was not implemented, and the boards continued to fix a minimum wage, at a rate it was felt the industry as a whole could afford.

With one exception, the history of the trade boards continued without much change, until after the Second World War. This exception was the Holidays with Pay Act 1938, which gave the boards power to allow a mandatory week's paid holiday to all workers coming under their jurisdiction. One indirect, and surprising, result of this was that all wage negotiating bodies began to press for similar concessions, and holidays-with-pay were voluntarily accepted throughout industry. Quite apart from this Act of Parliament, trade boards, like any other social institutions, were affected by the social and political attitudes of the times. Administrative action, the fortunes of the boards, and the industries that might be thought suitable for the establishment of statutory machinery, were affected by the ebb and flow of public opinion during the inter-war years.

In 1945, with the end of another war in sight, the government, and particularly the Minister of Labour himself (Ernest Bevin) were considering plans for the post-war period. If experience after the first war was to be repeated, Britain was likely to suffer great economic hardship, unemployment, and wage recession. In consequence, the need to safeguard collective bargaining, and cushion the lot of the lowest paid, became the Minister's most urgent consideration. He therefore turned to the trade boards, to see how they could be re-fashioned to fit in with the climate of opinion that prevailed just then. For one thing, the level of wages was much higher, and to be satisfied with a minimum wage that the industry could stand was not good enough, if it meant keeping the minimum wage low to safeguard inefficient employers. For another, to wait till negotiating machinery had proved ineffective was to wait too long, if workers were to be saved from a prolonged depression of their wages. Also, if both sides of industry were united in wanting a statutory body, it was thought inexpedient for the government to have the power of veto, which they had used in certain instances in the inter-war years. A Bill was accordingly drafted to give a 'new look' to the trade boards, and one way of doing this was to give them a new name. The 1945 Act became the Wages Councils Act, and the term, trade board, was abolished. A few amendments were made in 1948, and the whole legal position was consolidated in the Wages Councils Act 1959.

The philosophy behind the legislation had greatly changed. Whereas the 1909 Act had been introduced as an anti-sweating measure, wages councils were an alternative to inadequate negotiating machinery, low wages being a secondary consideration. Trade boards had fixed a legal minimum wage that all but the most marginal firms could pay. Wages councils were expected to negotiate a minimum that was 'reasonable', having regard to all the circumstances, including the wages current in industry as a whole. Wages councils were therefore more ambitious, perhaps more 'heroic' in intention, than trade boards could ever be.

Meanwhile, certain trades were developing parallel systems of statutory wage regulation. Road haulage, for instance, was governed by a Wages Act 1938, and operatives employed for the carriage of goods, wholly or partly for hire or reward, came under its jurisdiction. As it was superseded in 1948 by an ordinary wages council, it will not be dealt with separately. Similarly, the Catering Wages Act 1943 set up a complicated system of statutory control over the wages, conditions, health and welfare of workers in various branches of the catering industry. These too were abolished, and four new wages councils were incorporated in the 1959 Wages Councils Act, to cover the various aspects of the industry.

Agriculture. The wages machinery in farming has not been embodied in wages council legislation, though its constitution, methods and results have been similar. The legal control of farm wages, which accompanied guaranteed farm prices during the First World War, was abolished when the war ended. As the abolition coincided with a slump in farming, the position of employers and workers was unenviable. So low were farm wages, that by 1924 a new Act made the payment of a legal minimum obligatory, but the minimum itself was decided on a local basis, and County Agricultural Wages Committees were set up to negotiate the local minima. These continued until 1940, when with the possibility of impending hunger in the Second World War, agriculture became a major priority, and farm wages a national concern. Thus the Agricultural Wages Board took over most of the functions of the County Committees, though county areas still maintained the right to be consulted. Even this was abolished by the Agricultural Wages (Regulation) Act 1947 (consolidated by the Agricultural Wages Act 1948), and the centrally organised board became completely responsible for fixing minimum wages, time and piece rates, holidays-with-pay, hours of work, and overtime rates for the whole country. (The Agricultural Wages (Scotland) Act 1949, setting up the Scottish Agricultural Wages Board, was passed to govern the situation there.)

The county committees were not abolished, as they still had the power to make representations to the Board about general matters, and the function to make a valuation of local tied cottages, to issue certificates of exemption to workers unable through handicap to earn the minimum wage, and to approve payments in kind, according to the customs of the area. Compared with their earlier authority, the power of the local committees became but a shadow of its former self, and the method of controlling farm workers' pay and conditions became almost indistinguishable from that of other wages councils, with two exceptions. One was that enforcement lay with the Ministry of Agriculture, and not with the Ministry of Labour; and the other that the board's decision was final, needing no ratification by a Ministry.

Establishing a wages council. Compared with activity after the 1918 Trade Boards Act, the number of wages councils brought into being since 1945 has been relatively insignificant. Yet the steps to be taken in establishing a wages council have been clarified. Three methods have developed: the Minister himself might make the Order without the consent of the industry, if he decided that wages were low and negotiating machinery ineffective. Or both sides of industry might petition the Minister to set up a Council, because negotiating machinery was not good enough, or was likely to break down within months. At this stage there was no need to prove that wages were low, and the Minister had no alternative but to refer the request to a Commission of Inquiry. Thirdly, if the Minister was of the opinion that some or all the workers in a particular industry were being paid too little, and seemed to have poor wage negotiating machinery, or might find themselves in that position before long, then he could himself refer the matter to a Commission of Inquiry. In practice, the last two methods have been the way wages councils have been established since 1945.

The Commission of Inquiry. This has consequently become the significant factor in the chain of events. Appointed *ad hoc* by the Minister, the commissions have usually consisted of a chairman and two independent persons, with four others, half representing the employers and half the workers. The industrial representatives were drawn from industries not connected with the inquiry, though expert assessors have been made available for advice if needed. Their first objective was to examine the negotiating machinery, usually the crux of the problem. If it was inadequate, or likely to break down, or its decisions were not being observed, so that wages might be jeopardised, the report to the Minister was bound to advocate a wages council. But if the commission believed that with certain amendments the voluntary machinery might be improved, and informed the Minister of this, it became his responsibility to take such steps as seemed to him appropriate to strengthen the voluntary organisations. What in practice he could do about this, apart from advice and exhortation, or the threat to institute the legal regulation of wages, it would be difficult to see. He had no power to impose 'voluntary' negotiating machinery.

It is thus abundantly clear that the development of wages councils since 1945 has depended on the commissions. It was they who had to decide whether the negotiating machinery looked too shaky to be workable, and to assess whether remuneration was 'reasonable'—and more difficult still, whether it would remain so. By 'reasonable remuneration', they meant a level of pay that could have been freely negotiated if no legal sanctions were involved, and which the trade unions would freely accept. Having determined what this would be, they had to anticipate the future, and decide if it could be maintained. For example an inquiry into the retail trade was made in 1947, and the commission asked itself the question, will the relatively high wages continue? At that time they thought not, so the two requirements of poor organisation and potentially low wages seemed to be satisfactorily met, and wages councils for various branches of the retail trade were recommended.

Constitution and functions

The pattern of the constitution of the wages councils has not altered since we borrowed the idea from Australia in 1909, and created the trade boards. They have been appointed by the Ministry of Labour, and have consisted of equal numbers from each 'side' (that is, employers and workers), with not more than three 'independents', from whom the Minister has selected the chairman. Women were always eligible for membership. The independent members have commonly been chosen from the legal profession, or the universities, but not from industry. The 'sides' have represented their respective status in industry, their geographical interests, and the type of firm or class of worker with whom they have had experience. The Minister was expected to seek the advice of the appropriate organisations before making his selection, though in practice this was not easy, since wages councils were created because organisation on both sides was poor. Each appointment has been a personal one, and membership could be withdrawn if the Minister thought the person no longer fulfilled the purpose for which he was appointed, or had failed to attend regularly.

The function of the council has been to fix minimum rates of pay, either time or piece rates, and the terms and conditions of paid holidays, for all the workers within its jurisdiction. The draft agreement has then been widely publicised, including notices in the *London Gazette* and *Edinburgh Gazette*, and to each employer known to be in the trade. He in his turn had the responsibility to inform his employees, so that they too might lodge objections if they wished. The council, having received the protests, would, if necessary, meet again to amend or pass its original proposals, whereupon they would go to the Minister for ratification. The Minister's power has been strictly limited at this point; though he might send back the draft for further consideration, he has had no right to veto or alter the proposals. Even if the council refused to accept his suggestions the Minister was obliged to make the Order and abide by it. The Prices and Incomes Act 1966, and its successors, temporarily changed this, and gave the Minister power to refuse to ratify the Order, but it was understood that the position would return to the *status quo* later on. In any case the Minister was able to use the power of delay, which at times had quite far-reaching results.

Once the wage-regulation Order was made, and the employers informed, they were bound to display the Order on the premises at all times, and would be acting illegally if they paid less than the statutory wage (they could pay more if they wanted), or did not keep a record of their payments. The Order might be simple, covering merely the time rates for a specified number of hours each week, or complicated, including piece rates, or different scales for workers of different skills, age, or sex. It might include payment in kind, with its appropriate value in cash, and minimum pay for handicapped workers. Arrangements about holidays would certainly be included, and overtime rates for work done beyond the statutory week might be detailed. In most cases the Order has tended to be a lengthy and complex document, not easy for the ordinary worker to understand. Although a Wages Council has not been permitted to deal with other conditions of work, it has been encouraged to report what it knew, for instance, about health and welfare standards in specific instances to the appropriate government department, which might then enquire into the circumstances, and if necessary take action.

The Order might refer to the workers in the whole of a specified industry, or only to sections of it. Occasionally it would need interpreting to decide whether or not a firm, or a department, or a worker, came within its ambit. For instance, a packaging business might be concerned with two wages' councils, 'paper box', and 'paper bag', and problems of demarcation could arise. As a rule, such matters were decided by the councils themselves, and most problems have been settled without too much acrimony.

Enforcement. It would be of little use issuing orders for the payment of minimum wages, without a system of inspectors to visit the work-place to see if the regulations were honoured. Of course the worker might himself take action, either by summary proceedings against the employer, for the crime of infringing the order (he would have the right also to claim up to two years back-pay) or by suing the employer in the civil courts for breach of contract (when he could claim up to six years back-pay). More usually it has been left to the Ministry of Labour wages' inspectors attached to each region to enforce the legal minimum. Court action has been relatively infrequent, because the breaches in the regulations have usually been due to ignorance or apathy, and when brought to the notice of the employer, have been put right at once. Not only have the wages been brought up to the statutory minimum, but in most cases arrears have been paid in full, without prosecution.

Ending a wages council. It had generally been assumed when trade boards, and later wages councils were formed, that sooner, rather than later, they would work themselves out of existence. Most people believed that both sides of industry would prefer to be free to negotiate their own pay and terms of work, and that meeting together at the boards would give each side both the experience, and the incentive, to throw away the crutch of legal control, and to embrace voluntary negotiation as quickly as possible. Up to 1959 the facts did not justify this view, as only about eight wages councils out of nearly 70 had been ended, and in some cases this had happened because the industry itself had almost ceased to exist. Before 1959, it had been left to the trade unions and employers' organisations to approve the abolition of a wages council, and though since 1953 there had been greater activity by the Ministry in encouraging the revocation of Orders, or even in suspending them for a time, in most cases the opposition of both the Trades Union Congress and the British Employers' Confederation prevented action being taken. The unions opposed because they feared for the pockets of the workers, and the employers opposed because they needed protection from the undercutting of their less scrupulous rivals. In 1959 the Wages Councils Act empowered the Minister, on his own initiative, to set up Commissions of Inquiry to examine whether or not certain wages councils were still needed. The Commission could recommend the continuation of a council, or its abolition, as for instance in 1962, when they proposed the suspension of the Scottish Baking Wages Council, in spite of the opposition of the unions, who feared that workers in small businesses would be jeopardised. Or they might compromise, and suggest the exclusion of one section of an industry from wages council control, leaving the rest intact. An example of this came in 1964, when the Commission sided with the railway refreshment rooms and train catering staff, against the Catering Wages Council. In this case, the unions claimed that the workers in the railway refreshment service were well organised, and had achieved a standard of wages higher than that provided for by the Catering Wages Council. The wages would have been higher still, the unions alleged, but for the council, whose minimum rates were often cited by railway management as a reason for keeping wages down. The British Transport Hotels Ltd, the management side of the industry, and an offshoot of British Rail, joined the Catering Council in opposing the plea, arguing that they valued the contact with other branches of catering. Nevertheless, the commission decided to recommend the exclusion of this part of the catering industry from legal regulation because it had well developed negotiating machinery, and therefore conformed with the spirit of the Wages Councils Act.

Working of wages councils. The legal minimum wage achieved by this means is not negligible when considered in terms of workers and firms involved. About one in six workers have been able to rely on the councils to guarantee them a 'reasonable' wage (in 1967 wages councils (57) covered three and a half million workers, and the Agricultural Wages Board a further half million), and over half a million establishments have been subject to control.

A vivid account of the functioning of this statutory alternative

to voluntary bargaining may be found in *British Wages Councils* by
F. J. Bayliss (chaps. VI and VII). Each Council has been manned
by equal numbers from each 'side', with three 'independent'
members. On the interaction of these three groups has depended
the effectiveness of the Council as a wage regulating machine. In
practice, according to Bayliss, each 'side' worked together as an
entity, with the majority view prevailing. To attain this, arrangements had to be made for opportunities to discuss the issues in
private, before and during the general sittings. At the private
meetings, each 'side' appointed a leader, who was its chairman,
spokesman, and representative on committees. Not that personnel
for these duties was easy to find. The employers, for instance, were
drawn mainly from small scattered businesses, neither easy to
identify nor to recruit; while the workers' representatives were
selected from industries which, by definition, were poorly
organised. In most cases they came to consist of full-time officials
of unions most closely concerned. For these individuals, particularly officials of the T.G.W.U., the G.M.W.U., and U.S.D.A.W.,
the unions most likely to be concerned, work on the wages
councils was simply an onerous addition to their other activities.
The T.U.C. developed an advisory department for such officials,
but there were occasions when they had to put aside other pressing
work in order to find enough time for all the preparation and
discussion involved at the council. Decisions were usually reached
more quickly than by voluntary negotiation, but the time taken
was still considerable.

The 'independent' members were perhaps the most interesting
of the groups. Appointed by the Minister for their experience and
objectivity, paid a fee for their services, each having a vote, one
would have expected them to dominate the council. In a sense they
did, but not as dictators, using a casting vote on one side or the
other, to resolve a deadlock. Their object was to achieve an agreed
decision. To do this, they listened to, and weighed up, the proposals put forward by each 'side'. Where there was a collision, they
pleaded for further thinking. Thus much of their effort was
concentrated on the private meetings of each 'side', where by
persuasion and argument they tried to help each to 'give', and thus
to reach a compromise acceptable to all. Their own strength lay
in their power to vote, for as each 'side' put its case, it was
conscious of the need to persuade the independent members, and

as discussion proceeded, a reasonable solution would be hammered out to which all parties could agree. Thus in practice it was seldom necessary to use the vote at all, but the fact that the independent members could come down on one side or the other, made their influence the key factor in many situations. An exception to this general experience was observed on the Agricultural Wages Boards, where the employers' 'side' deemed it unwise to compromise, since their position at the annual review of prices might be jeopardised. In this case, the independent members were obliged to vote for one view or the other. Bayliss has described the role of the independent members as a 'complex amalgam of conciliation and arbitration. Yet it is both more and less than that. It is a unique hybrid function, which gives them a very great power, when it is needed, to get a decision; but which reduces their importance in proportion to the ability of the two sides to find compromises for themselves.' (Bayliss op. cit., p. 129.)

Opinion

For many years during and after the First World War, there was general approval of the trade boards (a view endorsed by the wartime Committee on Reconstruction). It was said that the legal control of wages in certain industries had virtually abolished the grosser forms of sweating, and the workers had therefore benefited. Many of the workers were women, always a difficult group to organise, and most were scattered in little businesses, and in various parts of the country. Statutory minima for these workers, it was argued, was the only way. Nor were the employers antipathetic, at least if they were 'good' ones. Some had been obliged to pay low wages because their competitors did so, and they could hardly expect to make a profit for themselves if their rivals undercut them. By curbing the excesses of the unscrupulous, trade boards were welcomed by the majority of employers, particularly those whose wares were to be sold on the home market. There was not quite the same enthusiasm if the competitors were foreigners (especially from the Far East), whose low labour costs were said to be 'unfair'.

Though there was little criticism during the inter-war years about the idea of legal minimum wages for certain trades, some grumblings, particularly about the machinery, could be heard. It was said, for instance, that the delay was too great between an application for a change, and the time when the decision became legal. For though it was democratic to ask the workers and the employers to comment on a proposal before it was sent to the Minister for ratification, the process was lengthy, and there were delays at the Ministry before the Order was promulgated. The shortest time was seven weeks, the average ten, but it was sometimes four or five months before the new wage rate came into force, with the result that conditions might in the meantime have changed completely.

Shortage of wages inspectors was the source of another complaint (approximately one for every 5,000 establishments to be inspected). The enforcement of minimum wages among three and a half million workers, often scattered, and in small-scale businesses, was a herculean task. The number of employers found to be disobeying the regulations was high, and the number of workers receiving less than their due, seldom fewer than one in seven of those inspected, too high for anyone to feel comfortable about the fate of others who had not been inspected.

The complexity of the Orders caused certain misgivings, as these were legal documents, couched in legal language, and were therefore notoriously difficult for the layman to understand. Workers in ill-paid jobs, were often, by the nature of things, the least literate. To them, the Order setting out a complicated system of payments was difficult enough, but it became unintelligible when expressed in legal terms.

One other criticism, which has been heard more loudly since 1945, has been the use of the power of delay exercised by the Minister. Apart from the period during the operation of the Prices and Incomes Act 1966, and its successors, he has been able to hold up his ratification, sometimes for months. For instance, during the economic crises, and the 'wage pauses' of the 1950s and 1960s, he more than once ratified the agreements, but post-dated their operation by nearly six months (*The Economist,* 9 October, 1961)— a serious situation for low-paid workers in times of rising prices. 'It might well be' wrote Professor Wedderburn (*Worker and the Law,* p. 132) 'that a stubborn Minister of Labour, urged to operate a wage freeze by an enthusiastic Chancellor of the Exchequer, could run into severe difficulties with certain Wages Councils, many of whom greatly prize their independence from his control.'

The 1966 Prices and Incomes Act proved the truth of this assertion.

On the growth of organisation amongst workers or employers, the statutory system of wage negotiation produced a mixed result. The consistent policy since 1918 was that the lack of negotiating machinery should be the main reason for establishing councils; but it was equally widely believed that a general improvement in wages would lead to better organisation, and that to meet together round the table would help both sides to see the necessity. Organisation became the more certain, it was thought, when the two 'sides' were the focus of negotiation. Without a strong union, or employers' association behind them, they lost much of their force. That voluntary organisation did develop in certain cases has been well illustrated by the emergence of what has come to be called the 'two-tier' policy. In certain cases the trade union has successfully organised sections of an industry, covered by a wages council, and has negotiated a higher wage rate for the organised group, leaving the rest of the industry relatively unorganised, but protected by the statutory minimum wage. For instance, U.S.D.A.W. obtained a higher wage rate for shop-assistants in co-operatives and multiple shops than the minimum enforced among the smaller enterprises. In spite of this, many have suggested that the presence of legal machinery has been a disincentive to trade union organisation. Workers felt it unnecessary to go to the trouble and expense of joining a union when their position was safeguarded by the wages council. The unions were either too lazy, or thought it too costly, to make the effort to recruit marginal members whose wages were guaranteed and who therefore were neither in desperate need, nor likely to constitute a threat to the standards of the organised.

What the overall effect on trade unions has been would seem open to disagreement, but two points can be made. Where the union has been strong, its efforts to negotiate a higher wage have sometimes been impeded by the existence of a wages council, as in the case of the railway refreshment staff. Further, it has been ruled that the Terms and Conditions of Employment Act 1959 (p. 129) and the wages councils are not compatible. If an industry were subject to a wages council, and a rate of pay higher than the minimum were voluntarily negotiated, that rate could not be enforced, even for part of an industry.

A more fundamental objection to the whole idea of wages councils, and everything they stand for, has been voiced by F. J. Bayliss. According to him, the basic conception of wage negotiation in Britain has been its voluntary nature. Agreements voluntarily approved through the give and take of negotiation have a much better chance of being honoured responsibly on all sides than those imposed by a legal guarantee. No matter how similar in composition the council and the voluntary negotiating body might be, they are quite different in fact. Unions and employers would not be doing their job in ordinary negotiation, unless they represented, as widely as possible, the views of those engaged in an industry. Yet it has seldom been possible to recruit a really representative membership of both 'sides' on the councils. To give unrepresentative agreement the force of law would seem alien to the traditions of British labour relations.

Moreover, when wages councils (trade boards) were first started, the economic circumstances of the country were different. Trade unionism was weak, employment subject to violent fluctuations, and there were pockets of under-payment so serious that the public conscience was affronted. Since 1945, trade unions have grown in power, though very little in membership, and rising wages and full employment have transformed the picture. Yet few wages councils have been brought to an end. It seems that neither the unions nor the employers want to abolish them altogether; what was inaugurated as a temporary expedient has become a permanent part of the picture, with the 'two-tier' policy thrown in for good measure. The Minister, with his increased power to initiate proceedings for the withdrawal of a council, has been reluctant to press forward without the goodwill of both sides. A reluctance that is understandable, since he must rely on their willingness to work a voluntary system. The Minister's memorandum (in 1965) to the Royal Commission on Trade Unions and Employers' Associations contained a section deploring the 'disappointingly slow progress in replacing statutory wages councils with voluntary bargaining machinery'. He even suggested an alteration in the law enabling him to abolish a council, if a union applied, and if he were satisfied that the workers would not suffer.

Half a century after their beginning, a tide of opinion has been mobilised to withdraw the statutory bodies of wage regulation as soon as convenient. The view has not gone unchallenged; from

E. G. A. Armstrong (*British Journal of Industrial Relations,* March 1966) has come a counter-attack. In his opinion the very fact that wages inspectors were discovering so many breaches of the regulations, involving so many thousands of pounds of unpaid wages each year, was a serious comment on the position of wage-earners in Britain. If inspectors brought to light so much under-payment in the establishments they were able to visit, what would be revealed if they visited all? It was useless to suggest that full employment brought its own solution, and that an underpaid person would quickly move to a better job. His own researches in Birmingham 1962–64, where vacancies greatly exceeded applicants, had shown that wage inspectors had recovered an average of £5,000 a year in arrears of wages. Paradoxically, full employment on Birmingham's scale made violations more, not less likely, since industry has been obliged to draw on 'deeper layers of potential labour', than would be the case otherwise. Part-time workers, married women, the semi-retired, and above all coloured immigrant labour, all poorly organised, tending to be unsophisticated, knowing little, and perhaps caring less, about wage levels or the duties of employers—these would be the type of workers drawn into gainful employment in a highly industrial and prosperous area like Birmingham, in the mid-twentieth century. For them a statutory minimum wage, and the continued use of government inspectors, would seem essential. The criterion for abolishing wages councils, concluded Armstrong, was not the level of employment, but the level of voluntary collective bargaining, which was a factor that continually eluded a certain section of workers. Therefore the need to protect these workers from exploitation was likely to be a continuing one, and the need for the vigilance of government inspectors an ever present one, in the foreseeable future.

VI

ARBITRATION

IT IS THE purpose of this chapter to examine the complicated and piecemeal arbitration service provided by the State to settle industrial disputes. This is not to say that privately arranged arbitration machinery does not exist, and reference will be made to it later. But that which is available to all industries, albeit under differing circumstances, is what has been of prime importance in this study.

Arbitration has long been considered the civilised method of dealing with the intractable dispute. It is the alternative to the law of the jungle, where force is the recognised criterion. If industrial relationships, whether concerned with questions of remuneration, hours, conditions of work, status, consultation, or anything else, can be submitted to voluntary negotiation, and a compromise agreement hammered out, to which all can subscribe, why should not disputes be amenable to similar methods? Yet experience has shown that in the very interpretation of these agreements, or in the desire of one side or the other to change the agreement, or in the inability even of members of the same side to agree on how the settlement shall be implemented, have lain the seeds of disaster. And disaster might take the extreme form of work stoppage, initiated either by the employers, by all the workers, or by a small section of the workers.

Such a stoppage, whether by lock-out or strike, could have untold repercussions (see p. 190–91). It could mean loss of pay to those directly involved, and to their families. It could involve other workers not concerned with the dispute at all. It could result in loss of production, and inability to honour delivery dates. The general public, as customers, would then be faced with loss, through delay, and perhaps a rise of price. In the face of such all-round hardship, the provision of a workable arbitration service would seem plain common-sense.

Yet it was not until relatively late in Britain's industrial development that permanent machinery was set up; when it came it clung to the traditional doctrine that in industrial relations voluntary agreement was more likely to succeed than compulsion. It accepted, moreover, a common corollary of voluntaryism, that every case stood on its own merits, should be dealt with *ad hoc*, and could not form part of a coherent whole, or contribute to a national policy of labour relations. For though no arbitrator has been immune to the climate of the times, or has failed to sense the general policy of the country, this is a far cry from the close application to a generally accepted set of principles that form the basis of an incomes policy. Nevertheless the machinery, haphazard and fumbling though it was, provided a foundation for what might become an acceptable, and much needed, service in industry.

Industrial Courts

Like so many of the social services in Britain, the first tentative steps to set up State machinery were taken years before the full-blown scheme reached the statute books. The earliest was the Conciliation Act 1896, though it would be idle to claim much for that. It was enacted in the pious hope that the Board of Trade would be made aware of the arbitration machinery which industry had established for itself, and would supplement it with conciliation boards of its own, if either or both parties asked for them. Apart from this, the real contribution of the Act was to create a state of mind in industry that would be receptive to outside help. Further, it set a pattern of arbitrating personnel, a mixture of neutral members with those involved in industry, that was to become popular in all kinds of adjudication. Perhaps most important of all, it gave experience in the difficult task of arbitration to a number of workers, employers and lawyers, who were to provide the nucleus of all subsequent conciliation boards.

By 1908 the Board of Trade had been able to assemble panels of workers, employers, and chairmen, from whom could be selected arbitration boards, when they were needed. The boards were still temporary, and therefore suffered the serious drawback of not being able to build up a set of standards, or principles, to which cases could be referred. An ordinary court of law has had the yardstick of the law itself to measure by, but these bodies had nothing, except their own assessment of each situation, and the results were uneven and unco-ordinated.

Nevertheless, the early experience of conciliation courts was on the whole satisfactory, and since one of the recommendations of the Committee on Reconstruction during the First World War had been the establishment of a standing arbitration tribunal, it was inevitable that something more permanent should be set up as soon as the war was over. Accordingly, the Industrial Courts Act was passed in 1919. Already, in 1916, the Ministry of Labour had been founded, and had been active in trying to keep industrial relations harmonious. So it was natural that the new Act should be closely linked to this Ministry. The Conciliation Act 1896, and the 1919 Act, together gave the Ministry the power to intervene in trade disputes. The earlier Act imposed the duty to enquire into the causes and circumstances of a dispute, to try to bring the parties together, and to appoint single conciliators, arbitrators, or boards, if asked to do so. The later Act made the machinery permanent, ready to be used when needed.

The normal model of the industrial court has been three members, all full time, all appointed and paid by the Ministry of Labour, and all independent. One of the three was the Chairman, usually a legally qualified person; the other two were selected, one each from a panel of employers and workers. They have been described (J. R. Clynes, quoted by Amulree, p. 174) as 'persons of experience, of known impartiality, judicially minded, capable of estimating evidence and reaching a reasonable decision according to the revealed facts of the case'. To be so impartial had dangers of its own. If court members were to be full-time, with loyalties that were not to be deflected from their proper functions of weighing evidence, how was it possible for them to keep sufficiently in touch with their own 'side', to give them the understanding necessary to reach a 'reasonable' decision? The dilemma was partially solved by sometimes appointing part-time members from the panels, and by the precept that full-time panel members should seek every opportunity to keep in touch with their 'side', while maintaining their own impartiality.

During periods of pressure, the court has been held in several divisions, mostly in London, but sometimes in the provinces, though it has not always been necessary for a 'full' court to be called. The Minister has appointed the President, and upon him has rested the decision whether a single arbitrator, or several members should sit. Expert assessors have occasionally been called, and women have always been on the panels, and always asked to sit in cases affecting women workers. In practice, the President and the full-time representatives, have together carried the bulk of the work. Only in times of crisis, such as illness, have the other members of the panel been called. The court has appointed a permanent secretariat, with its own London headquarters. No charges of any kind have been made by the Ministry for the services of the industrial court, though the parties have had to meet their own expenses, such as those of being represented at the hearing.

Whether either side should be legally represented has rested in the discretion of the court, though in practice this has not been refused. The court has never been a court of law, in the ordinarily accepted sense, as there has not been a corpus of law to interpret and enforce. It has nevertheless been conducted according to statutory rules, which have included the power of the court to regulate its own procedure, and in fact this has not strayed far from the procedure of an ordinary court of law. No case could be submitted to the court without the consent of both parties, and it was the duty of the court to listen to the arguments, and reach a decision that seemed fairest in all the circumstances. If unanimity were impossible, the President became the umpire, and his decision was final. In time, the decisions came to constitute a number of precedents, and in a sense, they might be described as 'case law'. Thus, courts sitting in the latter part of the century, have been in a stronger position than the early ones, because they could refer to previous decisions and arguments when making an award. Unlike the court of legal appeal, it was not the practice of the industrial court to make available the reasons for its award, but a full statement of the rival arguments has been published in many cases.

When once the decision was taken, it was left to the parties to accept or reject it, though having agreed to submit to arbitration, both sides usually accepted the award. If there was doubt about its exact meaning, the court could be asked by the Minister, or by either party, for an interpretation, and this the court was bound to give.

Single Arbitrators and Boards of Arbitration. If the dispute was local, or not involving a whole industry, the parties have often preferred a simpler form of arbitration than the 'full' court, and the matter having been put to the Minister, he might suggest a Single Arbitrator (with or without assessors), to go to the site of the difficulty, to hear the case. A number of lawyers, university professors, and others experienced in this kind of work, have made themselves available to the Minister for assignments of this kind. In certain cases, the arbitrator might become the President of a temporary arbitration board, with representatives of employers and workers sitting as a tribunal. Such hearings have usually been held in private, though the actual procedure has rested with the arbitrator, who would in any case be the umpire, and would promulgate to the parties the decision reached. These awards have not generally been made public, as they were considered to be the property of the parties. In practice, a large number of these private hearings have taken place, and many small disputes, that might have become major conflicts, have been peacefully settled. Many have thought the method should be more widely used, so that small bonfires could be quenched before they became conflagrations.

Court of Inquiry and Committee of Investigation. The Industrial Courts Act 1919 contained two other provisions which, though seldom used before 1945, have grown in public esteem since the end of the war. The Court of Inquiry and the Committee of Investigation were devices for the use of the Minister of Labour himself. At his discretion, and in serious cases where deadlock seemed inevitable, and where the parties had appeared to refuse arbitration, the Minister has had the power to appoint one of these bodies, which might consist of one or more persons. If more than one, they would usually be composed of an independent Chairman, and representatives of the employers and the workers, normally selected from outside the industry concerned. The court, or committee, have had the power to ask those with knowledge of the facts (mainly the disputants) to give evidence on oath, though not to subpoena them to do so. It was left to the Minister to use his own discretion whether to appoint a Court of Inquiry or a Committee of Investigation, and he has tended to choose the latter, if the issues were more local in scope, and less liable to have wider implications. The Court of Inquiry was generally held in public, and presented a report to Parliament at the earliest moment. The Committee of Investigation was more likely to hold private hearings, with no obligation to present a report to parliament. Otherwise, they have both been equally used, at an average of nearly two a year since 1945.

The original purpose of the Minister's discretionary power to appoint a Court of Inquiry, or Committee of Investigation, was to inform Parliament, and through it, the public, about the causes of the dispute, and the facts of the situation. It was thought that since many disputes had arisen out of misunderstandings, and failure in communications, to illuminate the facts would dissipate much of the bitterness. Moreover, since it was the public which usually suffered by industrial conflict, they surely had a right to know the plain facts. A Court could be set up during a strike without the consent of the parties, and many have looked upon it as a way of using the public as a jury, with public opinion as a powerful means of settlement. Others have regarded the device as a factor in drawing the heat out of a dispute, and giving both sides a chance to 'cool off'. They have been encouraged in this belief by the fact that Courts of Inquiry have dealt with a much wider range of disputes than the Industrial Courts. The latter have tended to arbitrate on questions of wages and conditions of employment. But the Courts of Inquiry have considered disputes over demarcation of work, alleged victimisation of workmen, recognition of trade unions by employers, as well as the more usual problems of pay and conditions. As the wider questions have often proved to be more obstinate, the power of the inquiries to shed light on them, and give time for public influences to work, has been thought beneficial, though European and American experience might indicate to the contrary. There, 'cooling off' has been just as likely to harden opinion as to make it more tractable.

The reports of the more recent Courts of Inquiry have displayed interesting developments. For besides setting out the facts, they have included recommendations for a reasonable settlement. The public, as well as the parties, have been able to focus their thinking on positive steps to escape the impasse. It should be emphasised that there has been no question of either side being bound, either legally or morally, to accept all or any of the recommendations; but experience has shown that many industrial conflicts have been helped towards a settlement by this method.

An investigation[1] made in 1965, showed that of the 34 Courts of Inquiry (or Committees) held since 1945, 24 were settled on the lines recommended by the courts, eight of the others could not be decided, and in the other two, the Court had no effect. This seems a very high success rate. As the Minister has appointed a Court only in those cases where he thought it would help, it might be argued that if he were to take the risk oftener, his success rate would go down but the number of settlements might rise, to the benefit of all.

It has been emphasised so far, that the findings of Industrial Courts, and Courts of Inquiry, though often successful in settling a dispute, were in no sense legally binding. Certain exceptions to this generalisation have made their appearance. For instance, the Road Haulage Wages Act 1938 laid the responsibility for guaranteeing fair wages, in the last resort, on the Minister of Labour, which in effect meant the Industrial Court, but it became a Wages Council in 1948, and rates of pay were legally enforceable thereafter. Similarly the Fair Wages Resolutions, applying to workers on government or local government contract, especially the Resolution of 1946, depended on the Industrial Court to arbitrate in cases of difficulty. But the most important break with tradition was the 1959 Terms and Conditions of Employment Act (p. 129), in which the Industrial Court became the arbiter, with legal backing for its decisions, where negotiated agreements had been flouted. By the same token, the ordinary awards of the Court made after 1959, and accepted by both sides, became legally enforceable as part of the terms and conditions of employment.

Industrial Relations Officers

Besides the permanent machinery to adjudicate on industrial quarrels, the Ministry of Labour has developed a preventive service of experienced officers, ready at any time to try to smooth out industrial disharmony, and promote good relations. Up to the early 1960s, one set of officers concentrated on promoting good personnel management, and another group was called upon in cases of dispute. By 1961, it was thought, the officers could be best used on the combined function, and the two services were consequently united.

The essence of the Ministry policy has been to stand aside, and

[1] McCarthy and Clifford, *British Journal of Industrial Relations* March 1966.

encourage industry to make agreements, settle differences, and develop its own machinery if possible. The Ministry has always hoped that the knowledge that skilled help was there for the asking—that each regional office had its own industrial relations officers, well primed by local officials about the facts of the situation, experienced in the ways of industry, and the arts of industrial relations—would have a softening effect on both sides. At first they were disappointed; but later, confidence grew, and with it the quality and qualifications of the officers improved, till by the middle of the century they were accepted both in their constructive work, and as a useful standby when difficulties occurred. Many hundreds of disputes which seemed insoluble have been dealt with in this way, mostly behind closed doors, and without the publicity that more overt methods would attract. Their work has been described as the most valuable service the Ministry has been able to provide. (Wedderburn, p. 123.) (Leaflet P.L.410.)

Industry's own arbitration service

It was earlier stated that industry had developed schemes of its own for settling disputes, and undoubtedly the bulk of industrial disharmony is smoothed out through the 'recognised channels'. Only when it got out of hand was it necessary to fall back on the Ministry machinery. No adequate study of all sides of private provision has yet been undertaken, but one authority has estimated that about 70 industries (Ince, p. 120) have made provision for arbitration where disputes have not been settled by private agreement. One example has been the engineering industry, especially that part of it linked together on the trade union side by the Confederation of Ship-building and Engineering Unions, and on the employers' side by the Engineering and Allied Employers' National Federation. By the 'York Agreement', for instance, a dispute in a factory should be tackled in the factory first—if necessary with the help of officials from the trade union and the employers' association. Failing this, the matter should go to joint meetings at the district or at the national level. The presence of recognised procedure has meant that no other action, such as reference to an outside arbitrator, or, at worst, a stoppage of work, was to be considered until the proper channels had been used.

Nationalised industries are another example, as they have been given a statutory duty to establish satisfactory arrangements for collective bargaining, and the settlement of disputes. Rail transport has had its own arrangements since the First World War, and these were continued without much change, after it became state-controlled. Coal-mining, too, carried over the old machinery into nationalisation. Most disputes in mining have been started at the pit, and have been settled at the pit, with or without the intervention of trade union and N.C.B. officials. Unsettled difficulties, and those with wider significance, have been sent to the District or the National Committee. Through the years, details have been worked out about time limits, umpires, which decisions should be final, and which might go on for further consideration.

The draw-back with many of these arrangements has been the delay; patience then breaks down, followed by a tendency to refuse further to explore the problem through industry's own conciliation machinery; direct action then, only too easily, takes over.

Joint Consultation (leaflet I.R.L. 1)

One thing above all else that experience has taught is that disputes seldom become serious without a background of misunderstanding, frustration, and accumulated abrasiveness between the parties. For this, the most widely supported remedy has been joint consultation, or an adequate system of communication and discussion between the various parts of one firm. If properly devised, and honestly prosecuted, it is argued, such a method could help to pool the thinking about the future prospects of the plant, to assess how all ranks might react to change, and to increase understanding of the way the shoe was pinching under existing circumstances. No-one would claim that the remedy was an unfailing panacea; indeed it has as often created conflict (Jacques) as resolved it, but it could be regarded as one way of trying to foresee, and deal with, possible causes of dispute.

Whitleyism

A more organised system of joint consultation was envisaged by the Whitley Committee on Reconstruction, during the First World

War. One of their recommendations was to organise, in every industry, a structure representing employers and work-people, and to consider matters affecting the progress and well-being of the trade, from the point of view of all those engaged in it, as well as of the general interests of the community. In the minds of the Committee the structure for each industry was shaped like a pyramid, with one National Joint Industrial Council of equal representation from employers and workers, several District Councils to consider matters of regional interest, and as many Works Committees similarly constituted as there were plants. At a time when 'workers' control' was preached by a few socialists, heartily opposed by the leaders of industry, and little understood by the rank and file, it was remarkable to find a government committee, led by the Speaker of the House of Commons, proposing that the employees of a whole industry should sit down regularly with the employers, and thrash out matters affecting the progress of the trade from all its angles. If it had been carried out in the spirit of the recommendation, as thorough-going joint consultation, 'Whitleyism' might have avoided many of the great industrial disputes of the inter-war years. But this was not to be, as its progenitor, J. H. Whitley, sadly complained. Instead, the Whitley Committees, that came into being, were almost exclusively wage negotiating and conciliation bodies. Nevertheless in those industries that adopted the Whitley structure (there were 73 in 1923, 40 in 1931, but 114 in 1947), a viable method of settling wage rates, and solving some of the knotty problems of dispute, was created. The Civil Service, Local Government, many of the social services, and a number of industries such as pottery and printing have adopted the pattern, and the Whitley Councils' reputation for dealing with disputes has been fairly favourable.

Other developments and ideas in arbitration. It would be unwise to claim more for the State arbitration service than it deserves. An analysis (*The Times*, 15 January, 1962) made by the Ministry of Labour into the methods used to settle wage changes from 1952 to 1961, showed conclusively that arbitration played a small and diminishing part. In 1953 as many as 20 per cent of the wage settlements were decided by this method, but subsequently the percentage declined, due mainly to changes in government policy, until by 1960 it was less than half of one per cent.

As for the principles activating the various arbitration bodies, it has been said (*The Economist*, October 1953) that before the war the members considered such well-known factors as the cost of living, the ability of the industry to pay, and comparable wages in other industries. But they never omitted the power element. They tried to prophesy who would have won in a strike, and avoided giving a decision that would have offended the interests of the winning side. This policy, it was thought, gained general respect, as both sides got approximately what they would have done with a strike, only more cheaply. After the war the power element was not the guide, otherwise the trade unions would have won much higher wages. Instead, arbitrators tried to stress the importance of 'real' wages, and the need for the unions to restrain their desire for higher wages and discourage the inflation spiral. Undoubtedly much restraint was shown, particularly by union leaders. But it was not always so, and in the absence of a recognised body of principles upon which wages should be judged, the temptation to pursue a 'free for all' has sometimes appeared, with the inevitable agitation, and liability to strike, that such a situation engendered.

'Unofficial strikes', the ones not recognised by a bona fide trade union, have been occasioned by a multitude of causes, worthy and unworthy. Where they have been 'lightning' strikes happening suddenly, and without the representatives of either side having a chance to consider the issues and find a peaceful solution they have caused the maximum dislocation, and some alternative has not unnaturally been sought. The solutions most readily put forward have been punishment of the strikers, or compulsory arbitration, or both.

Compulsory arbitration—labour courts

Focusing on arbitration, the notion that it might be compulsory has long been attractive to many people. If a society is rational enough to abide by the decision of an impersonal court in pursuance of private justice, there is no reason why it should not do so in its industrial disputes. Attractive as the theory is, there may be some doubt whether it would hold water in practice. A short examination of the British experience might illustrate the problems.

In the 1914–18 war, as in its successor in 1939–46, the country was faced with the necessity of winning at all costs; and one means was the avoidance of labour disputes. Accordingly in 1915, as in 1940, a system was enacted to make strikes and lock-outs illegal, and compulsorily to refer difficult disputes to an arbitration tribunal. If a dispute arose, and either side wanted to refer it to arbitration, it could do so, even if the other side disapproved. Decisions so taken were legally binding on both sides, even when both sides disliked them. Refusal to abide by a decision could bring punitive action by the State. In practice strikes did occur during the Wars, and action was seldom, if ever, taken.

This was compulsory arbitration in its crudest form, tolerable in war-time, but open to criticism in ordinary conditions. Nevertheless, when the second war ended, instead of abolishing the emergency legislation (as happened to a large extent in 1919), it was decided to continue the experiment of compulsory arbitration for a limited period. Accordingly, the two Industrial Disputes Orders (No. 1217, and No. 1304) were re-enacted over a further five years. By the one, if wages and conditions of employment were negotiated by the recognised representatives of both sides, the agreements became legally binding on all the employers and workers in the trade or industry. But, in return, strikes and lock-outs were prohibited. By the other, if a dispute arose, it was to be referred to the National Arbitration Tribunal, on the application of either side, for a decision, which automatically became part of the contract.

The year 1950–51 was crucial. Compulsory arbitration had already lasted longer than the experimental five years, and criticisms of its working were heard more loudly. Some of the unions were chafing under the prohibition against strikes, and were suggesting that the National Arbitration Tribunal had become a mere adjunct of government. If the government, for instance, asked for restraint in wage increases, the tribunal seemed to pay more attention to that than to the merits of the individual case they were asked to decide. It was also alleged that wages were being artificially pegged, but that profits and dividends were not.

In spite of the objections, compulsory arbitration was not dead, though clearly some modification had to be made. In 1951, Order 1305 was replaced by Order 1376, by which the right to strike or lockout was revived, and each side was encouraged to find a negotiated solution. If either side wanted arbitration, they could seek it from the Industrial Disputes Tribunal (replacing the National Arbitration Tribunal), whose decisions then became legally binding. But the right to seek arbitration was limited to those who were recognised by both sides as *bona fide* parties to an agreement—in practice the trade unions and the employers' organisations. Small groups or break-aways were debarred from making such a request. This was the situation up to 1959, but dissatisfaction with compulsory arbitration was growing still further, and was being expressed from another quarter. It was the employers who felt aggrieved. They claimed the Order worked unequally. When a decision became enforceable, the employers were easily identified, and obliged to accept the findings, whether they liked them or not. The workers, it was alleged, were not so easy to locate, and even if they were, their numbers made it impossible to enforce something of which they disapproved. In the last resort, it was said, no-one could condemn thousands of people to prison. In the face of this, and the luke-warm attitude of the unions, the time to end compulsory arbitration had arrived, so in 1959, Order 1376 was revoked.

What had appeared logically just and fair to all parties, including the whole community, had proved unworkable. It was objectionable to the workers, because they did not manifestly see justice being done by the Tribunal; and it was unfair to the employers, because, in the last resort, enforceability was only possible for one side.

Terms and Conditions of Employment Act 1959. Meanwhile another item of the war-time emergency, closely linked to compulsory arbitration, was in jeopardy. This was the legal right of properly negotiated agreements to be honoured by all parties. When the Industrial Disputes Order 1376 was abolished in 1959, it required a new Act to safeguard agreements and ensure that every employer enforced them. For instance, N.A.L.G.O. had been very concerned in case some of the local authorities failed to pay their officials on the nationally negotiated scales. The Terms and Conditions of Employment Bill was therefore introduced. It built on earlier experience, for though it did not automatically make every agreement legally enforceable, it did enact that if a collective agreement, which had been recognised by the Ministry of Labour, was not honoured by an employer, and if the authorised representatives of a substantial proportion of the employers or workers reported this to the Minister, he must take action.

The decision to take piece-meal action in this way gave both sides what they wanted, indirectly, without reinstating compulsory arbitration, or upsetting the voluntary nature of the agreement. The Act did three things: it continued the twenty-year practice of recognising only those agreements negotiated by bona-fide representatives of employers and workers. Secondly the power of complaint was limited to them. Thirdly it distinguished between major and minor problems, or what the compulsory arbitrators had called 'disputes' and 'issues' (now to be called 'claims'). A 'dispute' had been defined as a disagreement over the negotiation of a new agreement, or the modification of an old one. An 'issue' was concerned with the way each employer used the agreement that had already been made. If he were accused of a breach of the agreement, this was an 'issue'.

The new act turned its back on 'disputes', because by this time, both sides wanted agreements to be voluntarily negotiated, without the danger of the process being interrupted by a one-sided appeal to arbitration. Only if both sides wished it could a 'dispute' go to arbitration (for example the Industrial Court). But 'claims' arising out of agreements already made came within the jurisdiction of the Act.

In no sense has the Act proved a major measure, either to provide an 'incomes policy', or to reduce industrial conflict, but it has introduced several interesting points. One of these has been how to distinguish the appropriate representative bodies. The Act has given legal recognition to trade unions and employers' organisations, but has not given a definition of either group. It has been left to the Industrial Court to decide when, for instance, a 'break-away' union could be regarded as the substantive representative of the workers. Further, if the Minister were appraised of a 'claim', he was obliged to submit it to the Industrial Court, whose decision was then final and legally binding. The Industrial Court, which had been by-passed by the war-time compulsory arbitration system, was now brought into the limelight, and given the power to make legally binding decisions.

Labour courts. In Europe and a few of the Commonwealth countries, labour courts have been appointed, like any other court, to adjudicate in industrial disputes. Not that there has been any uniformity in their constitution and functions, except that where they have operated, they have decided where the balance of the argument lay, have issued their decisions, and have made them legally binding. Many of the courts, such as those in Germany, have a constitution similar to that of some of the British tribunals, or the industrial court—with a legal chairman, and a representative each of employers and workers.

Britain has tended to create a new tribunal whenever the need arose. One was enacted by the Industrial Training Act (p. 28), and this has been used for the Redundancy Payments Act (p. 137), the Contracts of Employment Act (p. 135), and others, including disputes, mainly concerned with employees of nationalised concerns, that were previously heard by various referees and boards under 23 different statutes. Quite separate tribunals were created to hear disputes under the National Insurance Acts (p. 225), and for many years, until 1966, there was a different one to hear appeals against the operation of the National Assistance Act. Then there have been all the possibilities under the Industrial Courts Act (p. 118). The variety of tribunals, from whom there was often no appeal, except on points of law, has been phenomenal. Whether they should all be replaced by local Labour Courts has aroused considerable controversy. Some have advocated this[1] in the hope that they would strike a balance between the interests of the worker in maintaining his livelihood, and the interests of the employer in promoting the efficiency of his firm. Others (for example Wedderburn in *New Society*, 9 December, 1965), have been more cautious about what has been called 'picking a ready-made package off some fashionable foreign shelf', in order to tidy up the clutter left by successive statutes.

The crux of the problem seems to lie in how far all disagreements should be subject to arbitration, and how far the findings of the tribunal should be binding on all parties.

One idea has been to use Labour Courts for a limited field of industrial difficulty only, and there are fruitful possibilities here. It might well be that to decide disputes over national wage rates or conditions of employment in this way would be an inappropriate use of the method, since the outcome of one dispute could become the precedent for the next. And this might set off a chain reaction

[1] Kahn-Freund 'Labour Management and Legislation', *Progress* March 1964.

that would be only a disservice to industry in the long run. But where 'issues' are at stake, or where individuals feel themselves unjustly treated (for instance, dismissals), the presence of an easily accessible Court might have a useful function. This was recognised by a Committee of the N.J.A.C., which examined the whole problem in their report on 'dismissal procedures' (1967).

VII

LOSING ONE'S JOB

THE ONE FACT the 'industrial revolution' in Britain made clear to the ordinary working man was the impermanence of his hold on any particular job. If he wanted freedom, the argument ran, freedom to work in the job of his choice, for the employer of his choice, in the venue he preferred, and to leave and go elsewhere when it suited him, then he must recognise an equal freedom on the part of his employer to take him or sack him. If this meant that his services were sought when trade was good, but he was cast on the industrial scrap-heap when it was bad, without a livelihood or means of getting one, it was better than a feudal society, where the labourer was tied to his master, without the right to better himself, or to order his own life in freedom and hope.

Thinking has moved some way from the extreme laissez-faire doctrine of the early 19th century, largely because of the inequalities and hardships the system produced, and partly because of a growing sense of the responsibility people had one for one another, and that the community had for all its members. It was said for instance, that everyone not only had the duty to work, but the 'right to a job'. Perhaps, in the minds of some, this meant no more than the chance to work if a job happened to be there, but as a battle-cry of the unemployed in the early 20th century it was more than that; it meant the right to a job, even if one had to be made for the purpose. From this there gradually grew up the view that a worker had a certain inherent right to a job, that for him it represented a 'property', from which he should not be parted without his consent or without compensation. Not everyone would go as far as this, but increasingly it was being claimed that 'stability of employment' (as the French would say) or 'job-security' (as in

133

America) meant that if a firm could not keep a man for life, in the one job, it was their duty to find him another as good, or better. Failing this, they should ease the parting in some material way. Others said that since many jobs might be lost through a firm contracting its payroll to meet the demands of price competition, labour had the right to a say in the process, since to them it might well be preferable to suffer a diminution in their own economic reward than to lose their jobs altogether. Short-time working could well be better than no jobs, and instances would not be difficult to find of workers and their representatives offering to abolish over-time, or reduce piece-work earnings and bonuses to avoid redundancies and excessive short-time working.

If it is argued that a worker has special rights in his own job, and if any changes in the job, particularly its abolition, have given him rights to a say in what should be done, and how the change should be handled; and if, in the last resort, the premature ending of a job has given him the right to compensation for loss—what would be his position if he lost his job for other causes? There may be many reasons why a man is dismissed, even apart from those who are employed temporarily or on a casual basis. For instance, he may be sacked through indiscipline or poor work, but on occasions he has had to go without any reason at all being given to him. The traditional right of employers to 'fire' their men without explanation was challenged by the I.L.O. in 1963, in Recommendation 119 (Cmnd. 2548 'Termination of Employment by the Employer'). The principle laid down here was that dismissal always required a 'valid reason', and that the most 'valid' related to the conduct or work capacity of the employee, or a firm's necessity to review its labour force. The I.L.O. went further than this by listing the reasons they thought were intolerable, or 'not valid'. These included membership of a trade union, seeking office as a workers' representative, filing a complaint (in good faith) against an employer alleging violation of the law, as well as dismissals because of race, colour, sex, marital status, religion, political opinion, national extraction, or social origin. When the British Government accepted the recommendation as a basis for discussion, it did so with certain reservations, stating that security of tenure could not be guaranteed to temporary or probationary workers, and that merchant seamen, fishermen, and temporary civil servants would have to be excluded. It also recognised that apart from such industries as docks and mines no convenient machinery was in general operation in Britain to hear appeals against dismissal, or to decide whether a reason given was valid or not. More often the matter, if it were raised at all, would be negotiated between the union official and the management.

The development of this new thinking on the relationship of a worker to his job has resulted in new social services to deal with this aspect of the problem of change. In order of appearance, they have been the Contracts of Employment Act 1963, which made it obligatory to give notice of severance, and the Redundancy Payments Act 1965 which outlined a system of compensation for those made redundant through industrial change. Industrial Tribunals were created to consider how far dismissals came within the meaning of the Acts.

Contracts of Employment Act 1963 (leaflet I.T.L.3)

This modest piece of legislation, applying to the whole of Britain (except N. Ireland), came into force in July 1964, and was intended to give workers some idea of the terms of their employment. The details, to be set down by the management for each employee to read, concerned wages, how calculated, and how often paid; working hours; holidays; schemes for payment during sickness, injury, or old age; the date at which the employment commenced; and the periods of notice. The Ministry of Labour may add other items to the list. Except in one particular, it was not the government's intention to lay down the terms and conditions of employment, which were to be left to the customary processes of negotiation. The one exception concerned the traditional right of the employer to dismiss at will, and the worker to leave without notice. For though in any dispute about the period of notice the courts have never let the lack of a written contract stand in the way of their interpreting the general practices of the industry, the position was not always clear to the worker himself, until this Act was passed. The Act has stated that if a worker has been continuously in his employment for 26 weeks, the employer must give at least seven days' notice of termination. This was raised to two weeks for employees of two years' standing, and to four weeks for those of five years' standing. Thus was established a general principle, that the longer a man remained in his job (within limits),

the longer the notice to which he was entitled, should the employment end. The worker in his turn was legally obliged to give a
week's notice, if after six months in the same job he wished to
leave. But in his case, no legal increase in the period of notice was
required, even if he had been in the job all his working life.
Voluntary agreement might modify these terms, but could not
undermine them. On the other hand, certain groups of workers
were exempted from the requirements. Civil servants, the merchant
navy and fishermen, close relatives of the employer, and part-time
workers (under 21 hours a week), were exempted from all the
provisions of the Act, including the receiving of a written contract
and the obligation to give or be given notice of ending it. Two
additional matters should be mentioned; the right to discharge or
leave the job without notice was safeguarded 'if the behaviour of
the other justifies it'; and a system of appeals was established
should either side think he had not been properly or sufficiently
informed. The same tribunal as for disputes under the Industrial
Training Act (see p. 28) and the Redundancy Payments Act (see
p. 140) was charged with the duty of settling disputes under this
Act.

The Act has not lacked critics, and many have thought it a great
waste of paper (and employers' time and money), achieving very
little. For instance the particulars of the terms of employment set
out in the document were in no sense a 'legal contract', but simply
an indication of the workers' entitlement. Nor was his 'document'
kept up to date. His employer need not supply him with any details
at all until he had been working for thirteen weeks, and changes
thereafter had to be notified within four weeks. It was not even
essential for him to receive a piece of paper of his own, provided
the information was lodged in a convenient and accessible place
(for example, the foreman's office) where he could read it during
working hours. These provisions were said to lead to delay over a
worker knowing his true position at any one time, and, if the document were lengthy and difficult to understand, it might even
discourage him from finding out. But what worried the critics
most was the absence of enforcing officers, appointed by the
Ministry of Labour, to see that the Act was carried out. It seemed a
curious imperfection for an Act, which in an aggravated case
could lead to a £100 fine, to have made no provision for an
inspectorate.

In spite of this, the Act has made a beginning in regularising the position of the manual worker, and bringing him into line with 'white collar' workers, who have normally expected a 'contract of service', when entering a post. Though 'on the spot' dismissals have not been abolished, some progress towards the I.L.O. recommendation of 'no dismissal without valid reason' has been made. Moreover, recognised periods of notice, with 'minimum pay' have been legally accepted and defined.

Redundancy

The circumstances under which a worker lost his job may have varied, but redundancy was picked out for special attention on two counts: it involved no blame to the worker himself, and it was inevitable and even desirable as part of industrial progress.

The word 'redundancy' was defined by an Acton Society monograph in 1958. It was 'the involuntary loss of a job through no fault of the worker concerned'. It was therefore different from unemployment, where the worker might have left his job voluntarily, or been sacked for incompetence, or misdemeanour.

Redundancy is apparently inseparable from modern industry, one of whose conditions for success is the capacity to change. This might arise out of the far-sightedness of a firm which has developed new processes, or new materials, and has sought to extend its business to incorporate the new ideas and new discoveries. It is a position that would not necessarily lead to redundancy, but it might do so if certain workers, skilled in the old processes, were no longer required for the new; or where mechanisation had supplanted labour. Since World War II, changes of this sort have not led to much redundancy as workers displaced in one area of a business have tended to be absorbed in another, particularly if the firm was able to grow as a result of its efficiency. A more common reason for dismissal has been when firms have amalgamated, and the whole undertaking has had to be reconsidered as one unit. In some instances, the opposite processes have been at work. Heavy competition, for instance, from other firms has sometimes led to contraction; or changes in the government policy (for instance, a credit squeeze) may have reduced the firm's capacity to maintain stable employment.

The attitude of employers to these changes has varied greatly, depending on the size and success of the enterprise, the general philosophy of those in control, and the age and nature of the labour force. At one extreme would be the man who has regarded the sole purpose of his firm as the making of profit. In his case, he might argue there was no place for human or sentimental interest, and if the firm changed to new methods, replacing labour, he would neither inform his workers of his intentions, nor think it any business of his to facilitate their transition to employment elsewhere. Others, though still wedded to the notion that the purpose of private industry was to make private profit, would argue that to present a group of workers or a whole factory with a few days' notice of the termination of their employment, and not to explain the reason, or to give longer warning, or to show some evidence of human understanding, would be irrevocably to damage the firm's reputation. Damage of this sort might rebound on the firm long after, as they would have lost the power to attract 'good' labour, when they needed it, and could scarcely expect the maximum of loyalty and responsibility for good workmanship from the labour they had. Other employers have gone even further, and argued that not only did it pay them to build up an image as 'good' employers, but that they had a social responsibility, which included their shareholders and their workers, as well as the consumers of their products.

The net result of a more enlightened attitude to the workers, and the acceleration of change in British industry has been the appearance of a number of interesting examples of private severance schemes.[1] The analysis and comparison of three such schemes have shown some common elements, though others have been clearly divergent. Thus in 1962 English Electric Aviation Ltd (see D. Wedderburn, 'White Collar Redundancy', 1964; A. Fox, 'The Milton Plan', 1965; 'The Fawley Plan', 1965) had to reduce the number of workers in their Luton and Stevenage factories by about 2,000. This was due to a reversal of government policy on the Blue Water Guided Missile contract, and meant that engineers, draughtsmen, and other skilled workers were most affected. The British Aluminium Co Ltd was affected by more general considerations of competition and technological change in 1962, as was the Esso Petroleum Company in 1964; but whereas

[1] In 1963, the Ministry of Labour had been notified of 371 private agreements covering about one and three quarter million workers.

British Aluminium had to close one factory and concentrate production in another, Esso reorganised its productive processes at Fawley, and reduced the payroll there. The very different circumstances of each case underlines the view that each redundancy is unique. Nevertheless, the common factors are instructive. For instance, all went through a period of initial secrecy, wherein management worked out plans for dealing with the problem. None brought in the trade unions in the early deliberative stages, though one explained in great detail to the trade union the reason for the redundancy, and the proposals being developed to meet it. This was about two months before the news broke. All made early contact with the employment exchange, and invited the Ministry to send officers to the plant. One encouraged the establishment of a temporary office on the site. All used their own personnel staff to help redundant workers to find alternative employment, and in two of the cases, where transfer to other departments in the same firm was possible, workers were moved. But it was common experience that if re-employment meant moving to another area, with its attendant disruption of social ties, children's education, re-housing and the like, the maximum reluctance was met, in spite of such incentives as removal grants and settling-in allowances. All gave redundant workers compensation for displacement, and the amount was, in each case, dependant on the years of service to the firm. One of them based the gratuity on a fixed sum, but the other two used the man's average income as a variable, though all of them made a difference between monthly paid staff and other workers. Early retirement under special conditions was a feature in two of the schemes.

The biggest difference lay in the fact that the two earlier schemes were compulsory, in the sense that the firm chose which workers to lay off, while the Fawley one was voluntary.

In the Esso scheme the company indicated which departments, and which areas, were not redundant, and where a man leaving would not qualify for benefits. It then delineated the areas where a reduction in man-power had to be made, leaving it to the workers themselves to choose whether to go or not. In the event, the voluntary scheme reduced the labour force by almost the exact number required, and to everyone's surprise, the ones to leave were not necessarily the most able and efficient, or even the young, since the average age was 46. The latter fact might probably be explained by the additional gratuity for those over 40, and the arrangement for anyone with ten years service up to the redundancy period to retire at 55. The period of readjustment was four months, and every effort was made to explain the scheme thoroughly. A member of each department, for instance, was designated as 'co-ordinator' to help and advise any worker who needed it.

The voluntary system has not been tried out very often, but it seems to contain, in its essence, the answer to one big problem in redundancy. Who shall choose the workers to go? If management has made the decision, the commonest criterion (and the one favoured by the unions) has been 'last in first out', a logical, but often unsatisfactory, policy, as it might mean the redundancy of key workers, or a man finding it impossible to stabilise himself in employment at all, if he has had the bad luck to enter successive firms that were on the point of cutting back their labour force. The worst of all was if management failed to explain the reasons for their selection, and gave no more than the minimum notice of their intentions. The voluntary plan, coupled with extensive explanation and assistance to find other work, with sufficient time for people to make up their minds and look around, and an attractive 'golden handshake', appears to have worked with the minimum of dissatisfaction. Whether it would work as well in areas without alternative employment, or in times of bad trading conditions, is more doubtful.

The Redundancy Payments Act 1965 (leaflets I.T.L.1 and 2, R.P.L.1). How the firms have reorganised or reduced their labour force has been their own responsibility, and is likely to remain so. But the idea that no man shall be dismissed through no fault of his own, without recompense, has been gaining ground. At first it was opposed by the B.E.C., and the T.U.C., who preferred more attractive unemployment pay to any special redundancy compensation, since they believed the lump sum would restrict mobility, as workers would not seek alternative employment until the last moment in order to qualify for redundancy pay. Even when the draft of the Bill was laid before them (as members of the National Joint Advisory Council), the T.U.C. members hesitated to support the idea, fearing in addition that the prospect of redundancy payments would prejudice the employers against claims for ordinary wage increases. Another point that bothered both sides of industry was the minimum service requirement. Certain industries (particularly building) would be subject to special hardships, since short-term employment was their traditional system of work, and most workers in such industries would therefore be unable to qualify for 'compensation'. The solution of that problem proved insuperable for the time being, and the government had to proceed with their plan, leaving this and several other questions to be dealt with later.

When the Bill was finally presented to parliament, it was seen to be founded on two principles. Firstly, the compulsory responsibility to provide 'compensation' for workers losing their jobs through redundancy was placed squarely on the shoulders of the employers, instead of the tri-partite contributory method of ordinary unemployment insurance. But it was placed in such a way that part of the expense was pooled, through a weekly contribution to the National Insurance Fund of a few coppers for each insured worker on the pay-roll, the rest (about 30 per cent) being met by the firm whose workers were affected. The advantage of splitting the cost, it was argued, was to discourage employers from frivolous sackings at the Fund's expense, and to reduce the expenses of any one employer to bearable proportions.

Secondly, the actual compensation depended on three variables: wages earned; years of service; and the age of the worker, with an extra amount given to those over forty. The argument supporting this privilege for age was that, if firms were more highly reimbursed when dismissing older redundant workers, they would not be discouraged from employing the older worker in the first place. Further, if the older worker received bigger compensation, when found redundant, this might offset his difficulties in finding another job, since age has been found a barrier to employment in some cases.

The Redundancy Payments Act came into force in Great Britain in December 1965 (a similar scheme was applied to Northern Ireland early in 1966), but excluded the Channel Islands and the Isle of Man. Its object was to provide the 'golden handshake' to all workers over 18 years and under 65 (60 for women), who had been in 'continuous' full-time employment for two years or more with the same employer, or his heirs and successors, provided the business was carried on substantially as before, and who had been dismissed through redundancy. Those not eligible for compensation were part-time workers (less than 21 hours per week), those of pensionable age, dock-workers and share-fishermen, servants of the Crown (including Health Service employees, and the Armed Services), and near relatives (usually husband or wife, though in the case of domestic work, including grandparents and grandchildren).

If the employer had no more need for his services—and gave him notice in writing, a notice he must work, unless given permission by his employer to leave earlier—he became eligible for a redundancy payment, even though the firm might be taking on more (though different) labour. But if he were offered 'suitable' alternative employment, without a break, in the same firm, or that of an 'associated' firm, and refused it, he might well have made himself ineligible. There was a fairly strong view, held in some quarters, that severance pay should not be given if a man were on strike when his job ended, but it was finally held that he would still be eligible provided he made up the lost days, if the employer demanded it; and his days out on strike would not count for severance pay.

The pay itself was calculated from the date a worker entered the firm, or from his eighteenth birthday, whichever was the later. No-one could claim until he had worked continuously for two years, and therefore the earliest age an employee could be eligible was his twentieth birthday. The pay (leaflets I.T.L.1 and 2) was free of income tax, and calculated according to his weekly wage, his age group, and length of service. But there were limitations on what a redundant worker could receive, since there has always been a wage ceiling and a maximum length of service on which his claims could be based. If a person were declared redundant at pensionable age or over he would not be eligible, and if redundancy occurred within twelve months before retirement, compensation would only be paid at a reduced rate (leaflet R.P.L.1). The position of the worker in the bankrupt firm was safeguarded, as was that of the man whose employer refused to pay. In these cases the Fund itself investigated eligibility, and made a 'guaranteed payment', while sorting out the employer's position.

As for the employer, he was liable to contribute, through the National Insurance stamp (leaflet N.I.140A), to the Redundancy Fund set up by the then Ministry of Pensions and National

Insurance (later the Ministry of Social Security). But the onus was on him to make the actual payment to the redundant worker, and then claim rebate from the Fund. This allowance was calculated at two-thirds of the total sum if the redundant worker were forty or under, but seven-ninths if he were an older worker. Early warning to the Ministry of Labour of impending redundancy was an integral part of the scheme, partly to give the officers time to clear up any queries about claims before the dismissals took effect, and partly to give the exchange time to find the workers other jobs. Employers were urged to give at least 14 days' notice, and might even find their rebates reduced by as much as 10 per cent if they failed to do so without reasonable excuse. Claims for rebate had to be made within three months of the date of payment.

In certain cases the employer was already running his own private scheme of severance pay, such as those examined earlier, and since redundancy has tended to be unique to each industry, it was argued that these private schemes ought to be recognised for rebate purposes, and as alternatives to the national one. The relevance of this contention was recognised by the Act, and provided the occupational scheme were approved by both sides of industry, and that the employer kept up his weekly payments to the Fund, he could claim his allowances in the usual way.

A scheme as complex as this has naturally led to dispute and uncertainty about interpretation, and the Industrial Tribunal set up to settle questions arising out of the Industrial Training Act 1964 (p. 28) and the Contracts of Employment Act 1963 (p. 135) was given the further duty of adjudicating on the Redundancy Payments Act too. In this case, either the employer or the worker could bring the appeal, but it was the employer's responsibility to show why the worker was not eligible. In the first year (1966), about 6,000 appeals were heard, and nearly all were from workers wishing to establish their right to payment. The average compensation for the 137,000 workers receiving redundancy pay in 1966 was £190, which with unemployment benefit (where appropriate) must have considerably eased the hardship of those losing their jobs.

The whole principle of the Redundancy Payments scheme did not go unchallenged. Most serious was the allegation that there was no relationship between the lump sum received and the loss sustained. Letters began to appear in the press about workers declared redundant on Friday night, receiving their 'compensation', only to be taken on by another firm on Monday morning, at an increased wage. Why, it was argued, should employers be asked to pay out substantial gratuities of this kind, when the worker suffered no loss at all? It was not the practice in other countries which had developed severance schemes, and there seemed little justification for it here. The only convincing answer lay in the fact that other countries, notably members of the European Economic Community, had evolved severance payments as part of a general scheme, including adequate family allowances, wage-related unemployment pay, and good re-training facilities. The lump sum in their case was modest (about £105 in Belgium after 20 years' service) and was regarded as a solatium only. The Redundancy Payments Act in Britain was introduced as a solitary measure, when unemployment pay was below subsistence level, family allowances negligible, and re-training facilities only in embryo. 'Compensation' was therefore more than a solatium, especially for the older worker, with long service, who might find re-employment a difficult process, and who would need the maximum he could get to tide him over the lean period that was almost sure to follow his redundancy. Moreover it had not gone unnoticed that higher staff, declared redundant from lucrative jobs, were helped on their way by the 'golden handshake'. So, though the Act did not gear the payment to the actual loss, at the time of its passing there were reasons, both economic and social, for the payment of a lump sum, even a substantial one.

Thus a new social service to assist the movement of labour from one job to another, and to reduce hardship, has been created. But the position of the man who has lost his job for reasons other than redundancy remains to be dealt with. He needs three things: (a) the feeling that justice has been done, and that no job would be lost without there being some impartial body to whom he could appeal; (b) adequate remuneration for the period between one job and another; (c) appropriate training and the facilities to find new work. This would mean a system of labour courts, wage-orientated unemployment pay, and a much more dynamic system of re-training and job advice. Of these three, the third is developing quickly (p. 18), and the second will be dealt with in the next chapter. Only the first has still a long way to go.

VIII

INCOME MAINTENANCE FOR THOSE NOT WORKING

Early development and principles

THE INTERRUPTION OF earning power has been a major cause of poverty from time immemorial, and an even more calamitous one with the development of the factory system. Factories have meant urbanisation, and town-dwelling has separated people from the kind of self-sufficiency associated with the land, and the resources (limited though they might be) of the extended family, common to a settled rural community. Technological change and the need for labour mobility have accelerated the process, and most workers know that once they have lost their earnings, they have neither a family group able to absorb them, nor alternative resources to accommodate them.

The problems of self-dependence and the need to provide the maximum incentive for everyone to earn enough to meet his own responsibilities by himself, were fought out in the 19th century in the face of massive unemployment, ignorance and ill-health. It is not surprising therefore, that the solutions tended to be incoherent and inconsistent. The Poor Law had survived from the end of the 16th century, and was the sole communal attempt to deal with poverty. But under the new conditions of the 19th century, it required radical reorganisation to make it viable. As this reconstruction happened to coincide with the hey-day of the 'laissez-faire' doctrine, the new Poor Law was founded on the belief that 'self-help' provided the greatest good, and that public aid should be avoided as much, and as long, as possible. Thus, the Poor Law (Amendment) Act 1834 enlarged the size of the administrative unit from the parish to the area of the Board of Guardians, so that each would have financial resources (from the rates) to meet the demands of a growing industrial society. But it assumed that such resources would be used only in the most compelling circumstances, that the family was legally responsible for the maintenance of its members as long as it could, and that only the completely destitute, and those without relatives to support them, could become a charge on public funds. There was to be no question of subsidising a person in temporary difficulty, if he had resources of his own. Only when he had reached the bottom could he be helped—at a price. Paupers were to be penalised and deprived of many of their rights. The 'theory of less eligibility' was meant to be, and in many areas became, a harsh deterrent against losing one's self-dependence. One aspect of the theory was expressed by the 'work-house test', and the abolition of 'out relief', which made the destitute give up their homes, and enter the work-house. It is a curious side-light on the theory of the times, that Boards of Guardians spent more money on buildings, equipping and maintaining work-houses, than would have been spent on relieving the poor in their own homes; and that an age which believed so profoundly in the sanctity of the family, felt no compunction in scattering it when called upon to give public aid. For the work-house was rigorously segregated into male and female (and sometimes children). It is hard to believe that many families so divided could ever find the money, or the initiative, to set up house and unite once more.

The Poor Law was not the only method of providing income during loss of earnings in the 19th century. A second was charity. Many factors[1] were at work to influence its growth. The largest was probably the growing affluence and leisure of the upper classes. Where many enjoy surpluses, some are concerned by the plight of the needy, and are prepared to use their time and wealth to relieve distress. Coinciding with the growth of affluence came a development of the social conscience, and a humanitarianism that had not been so observable before. If this new spirit degenerated, in some, to a mere desire to follow a fashion, or to store up 'treasure in heaven', by good deeds on earth, it should not blind us to the deep sincerity of the many who strove to reform society, and thus get rid of the conditions that made poverty inevitable, or to work among those who could not help themselves. On the other

[1] See Young and Ashton, *Social Work in the 19th century*.

hand, the characteristic of charity was the perpetuation of 'two worlds', those who gave and those who received, and it was understood that neither changed places with the other, or over-lapped at any time.

But the 19th century evolved a third method of meeting the problem of the interruption of earnings—mutual co-operation. The growth of the friendly societies, and other means of mutual aid, such as building societies, and the consumers' co-operatives, was due partly to a fundamental belief in 'self help', and partly to the knowledge that the individual by himself could not hope to provide against every rainy day. By joining together there might be hope of survival. If the association were big enough, there was a guarantee that when some were in need, the rest were not, and if all paid, all were potential beneficiaries; therefore none would feel himself demeaned by resorting to charity, or the Poor Law, but each could accept his due in times of hardship, knowing he had paid for the right when times were better.

These three, the Poor Law, charity and insurance, helped, with other factors, to formulate thinking as the 20th century came in; and were to produce the basis of a new method of dealing with some of the causes of poverty. At least, it was a new method in Britain. Europe, notably Prussia, was already experimenting with the idea of insurance, and had introduced schemes of unemploy-ment and sickness benefit which recognised the need for working people to contribute a percentage of their earnings to a fund out of which income could be maintained when earnings ceased.

In Britain, the first unemployment and health insurance Acts came into operation in 1912, but applied to a limited number of industries only, including building, mechanical engineering, iron founding, vehicle construction, saw-milling and ship-building. It was not until after the First World War, in 1920, that other industries (with a few exceptions, such as agriculture) were added. From the beginning, certain fundamental principles had to be decided. The first was whether to follow continental precept and aim at relating benefit in adversity to the wages earned during affluence, or to accept the Poor Law principle of benefit at the basic minimum, which the individual could supplement for him-self out of his savings. The latter alternative was chosen. It satisfied both the traditional concept of the State's function, that it should interfere as little as possible, and the general aspiration towards 'self-help', the belief that individual saving was a 'good' in itself.

Secondly, a decision had to be made on how to finance the scheme. It could well have been out of taxation (including rating), which broadly meant that payment would come from everyone in the country, according to his ability to pay. Many would have preferred this, since it appealed to their egalitarian consciences, and satisfied their feelings of justice. But it suffered from one over-riding drawback—it substituted a tax-financed scheme for a rate-financed Poor Law, with all the overtones of State charity, and public stigma, that people wanted to avoid. Alternatively the employers might have been called upon to pay for it. Already Workmen's Compensation (p. 169) was run on these lines, and since loss of earnings through unemployment and sickness was of direct interest to the employers, it might be thought desirable that they should be responsible for the new schemes too. Here again, the general feeling was too strong. Workmen's Compensation was already running into difficulty, and encountering the complaints and disapproval that were to dog its steps until its ultimate dissolution in 1948. Moreover, the belief was gaining ground that to put a scheme of income maintenance into the hands of the employers was to deliver up the workman to all that was worst in charitable effort, and to maintain him in a subjection from which by education, by trade union action, and by an improving standard of living, he was striving to be free.

The answer lay in a form of insurance to which the three parties could contribute. Firstly the workers, who, by the friendly society schemes, had proved their capacity to join together in mutual aid. Contributions from them were essential to guarantee that benefit was paid as a right, and not as a charity—and also to relieve the rest from having to foot so large a bill. Secondly, contributions from employers were supported as a means of recognising the part played by industry in unemployment and sickness, and of under-lining the employers' interest in the welfare of their workers, even those no longer in their employ. In a sense, this was the perpetuation of the 'two worlds', though there is no evidence that the workers had negative feelings to match those so often roused by charitable effort in the 19th century.

The third party to the fund was the State itself. In performing this function it accepted the community's responsibility for income maintenance as a means of redistributing income from the wealthy to the poor and it assured a continuation of a social contract that had persisted since 1601. Thus were the three streams of the 19th century blended into a new method of coping with the age-old problem of poverty.

Whether there should be a fund built up over good years to provide resources for the bad was another of the problems. The alternative was a system of 'pay as you go', the essence of the Poor Law scheme. Everyone had experienced the difficulties of this—of the way a depression could hit certain areas, intermittently creating an intolerable burden that might have been ironed out over the years if there had been a reserve fund for support. Though subsequent experience of rapid inflation showed the futility of building a fund, in 1910–11 the arguments against the old Poor Law experience seemed overwhelming, and as private insurance, and the friendly societies, had based their finances on adequate capital resources, the best answer, at the time, seemed that the scheme should be funded.

Another aspect of finance concerned the rate of contribution. It might have been on a graded basis—'from each according to his capacity', even though benefit was to be at a minimum flat rate. But opinion was against this. If all were to benefit alike, all should pay alike, and the flat rate of contribution was decided upon. Thirty years later when Beveridge was writing his report on the social insurances (Cmd. 6404), he defended this method, because it was administratively uncomplicated, and had been demonstrably workable. Nevertheless, its critics argued that it had to be fixed at a level the poorest could pay, which artificially depressed the benefit rates; and that in periods of depression, such as were experienced in the 1920s and 1930s, the very poor were severely handicapped even by the rate that was fixed. It was said that while the better off could easily have afforded higher contributions, to the poorest-paid the contributions demanded were an alternative to bread. It was a tax, and a regressive one.

Of the many other principles that had to be decided before the scheme was launched, four were outstanding: membership, compulsion, administration, and conditions. On the first point, a comprehensive scheme of membership, covering everyone, could not have hoped to succeed at that period. It was the Royal Commission on Poor Law (1905–9) that had unanimously recom-

Income Maintenance for those not Working

mended the initiation of social insurances, to remove certain claimants from the Poor Law. It would have been inconceivable for a scheme to have covered persons other than those likely to be at risk. Membership was therefore selective, and confined to manual workers, and those within a low salary limit. The coverage was not quite the same for unemployment and sickness, but the general principle of selectivity operated, until it was amended in 1948.

Secondly, the question of compulsion has always been a fertile ground for discussion. Many were against it, on the grounds that workers should be free to use their wages in the ways that seemed best to them, and not be forced into a national arrangement against their will. Moreover, it was said, people should be free to set up alternative plans if they wished, as a free market has the additional advantage of greater efficiency and more effective provision for everyone. These arguments were weighty, but the counter-arguments could not be ignored. If people could choose whether or not to join at all, the very ones most at risk were likely to be the ones to avoid joining, and the result would be that the Poor Law would once more have to shoulder the burden, when earnings ceased. Also, compulsion would guarantee that the maximum number would be contributors, with beneficial results to everyone. Other things being equal, the larger the membership, the smaller the contributions, and the greater the benefits. So the principle of compulsion was accepted.

Next, claims that competition promoted effectiveness did not go unheeded. Though the administration of unemployment insurance was nationalised from the beginning, national health benefit was not. One of the outstanding factors favouring the establishment of social insurance schemes had been the alleged success of the Friendly Societies. These Societies had been popular among working men during the 19th century, and though Professor Gilbert has revealed how insecure the funds of many of them were by the early 20th century, they were regarded by many people as an example of working class saving that could well be continued. Insurance companies, too, were developing quickly, and offering income maintenance for loss of earnings through sickness, accident, death, and sometimes unemployment. A ready-made administrative organisation seemed therefore at hand. It enjoyed the support of all ranks of society, and in the case of Friendly

Societies, had the additional advantage of democratic control by the members. Influences were strongly in favour of using these bodies to administer at least one of the new insurances. Thus it was that in 1912 the National Health Insurance scheme came to be administered by those selected insurance companies or Friendly Societies thought to be capable of the work. The 'Approved Societies', as they came to be called, set up non-profit-making sections in their organisation, to run the National Health Insurance, and workers compulsorily insured were then invited to join one or other of the approved societies, which in turn had the right to refuse applicants who failed to meet their requirements of membership. The government (through the G.P.O.) established a residuary society, which those not able to find membership elsewhere could join. Thus all were covered, and a competitive scheme, offering a fair amount of freedom of choice, was established. The arrangement had many advantages. For instance, apart from the self-government that was so strong a feature of the Friendly Societies, and the fraternal interest taken in the members, many societies became wealthy. They achieved this mainly through a membership that was large, composed of healthy men and women making few demands on the funds, and creating surpluses to be divided out as bonuses for those of its selected members in need. The weekly cash benefit for sickness could rise to more than 50 per cent above the minimum laid down by the government. Additional benefits, in the form of free dentures, spectacles, and other medical aids, were made available. And since each society was subject to a quinquennial review, one that failed to provide these extras in one five-year period might be wealthy enough to do so in the next. Thus N.H.I., a benefit limited to the contributor, and, unlike unemployment insurance, excluding his dependants, was no bad thing, if you happened to belong to a wealthy society. But there lay the rub, and murmurings against the arrangements were soon to be heard. If all were obliged to pay the same, it was said, why should some workers be so much better rewarded in sickness than others? It was not as if all were equally free to join whatever society they wished. Had this been so, contributors would have flocked into the wealthy ones, such as that associated with the Amalgamated Society of Woodworkers, and avoided others like the Miners' Federation, whose members suffered much sickness which kept the benefits at the minimum. The quinquennial review itself caused irritation, as it became a matter of luck whether one happened to apply for, say, one's free spectacles, during the period when the society was in funds, or when it was not. A few days either way could make all the difference. So, apart from the grumblings about the alleged ill-service from the panel doctors, and the omission of any service at all to dependants, the administrative arrangements which allowed so much freedom of choice for contributors had many disadvantages, and outraged the sense of fairness among the workers.

Fourthly, it was evident that rules there would have to be, if the scheme were to be workable. It was decided, for instance, that each person had to qualify for benefit by a minimum number of contributions, that in the case of unemployment, an applicant had to be genuinely unemployed, and 'able and willing to work'; and that for sickness benefit a doctor's certificate had to be produced as evidence. Nor was benefit to be unlimited in duration; after a recognised period it would end, being revived only by further contributions. The actual interpretation of these and other rules became a serious matter, particularly for the unemployed during the depression of the inter-war years, and contributors anxiously counted the number of stamps on their two cards (unemployment and N.H.I.) to calculate whether they were in benefit or not. Nevertheless, the experience of working the schemes—of what jobs a man could refuse without losing benefit, or of when a worker could be regarded as sick even though he was out and about—all this experience was invaluable later, when the whole scheme was altered.

In the working out of these principles, two additional ones emerged to cause considerable controversy and concern. They were the questions of supplementation and insurance. It was earlier stated that the principle of wage-related benefit was jettisoned in favour of a minimum rate on the lines of (though usually better than) the Poor Law. In certain cases (particularly sickness benefit, which ignored dependants) the rate was lower than subsistence, and the problem of supplementation had to be faced. For the most part, the only body able to make discretionary payments of this kind was the Poor Law authority, and insured contributors were therefore driven to the very body from which, by their payments, they had hoped to escape. The rate-payers, in their turn, were faced with serious inroads on their finances owing to the poverty of their neighbours. When, later, old age pensions came to be tacked on to the scheme, and the number of old people in the population began to swell, the position was exacerbated. Rate-payers in areas where the average age of manual workers was high were obliged to pay out more in supplementation than those in other areas with a smaller proportion of old people. The elderly themselves frequently preferred to live in want rather than submit to the stigma of the Means Test and the Poor Law. Though the problem was, to some extent, met for old people and widows, in 1940–1, by the transfer of supplementation to the Assistance Board (a government body created in 1934 to deal with the long-term unemployed, and financed out of the Exchequer), the problem of supplementation, where benefit was insufficient, remained to plague us (p. 162). Later it was to be considered in relation to low wages too. Though it had been a maxim of the Poor Law from 1834 onwards that public money should not be used to supplement low wages, and though the maxim had been adopted categorically by later schemes, including the social insurance schemes, opinion was beginning to change by the late 1960s. It was being stated that some wages were so much lower than the lowest benefit prescribed by the government that the only alternative was to use public money to raise them. A direct dole to the wage-earner was not necessarily the right method, but considerable interest was taken in the idea of differential children's allowances according to family income.[1]

The other problem was the insurance principle, which was something that had brought the working man out of the demoralising shadow of the Poor Law, and made it possible to hold his head high when accepting benefit. The purists have declared (see Macleod and Powell) that his insurance was not self-supporting, or something he and others similarly at risk, had paid for, as had been the case in their mutual help schemes, or as others were doing through private insurance. On the contrary, it was argued, he had little more right to his benefit than to the doles provided by the Poor Law. From the beginning, the schemes had been subsidised by the employers and the State, and though one could suggest that employer-payments were an alternative to wages, the same could not be said of exchequer contributions. Further, by 1922, with the inclusion of vastly increased numbers in the scheme as potential

[1] See Family Allowances and Social Insurance Bill 1968.

beneficiaries, and with the post-war depression, the unemployment fund had run into difficulties, from which it had to be rescued by extensive loans and grants from the Treasury. Throughout the whole of the inter-war period, this situation continued and worsened, until by 1939 the fund was loaded with a huge burden of debt, and no-one could have legitimately stated that his benefit was an insurance, in the ordinarily accepted sense of the word. Much has been made of this fact, and it would be idle to suggest that social insurance, as it was practised up to 1948, and indeed for a dozen years thereafter, was anything but a series of funds, to which workers contributed directly about one-third, and a further unknown proportion through taxation. (After 1948 unemployment and sickness did not bring the fund into imbalance but retirement pensions did.)

Returning to the coverage, unemployment and sickness, the two premier risks of a worker's life, were the first to be included. In 1920, the relevant workers in nearly all industries were brought in, and the next groups were widows, orphans and old age pensioners at 65 years. New national funds were created for them in 1925, though to the workers and employers there was little change, since they contributed through the existing (though more expensive) N.H.I. stamp.

The development of old age pensions has been a curious one. They began in 1908, paradoxically enough, with a non-contributory scheme for people over 70 years. It had long been thought that the elderly, who had not managed to provide enough for their retirement, should be shielded from the rigours of the Poor Law, if at all possible. The Royal Commission on the Poor Law 1905–9 had unanimously agreed that a separate scheme should be started urgently; and since there was not enough time to build up an insurance fund, the pension was started as a direct payment out of taxation. Facilities for administering it were totally lacking, and as it needed some local arrangements to apply the Means Test, for which the Poor Law authorities were clearly unsuitable, the government had to fall back on one of its departments with local offices, viz: the Customs and Excise. So for nearly 30 years, old age non-contributory pensions shared offices with wines and spirits. The Means Test itself was *ad hoc*, and even when the administration was handed over, after 1948, to the N.A.B. (with a Means Test of its own), the pensions at 70 test was quite different, and in some ways more generous, as old people could claim pensions even though they were earning. It was not until 1966, when the Means Test for supplementary pensions was re-organised, that the old age non-contributory pension was abolished, and all old people, whether contributors or not, could apply for supplementary benefit via the G.P.O. to the Ministry of Social Security. The old age non-contributory pension was really an anomaly, but it served a useful purpose, and when it came to an end there were still about half a million beneficiaries.

What was surprising was the length of time that elapsed before a contributory scheme was introduced. But in 1925, contribution was made compulsory for those in the N.H.I., and this could be maintained voluntarily if a worker ceased to lie within the compulsory category. As there was no 'earnings rule', all who had a good contribution record obtained the pension, and either went on working, or retired. Up to the war, supplementation could be obtained from the local P.A.C., but after 1941 it was passed to the Assistance Board. It was expected that about half a million pensioners living in 'proud poverty' would reveal themselves at this change, and it was a shock to find that more than three times that number came forward, and were found to be eligible. This experience, and social research among the elderly thereafter, gave rise to a strong suspicion that many more had failed to apply. In 1966 an all-out drive was started, to persuade retired people to enquire whether they came within the 'supplementary benefits' scheme of social security.

The Beveridge Report 1942. New principles analysed

Already a comprehensive scheme of income maintenance had been developed in the United Kingdom. It had grown up piecemeal, but it provided cash benefit, without a Means Test, to those groups of workers least able to provide it themselves, when they lost their jobs, fell sick, suffered an industrial injury or disease, became too old to work, or died leaving widows and young children. Beveridge claimed that much of the old arrangement was good. Gaps need filling, and improvements made, but withal he preferred to build on the well-tried principles, instead of creating an entirely new plan.

For instance, compulsory membership was essential. So was the tripartite system of payment, with the employer, the worker, and the State creating a joint fund. Similarly, flat rates of both contribution and benefit were to persist; and he knew that no scheme was viable unless certain conditions, particularly of contributions, were accepted.

It is not intended to discuss here the three postulates without which the Beveridge plan would have been unattainable—a national health service, children's allowances, and full employment—though each is of profound and fundamental importance both to the satisfactory working of the social insurances, and to the individuals within the scheme. But some analysis of his new principles must be made, to understand the thinking of the mid-20th century, and to appreciate the factors that have led to further change.

Four of his principles, though important in their way, were not so fertile a medium for change as two others. Nevertheless, the suggestions—(a) to provide income maintenance during all the inevitable risks of industrial life, (b) to see that benefit lasted as long as the contingency, (c) that there should be equal benefit for equal need, and (d) that a thorough-going overhaul of the administration should take place—brought much needed changes, and became the blue-print of the National Insurance Act 1946.

(a) Most of the inevitable risks of industrial life had already been recognised before the Beveridge report. To unemployment, sickness, maternity, widowhood, orphanhood, industrial injury and retirement, he merely added a funeral grant. His tentative proposal for a marriage grant was not accepted. It was not until later that a grant for work severance was added, and it was financed in a different way (p. 140). Industrial training as a means of solving some of the problems did not become part of the national scheme of provision until nearly twenty years later (p. 28), though it had been visualised by Beveridge as an important adjunct to his scheme.

(b) Re the principle that benefit should last as long as the contingency, Beveridge was not prepared to sit by and let the contingency continue indefinitely. Certain circumstances, like retirement or orphanhood, only time could remedy. But in sickness, he urged the responsibility of the State to provide the means to cure people, or at least as far as circumstances and medical science could do this; and that of the individual to take advantage of all the means available to get well as quickly as possible, and to keep well.

Meanwhile, if a person was unable to work through sickness, his social security benefit should continue unabated for as long as he needed it. This was a vast change from an earlier period, where sick benefit lasted for a limited period, usually six months, and was then stopped altogether, or severely reduced. The case of unemployment was a different matter. Much of it was short term, fluctuating with the season, or the state of trade, and a man could expect to return to his old job when times were better. But some of it was structural (this had been common in the inter-war period) and a job might end, never to be revived. In such cases, a man might become unemployed for the rest of his life. It was Beveridge's view that during short term unemployment a man should receive benefit as long as he needed it, while being encouraged to accept 'suitable' work if it were offered. The employment offices, which he had helped to establish in 1910, were to be the chief instruments for that. But where the prospects for employment were remote, unemployment benefit should not continue indefinitely, but should be replaced by a 'training allowance' (leaflet P.L.394), and a man should be as willing to accept re-training as the State should be ready to provide it. The connection of training with unemployment benefit, in this way, met much opposition from those who opposed the use of training as a kind of 'test'. These critics preferred a more positive view of training, and insisted that training allowances should be larger than benefit, and should be used as an incentive. Thus up to the 1950s, government training was limited to certain groups, like the disabled (p. 60), and unemployment benefit depended on the number of contributions to the fund a worker had made. This was altered in 1966 (leaflet N.I.12) and a standard period of unemployment benefit became available for all who were eligible.

(c) A third principle, that there should be equal benefit for equal need, was aimed at remedying the injustices and inequalities that had found their way into the old patchwork provision—for example, sickness benefit had excluded dependants, and children were of different value according to which branch of social insurance their parents happened to claim. These were injustices that needed attention. The position of the gainfully employed woman was perhaps more anomalous than most, as her benefit was always a percentage smaller than that of a man. Beveridge argued that the overhead costs like training or rent, were the same for a woman as for a man, and there was little evidence that her food bills were smaller. Accordingly he advocated that men and women should receive equal basic benefit. And this became law, except for married women (p. 231).

(d) As for the administrative reorganisation, Beveridge had been appalled by the way people in need had been shuttled about from one office to another seeking benefit, and he advised the establishment of large multi-service offices, where all categories of applicants could be dealt with under the one roof, not only to establish their claims, but to receive benefit. This would have meant an enormous programme of new building, which post-war Britain was not in a position to undertake. Nevertheless, the need for greater concentration of service in one building was not forgotten, and attempts were made, particularly after 1966, when the Ministry of Pensions and National Insurance and the National Assistance Board were amalgamated in the Ministry of Social Security, to provide offices prepared to examine claims both for contributory benefits and non-contributory supplementation, though the difficulties proved more complex than were at first expected. Meanwhile, the G.P.O. had earned a favourable reputation in the actual cashing of warrants, and though urgent claims for non-contributory benefit were met in the Ministry offices, most other payments were made through the G.P.O.

Beveridge's other two principles of comprehensiveness and subsistence were to have more fundamental repercussions than those outlined above. Comprehensiveness meant that instead of selected groups of workers being compulsorily insured, nearly all those over school leaving age became contributors. He had been moved by the anomalies of those who were omitted from the old scheme, and he readily saw that a greatly enlarged membership would have a positive financial result, since the percentage of the better off likely to claim benefit would be smaller than the percentage of the selected groups who had formed the earlier scheme. There was one exception, the retirement pension, which Beveridge foresaw would be widely patronised if all the more elderly members of the population were to be 'blanketed' into immediate benefit. He suggested that new contributors should wait a considerable time (he thought twenty years) before being eligible for benefit. This advice was not accepted. Though an upper age limit was placed on those entering, a period of ten years' contribution only was demanded (it was three years for contributors who had been in before 1948). The financial results of this generosity were to be felt for many years. The comprehensive principle was not difficult for people to accept at that time. The common experience of living in war-time, of danger, of general shortages, of the need for a combined effort to prosecute the war, conspired to influence public thinking, and his slogan 'all in together', brought a ready response from most people.

The comprehensive principle was put into effect by creating three contribution bands: Class I, those under contract of service (leaflet N.I.20); Class II, the self-employed (leaflet N.I.41). These two made up the bulk of the population, and were defined on an industrial or occupational basis. It was recognised that apart from wives, whose insurance benefit was secured by their husbands' contributions, a group of non-gainfully employed people existed, and these formed Class III (leaflet N.I.42). In Classes II and III, those whose income was less than a stated minimum were exempt from either contribution or benefit. Thus, virtually all the inhabitants of the country became contributors directly or indirectly. It is possible this change in principle was the most far-reaching of all. It effectively eliminated one of the strands leading into the first of the insurances, by abolishing the class representing 'philanthropy' —the givers but not receivers—since all were now potential receivers. Redistribution of income from the rich to the poor continued (whether on the scale the egalitarians hoped, is not known), since the Treasury made direct contributions from the taxes, but became differently geared, so that its emphasis was on distribution from the well to the sick, the employed to the unemployed, the young to the old—rather than towards a greater equality of income. Because all were now potential beneficiaries, it brought into the actual experience of the scheme the better paid, the better educated, and the more vocal parts of the population.

Comment and criticism have been considerable, and proposals for change have been widely aired. Some, for example, would prefer to revert to the selective principle, on the grounds that their own likelihood of needing cash benefit for unemployment or sickness (though less so for pensions) was negligible, and the contribution tax an unnecessary imposition. Others have regarded the national scheme as less efficient, or financially productive, than occupational ones, the growth of which has been a feature of 20th century industrialism (p. 167). Moreover, though the costs of 'fringe benefits' are passed to the consumer, as are social security contributions, there is more room for manoeuvre in fringe benefits, which in any case have been lower in Great Britain than in most other industrialised countries. For example, in 1962 fringe benefits as a percentage of 'price' was 12 per cent in Great Britain, 17 per cent in the U.S.A. and 31 per cent in Germany. (*The Times*, 6 March, 1962.) Thus, universal personal involvement in the compulsory contributory scheme has resulted in a ferment of ideas, and a welter of discussion, which should ultimately evolve something better.

The other principle, subsistence, was a very different matter. In Beveridge's opinion benefit should be enough to live on, but no more. Because if it were higher than the minimum, it would counter the British propensity for thrift, a virtue the Victorians had nurtured, with advantage, it was said, to their greater national prosperity, and individual independence. Nothing, he thought, should be done to undermine this. At the same time, to offer benefit that was less than subsistence was to assume that those who had been unable to make private provision, and even some who had, would be forced inevitably to seek supplementation, with all that that meant in inquiry into means, and (as it was regarded at that time) interference with personal liberty. He recognised clearly the difficulties in implementing such a policy, since people varied in their expenditure, especially concerning rent. But there were requirements that were fundamental to all including food, clothing, fuel and light. Apart from rent, some balance could be struck that would meet the basic needs of everyone during interruption of earnings, and a standard allowance for rent might be included in the benefit. In practice, the National Insurance Act, when it came, excluded rent from benefit, and this, in effect, meant that the government repudiated the subsistence principle, and perpetuated the need to seek supplementation. Financially, there was justification for this, since only those who could prove need were supplemented, and large numbers, particularly of the retired, who enjoyed alternative means, received smaller benefit than if their pensions had been geared to subsistence. Substantial savings to the National Insurance fund resulted. Moreover, social insurance was still regarded as a 'poverty' service, an extension of the Poor Law, which people were willing to expend on the poor, who could prove their need, and who would be kept alive by means of minimum payments, but which had less to do with independent citizens of all ranks, who could be expected to look after themselves. Paying benefit at less than subsistence had of course the additional, though problematical attraction, that it might discourage malingering.

Whether it was the failure to accept the subsistence principle, or the difficulty many in the middle income group experienced, when they had to adjust their spending to the basic benefit, or a mixture of these and other causes, it was in this sphere that the greatest changes in thinking were to occur during the next ten years. Income-related insurance had been practised in other countries, and was inherent in most of the superannuation schemes that were developing in both public and private service. The fact that the schemes were mostly confined to staff, and excluded manual workers, stimulated the Labour Party to prepare a plan for a compulsory pension scheme, geared to income, and inclusive of all insured persons. By 1959 the Conservative Government had produced its own limited plan, applying to retirement only (p. 228)—the first real break from the Beveridge principle. Later, in 1966, the idea was extended by the Labour Government to other aspects of income interruption, such as unemployment and sickness—at first, for short periods only (p. 226).

Whether for short periods, or for the duration of the contingency, the pattern was the same. Benefit was divided into two: (a) the standard, or flat rate, being the same for everyone, according to his insurance class, and the nature of the contingency; and (b) the graduated rate, which depended on earnings, and was not available to those with low earnings. Similarly, contributions were divided into two: (a) the flat rate, which in the case of Class I contributors was paid by the employer, the worker and the Treasury, but for Classes II and III was confined to the contributor and the Treasury only. At first, the time-honoured method of stamping the card was used, but later cash was to be credited to the fund by the Inland Revenue through the P.A.Y.E. mechanism. (b) The earnings-related part of the contributions was paid in respect of Class I only, and was shared between the employer and the employee on the basis of his average wage, and in respect of those above a certain minimum wage. The P.A.Y.E. channel was used for this from its inception.

The earlier plans for graduated payments were limited to an income band. Later all incomes may be included, and perhaps all classes of contributor. Benefits have also been limited, and in general no beneficiary may receive more from the State scheme than he would have had in full-time employment. Thus has the principle of 'less eligibility' persisted.

Aspects of social security 1948 onwards

The Beveridge plan, though not accepted in its entirety, became the cue for a spate of legislation as soon as the war looked like ending. In 1945, the Family Allowances Act had become law, and a new government, elected in the same year, quickly introduced more Bills to change the old system. The year 1946 saw the passing of the Industrial Injuries Act and the National Insurance Act, as well as the Health Service Act. By 1948, with the National Assistance Act, the framework was ready for the establishment of a new policy of income maintenance. July 5th was the appointed day.

Details of the scheme will be found in the Appendix (p. 225), but a few comments on certain aspects of it need to be made—particularly on questions like supplementary benefit, retirement, the phenomenal growth of occupational schemes for income maintenance, and finally Industrial Injuries Insurance, which replaced the earliest social benefit, Workmen's Compensation.

Non-contributory supplement (leaflet S.1, S.L.9). Associated with the neglect of the subsistence principle has been the need for supplementation—at first from the Poor Law, but later from the Treasury. For those on unemployment benefit, this has always meant a close connection between the Ministry of Labour and the appropriate department responsible for the non-contributory additions (from 1948 the N.A.B., and after 1966, the Commission for Supplementary Benefit). Special staff, known as Unemployment Review Officers were appointed (the N.A.B. designated 50 in 1965) to concern themselves with problems of unemployment, particularly those thought to be 'intractable'. The essence of supplementation has been the requirement to prove need, and the 'needs test' has been the centre of the transaction. The test itself has been modified from time to time; but reminding people as it has of the Poor Law Means Test, it has had a hard fight to live down its unfortunate reputation. Though unemployment supplementation was linked so closely to the need to find another job, additional benefit on retirement has generally been viewed from another angle, with propaganda campaigns being conducted from time to time urging people to apply.

One of the strengths of the supplementary benefit has lain in the discretion officers have been allowed to exercise. For though they have had to work rigorously, according to the regulations, they have been allowed to plead mitigating circumstances in certain cases. For instance, a young man was found to be receiving a slightly higher benefit than he was entitled to. The officer discovered he had an incurable disease, and would shortly die, so a plea was put to the appeal tribunal that the amount should not be modified, and the tribunal accepted the officer's suggestion. The use of discretion in this case would seem fully justified.

The development of earnings-related benefit should eventually reduce the need for supplementation of social security payments. But a residuary scheme is likely to be indispensable for a long time.

There are always the exceptions, the individuals who slip through the mesh of the most carefully considered provision; seasonal workers; those without a settled way of life; those who find themselves faced with a sudden emergency; and largest group of all, housewives permanently or temporarily separated from husbands; all these are likely to need cash help, and to need it quickly. So the non-contributory side of social security is likely to remain, though perhaps as a casualty service rather than an integral part of an income-maintenance scheme.

The retirement principle. Up to 1948, payment of the old age pension had nothing to do with retirement, and industry was faced with the difficulty of when to dispense with the services of the old, just as the worker had to decide the right moment to quit. During the inter-war years, the presence of numbers of young workers without jobs had led to the demand for older workers to retire. This, in turn, raised the question for the individual about his own finances, as the pension was manifestly insufficient to keep him; and for the employer, whether it would pay him to allow an experienced skilled man to leave, without any guarantee that he could be replaced by another worker equally productive.

In a sense, the Beveridge idea, to make retirement a condition of

M   163

obtaining the pension, was a solution of the old dilemma, and people began to accept the convention that their work-span ended at 65 (60 for women). But the period after the war brought new problems. There came a universal desire, not only to repair the ravages of war, but to improve the standard of living (some talked of doubling it in 20 years). To do this productivity must rise, and labour, already a scarce commodity, must be put to the best use. In the light of this, the question was asked whether the community could afford to dispense with the labour of the elderly as prodigally as they were doing, especially when retirement increased the charges on the State. The fact that old people were both increasing in numbers, and in proportion to the rest of the population, and that improved nutritional and medical facilities lengthened their work potential, added to the controversy.

The problem resolved itself into three parts: there was the individual old person. Did he want to go on working longer? Could he afford to retire? There was the employer. Did he want to retain the services of the old in their former jobs, or in new ones? Was he prepared to develop schemes to ease the old out of their jobs, or to rearrange his productive process, or his man-power distribution, to keep them in his employment? And thirdly there was the community. Was it prepared to accept the cost of keeping the old, and trying to make their final years as happy and healthy as possible, or did it consider them a burden, which the old themselves should be expected to share?

A certain amount of research into these different aspects of the problem has been undertaken since 1948, and though the answers are not by any means conclusive, ideas have slowly developed as surveys have been made.

The worker. In 1954, a report[1] was published about the reasons people gave for their retirement, and it was found that nearly half the men, and more than half the women had retired at the minimum age. Of the retired men, more than half said they had done so because of their own ill-health, and another quarter because their employers had discharged them on reaching the age. Only four per cent felt the work too heavy, but about one in fifteen retired for 'rest and leisure'. Of the retired women, about half gave ill-health as the main reason. About one in eight left for family

[1] M.P.N.I., 'Reasons given for Retiring or Continuing at Work', 1954.

reasons, but very few said they had been discharged by their employer, and hardly any said the work had been too heavy for them.

The reasons for staying on at work were equally illuminating, and were much the same for men and women. More than half of them could not afford to retire, another quarter felt 'fit and well', and the rest 'preferred to work'. Ill-health has therefore played an overwhelming part in forcing people to retire, and lack of money has been a vital incentive in keeping them at work. It has long been thought that heavy manual jobs were more trying for workers than those requiring more skill than physical strength. Research[1] suggests otherwise. Provided an older worker is not debarred on medical grounds, heavy muscular effort has not in itself been the difficulty. Where the job has demanded knowledge, accuracy and stability, the older worker has been able to hold his own quite successfully with the younger. The same is true in the re-training of older workers, where the elderly have proved themselves quite capable of learning new skills. The real problem has been speed. If the machine, or the team, or the payment system have tended to increase the pace of his work, the strain has proved too great. Similarly, where he was asked to learn new skills, the older worker took more time than the younger one.

The employer. Measuring the attitude of the employer has been more difficult. But in the early 1950s the National Advisory Committee of the Ministry of Labour produced reports on the 'Employment of older men and women'. (Cmd. 8963 and 9628.) It was noted that there were wide variations in the proportions of older persons employed, even by comparable industries, and it was suggested that factors other than the suitability of the work must have influenced the engagement and retirement policies of the firms. The reports confirmed that the government and industrial retirement pensions made retirement at 65 (60) the normal procedure, acceptable both to workers and employers. They also pointed to the need for employers to offer opportunities of promotion to younger workers, and to consider whether the firm was suffering from an unbalanced wage structure. They recognised that industry must have a retirement policy, if the channels of promotion and change were not to be clogged. But

[1] H. M. Clay, 'The Older worker and his Job', *D.S.I.R.*, 1960.

the claims of the older worker should not be overlooked. The reports were well publicised throughout industry, though how far employers found alternative jobs for their own older workers, or actually engaged elderly employees, is not known. Investigations made by the Nuffield Foundation[1] suggested that about 20 per cent of men reaching pensionable age needed alternative jobs; how many jobs were available was doubtful. Firms were able to absorb a few of their own elderly workers, but taking on new ones of pensionable age would be another matter. No-one doubts the value of the special workshops for the elderly set up by firms, voluntary organisations, or local authorities. Yet this has more the flavour of philanthropic effort, than the independent production we associate with gainful employment.

The Community. Little direct research has been made, either about the community's attitude to the economic and social costs of old age, or its ability to meet the demands of a large retired population. The position was roundly faced by the Phillips committee (Cmd. 9333) in 1954, which pointed to the severe strains likely to be met. It could not envisage the aged being financed for the rest of the century (after which the problem might diminish, as the product of the low birth rates in the 'twenties and 'thirties reach retirement) out of a 'funded' scheme, since the annual sum required might seriously affect the economy, and the committee was left with the inescapable conclusion that the elderly of today must in large measure be financed out of what today's workers have produced. Moreover, as productivity increases, and the general standard of living rises, the old would want to enjoy the improvement too, and most people would sympathise with this. Yet it would be a lavish and expensive process, which the elderly should help to meet. Accordingly, the committee thought that retirement at 65 (60) was too soon, and that the older worker should prolong his work span for at least three years.

Certain members of the committee wanted to abolish the 'earnings rule', and the retirement principle altogether, making it possible for people to draw their pension, but to continue working. When Beveridge introduced the retirement principle, he believed the pension would be at subsistence level, and that it should be

[1] 1955 Le Gros Clark & A. C. Dunne, 'New jobs for Old Workers'; 1957 Le Gros Clark, 'Bus Workers in their Later Lives'.

raised higher with every year of full-time employment an individual worked after the minimum age. He emphasised that people should be encouraged to continue working if they could, both for their own sakes, and to lessen the burden they might impose on the community. But for them to receive a full-time wage as well as a pension at subsistence rate was, in Beveridge's view, an unnecessary and harmful load on all citizens below pensionable age. Further experience has suggested that the retirement principle has not worked in the way he expected, and that more have voluntarily retired, or been discharged at the minimum age, than he anticipated.

From time to time the rule has been eased by increasing the allowable earnings, and though many have opposed its total abolition (for example the T.U.C.) for fear it might undermine wage agreements, and create in old people a source of cheap labour, the increasing pressure to review the issue has continued.

Another question which emerged from the discussion was the part played by occupational schemes for income maintenance in old age (or in periods of earnings-interruption).

Occupational schemes. Employing bodies have shown a growing interest extending over many years, in the provision of income maintenance for their employees. The best known of these private schemes have been concerned with superannuation, though in the second half of the 20th century, the idea of providing pay during sickness or accident, and severance pay for unemployment caused through no fault of the worker has become more popular. A survey of these private schemes, published by the Ministry of Labour ('Total Labour Costs' 1966) revealed that 'private social welfare payments' represented just over three per cent of total labour costs; or taking manufacturing industries alone, about £27 per annum for each employee. Nearly £1 10s 0d of this was for redundancy, about 10s 0d for sickness and miscellaneous funds, and the rest for pensions.

During the latter part of the 20th century, national schemes of provision have tended to fall within the scope of wage negotiation, and have been more common in the public sector than the private, where 'fringe benefits' tended to develop on a company basis. The major concern of individual firms has been with 'white collar' workers, rather than manual, though in public enterprise both types have been included. Surveys of sick pay schemes in 1964

(Ministry of Labour: 'Sick Pay Schemes', M.P.N.I.: 'Inquiry into Incidence of Incapacity to Work') indicated that almost all workers were covered in the public sector; but in the private sector, though nearly all 'white collar' workers were included, only about a third of the manual workers were covered. Even so, more than half the gainfully employed (class I) of Britain were covered for sickness by an occupational scheme providing, for a limited period, supplementation of national insurance benefit, up to average income level.

The provision of superannuation has been a popular means of attracting workers to a firm or service, and in nationalised industry, and local and central government, it is practically universal. The growth of it in private industry has been rapid since 1946, and though the number of workers covered (about 12 millions) has been slightly smaller than for sickness (about $13\frac{1}{2}$ millions), pensions have obviously been more expensive, and more long-term.[1] Their importance was recognised by the first of the earnings-related social security schemes. In 1959, the National Insurance Act made it possible for employers operating a private plan to contract out of the national scheme (leaflet R.1 and N.I.114) if their scheme was at least as advantageous to the worker as that of the government and provided it safeguarded his pension rights, should he move to a different job. Within a short time, five million workers had been contracted out in this way.

By no means all the occupational schemes included worker participation. Some of them were not funded at all, though if they were cited as an alternative to the government pension, the presence of a fund that would guarantee the preservation of a worker's future pension rights was a condition of recognition. Others were taken out by the firm as an insurance policy, and the rest were mutually contributory, with the workers paying their share directly. Even where there was no employee contribution, it was agreed that workers paid indirectly in the form of deferred wages. Many firms carefully weighed the cost to themselves whether to fund or not, the different ways in which income tax was levied had a profound effect on the decision. In some cases a contributory scheme proved more expensive to the employer than a non-contributory one.

The nature of the schemes, and the part played by workers' payments, have created further problems. For besides the well-

[1] Government Actuary. Survey on 'Occupational pension schemes', 1966.

worn one of how to deal with inflationary tendencies, there has been the serious question of transferability, or 'vesting'. Most of the schemes in the private sector were introduced as a means of improving the firm's image as a good employer, thus helping to attract high quality labour. Vesting, or an encouragement to leave the firm, hardly entered into the calculation. When the government graduated plan appeared, and employers were given the right to contract-out in favour of their own, they were obliged to make provision for transfer to the extent of their obligations under the Act, but no further. As most contracted-out pensions were better than the national one, anyone leaving the firm might be faced with a real loss of prospects. The National Joint Advisory Committee, surveying the position in 1966, found that though about three-quarters of the workers in private schemes were covered by provisions for transfer on leaving the firm, only about eight per cent of those withdrawing actually preserved their rights. ('Preservation of Pension Rights on Change of Employment'. 1966.) The committee said this was 'largely on account of the way the options were exercised'. Clearly, the administrative problem of keeping a small number of pension schemes in suspension, as one changes from job to job, is daunting, but it should not be too difficult to solve if some national fund were created to deal with it.

One other industrially orientated scheme remains to be discussed —industrial injuries insurance. It has not developed through the main social insurance stream, but having entered it in 1948, and become one of the services administered by the Ministry of Social Security, it is considered by workers and management as thoroughly integrated into the plan for income maintenance during interruption of earnings.

Industrial Injuries Insurance.[1] What appeared to be a completely reorganised scheme was introduced by the Industrial Injuries Act 1946, and became operative in 1948. The changes at that time were indeed great, but many details of the new plan have been handed down from the first Workmen's Compensation Act 1897. This Act had stated: firstly, that workers must have suffered an 'industrial injury' (or, after 1906, a prescribed 'industrial disease'). This meant one that had occurred because of an accident 'arising

---

[1]For an analysis of the history and ideas behind this scheme see A. F. Young, *Industrial Injuries Insurance*, Routledge and Kegan Paul, 1964.

out of and in the course of' employment; or, in the case of a disease, one that was a hazard of the employment, and not a risk common to all persons, and one which could be presumed to have been contracted at the place of work because the sufferer had been employed there (p. 90).

Secondly, if the injury or disease were established as a *bona fide* result of the employment, it became the employer's responsibility to pay the compensation. The scheme had been introduced more than a dozen years before the first of the social insurances, and it is perhaps understandable that the tripartite method of contribution was not considered for workmen's compensation. The latter followed naturally upon the Employers' Liability Act 1880, which, in turn, had been a modification of the Common Law, requiring an employer to exercise 'care' in his relationship with his workers. At any rate, it was upon the employer alone that liability for compensation rested.

Thirdly, the selective principle operated, and manual workers, and those below a certain salary, were covered. This principle was later to be followed when unemployment and sickness insurance were introduced.

From the workers' standpoint, the calculation of the compensation was probably the most important part of the scheme, and this was based on the notion that when a man entered upon a contract of labour, he accepted certain responsibilities for the ordinary risks of the job. Thus, when an accident occurred, it was thought only fair that he and the employer should share equally in the liability. Accordingly, the weekly compensation was not to be more than half his average weekly wage; and since the employer needed some safeguard against unlimited claims, the principle of the 'maximum' was also accepted, and should half the wage exceed this, the 'wage stop' would operate. Sometimes weekly compensation was foregone in favour of a down payment, a 'lump sum'. This had the advantage, for the employer, that he could capitalise his liability, if the injury looked like going on for a long time; and for the worker, that it gave him a sum of money to meet outstanding debts, or perhaps start a business. It was criticised, when such payments were not registered in the county court, or were abused by employers, as a cheap way of discharging liability, with a less than satisfactory outcome for the injured man. Compensation according to a man's family responsibilities was not introduced until nearly the end of the scheme, and even in fatal accidents, many years were to pass before compensation related to the number of his dependant children was adopted as part of the calculation.

It was the original aim of the measure not to depend on the courts for its operation, but to create a system in which a man injured at work could simply and quickly receive benefit from his employer. In the majority of the accidents this spirit prevailed, and everyone hoped that if disputes arose, they could be settled by friendly negotiation. Only in exceptional cases was it thought likely that the matter would have to be taken to court. In practice, such early optimism was not justified, because employers increasingly covered themselves by private insurance. This meant that the number of court cases tended to rise, since a decision on one claim became a precedent for others.

Discontent about the working of the provisions began to grow among the workers, especially concerning the amount of compensation, and the litigation that so often resulted. The workers compared their lot with that in other industrial countries, and decided they were receiving less compensation than in most. Hardly any country allowed a payment as small as half the average wage, or put a ceiling on maximum compensation. The abuses of the 'lump sum' system were extensively quoted, and the absence of dependants' allowances widely deplored. Added to the general dissatisfaction was the difficulty so many experienced in establishing their claim to any compensation at all. Injured men were questioned as they lay in hospital, their recovery retarded by the worry of an impending court case, and their fear it would go against them. They were in a position of weakness, since they seldom had the means, except through their trade union, to be legally represented, though it was known the insurance companies employed full-time lawyers. There was considerable dissatisfaction too about the medical review that formed an integral part of the proceedings. It was widely believed that the dice were loaded against the injured man, even on an issue as fundamental as this.

The complaints so loudly heard from the workers' side against the scheme were, paradoxically, not echoed by the employers. Yet it was on them that liability for cash benefit fell. The answer probably lay in their recourse to insurance, which spread the cost, and afforded protection to all but the largest companies (who organised their own insurances) and the most careless (since there was, in general, no obligation to insure). On the other hand, the administrative cost of running the insurance came in for adverse comment by more than one Committee of Inquiry, including Beveridge in 1942.

Opinion was ripe for change, and though not all the Beveridge recommendations were accepted, it was his plan, in the main, that was adopted. An examination of the new policy, under the Industrial Injuries Act 1946, shows remarkable similarity in detail to the old. Benefit was payable solely on the basis of industrial injury or disease, which were interpreted much as they had been for half a century. The device of the 'lump sum' continued, in spite of the early grumblings about it. Though the courts were no longer the means of deciding difficult cases, the appeal tribunals were often conducted like courts of law, and claimants appearing before them felt at a disadvantage. Nor were the medical boards altogether popular, and the majority of appeals, by both claimants and the Ministry, were against the medical decisions.

The three major points of change that were crucial to the new scheme, and entirely altered its complexion were: Liability to pay benefit was passed from the employers to a government fund, to which the State, the employers and the workers contributed, as they did in other social insurances. Secondly, administration became the responsibility of civil servants, appointed for the purpose. This is not to say the scheme was less rigorously administered, but there was no longer the suspicion that cash was being paid by those whose interests were to keep it as low as possible. Thirdly, the plan of the basic benefit showed sensitivity and imagination, and compared with other social insurances, was reasonably generous. Later, some of the industrial injuries benefits participated in the 'earnings related' supplements, when these came to be grafted on to social security in 1966.

These three changes so altered the spirit of the scheme, that in spite of the superficial similarity to workmen's compensation, accident benefit ceased to be thought of as the Cinderella of the social services for income maintenance.

A brief outline of the social insurances appears in the Appendix (p. 225), along with some of the general principles under which they work. As the details are continually changing, reference to the appropriate leaflets makes it convenient for readers to apply to the Ministry for the latest information.

PART III

THE THEWS AND SINEWS

IX

THE TRADE UNIONS AND EMPLOYERS' ORGANISATIONS

THE THREE GREAT social institutions, the trade unions, the employers' organisations and the professions, have become so much a part of the British scene, that it would be hard to visualise the industrial social services without them. They have been in some senses the midwife, helping the infant service into the world; in another the handmaid, nurturing, criticising, suggesting new methods; always the watchdog, protecting and furthering the interests of their constituents, so that the service for the members has been improved; sometimes the hangman, killing off potential social services if they disapproved. The purpose of each of these social institutions has been self-regarding. If others benefited from their activity, it was a happy, though not a necessary outcome. As each has gained in maturity and success, perhaps it has realised that in the long run 'well-being' is indivisible. If one faction is to achieve its own greatest good, in the inextricable complications of modern society, others must do so too. Statesmanship of this sort has still a long way to go, but there is evidence that the objective has begun to be appreciated.

Whatever their future, some analysis of their structure and their problems needs to be made, since the initiation of social services in industry owes so much to the attitudes they display; and implementation depends almost entirely on their will to make them work.

We begin with the trade unions, because most has been written about them. They have been studied, analysed, and commented upon with far greater assiduity than have the other two. And they represent the employees of industry, on whose behalf the social services were formed; this is another reason to give them first consideration.

Definitions of trade unions cannot satisfy everyone, since the concept itself is dynamic. The Ministry of Labour has suggested that they comprise organisations of employees, salaried and professional as well as manual, and include among their functions negotiation with employers to regulate the conditions of employment. This excludes the notion of permanence, which most trade unionists would wish to emphasise, but it avoids the old mistake of limiting membership to manual workers. When unionism was legalised in the early 19th century, it was a working class movement, with a membership of a few thousands. Numbers fluctuated with the state of trade, improving in good times, but slipping in bad, though the solid core steadily increased, until after the Second World War it had reached about 10 millions. Even so, only about four out of 10 British workers have joined a union—a phenomenon not peculiar to this country. In Sweden, the Mecca for trade unionists, the proportion of members of trade unions to all workers has been four and a half in 10, while in the U.S.A. it has been little more than two and a half in 10 (*The Economist*, 3 September 1966).

Each country has developed its own trade unions to fit its own needs. Britain, with its long tradition of unionism, has studied the newer methods of other countries, and adapted them to its own use where possible, though it has been unable to transfer and absorb whole systems, no matter how successful they may have been elsewhere.

Trade unions in Britain were at first local in scope, but later became national, through the intelligence and drive of the craftsmen. Thus in any classification of the unions, it has been customary to separate the craft from the industrial and general unions.

Traditional categories

Craft unions (for example, the Amalgamated Engineering Union)[1] being the oldest unions, have often been the wealthiest. They have built up large friendly society funds, and in many cases, large amounts for general purposes. Some began as organisations of workers engaged in a single craft, later agreeing to include workers less well qualified, and few have failed to adapt themselves to the changes in industrial needs and methods that time has brought. Flexibility has been the strength of the trade union movement,

[1] 1968 A.E.F.

though craft unions have tended to be more conservative, since they have had most to lose. Thus if craftsmen have developed 'work-shop practices' (sometimes called 'restrictive practices') clearly defining what job each craftsman might do, or the number of apprentices per craftsman a firm might employ, they did so in self-defence. If a carpenter could do a plumber's job, or a white-smith take more apprentices than he could adequately instruct, or the compositor were to find himself working alongside a number of semi-skilled printers, where would be the advantage of an apprenticeship, and what the justification for a wage differential? Industrially, and in the long run, the inefficiency of such rules (which have always been easier to make than to alter) has been plain to see, and the struggle to upset the 'who does what' agreements, and to encourage the dilution of craft labour, has been one of the major sources of conflict in the 20th century.

Commentators have frequently classified unions as 'horizontal' or 'vertical'. The horizontal have tried to organise workers with similar interests, no matter which industry might employ them. The A.E.U. has sought out engineers and kindred tradesmen in light, medium or heavy engineering firms, and in a host of others not specifically concerned with engineering as such, and a broad band of A.E.U. membership has consequently stretched over the country, and over many industries. Craft unions, on the whole, have been more given to this kind of organisation than any other, though modern developments have conspired to broaden the band in some of the biggest craft unions, making them vertical, in the sense of including all grades of skill and un-skill in the membership, so long as there was some affinity between them.

General unions were an answer to the 19th century exclusiveness of the craft unions, since many unskilled, low-paid workers were unorganised, and would have been refused membership, even if they had sought it. Part of the extraordinary growth in public interest (and antagonism) towards unions, during the latter part of the 20th century has been due to the rise of the general unions, each having no theoretical barriers to membership, and three of them (T.G.W.U., G.M.U.W., and U.S.D.A.W.) have grown to be some of the largest trade unions in Britain. The general unions, particularly the T.G.W.U., have set out to attract every worker not already in a union, and to slot him into one of the divisions into which the union has been organised. (Ernest Bevin in the 1920s and 1930s reorganised the T.G.W.U. to make it possible for almost every worker to find a home in it if he wanted.) By their very comprehensiveness, the general unions have provided an answer to the fast changing industrial scene, and have been able to recruit in fields which other unions were obliged to ignore. Their increasing membership has enlarged their power and influence, and at the same time has brought advantages to the ill-paid and unskilled, for whom they were originally designed. One of the outstanding developments of the middle 20th century has been the improvement in pay and conditions of the 'poorer' sections of the workers, the consequential lessening of the gap between a crafts-man's and a labourer's pay, and the growing discontent that 'differentials' have not been maintained.

Industrial unions cut across craft barriers, and based themselves on the employing agencies. Thus the N.U.R., the N.U.M., the U.P.W., the Iron and Steel Trades Confederation, have been designed to conform in membership with employment in an industry. They have become 'vertical' unions, where all crafts and grades of workers in an industry have come under one umbrella. Britain, unlike America, has not seen the development of the 'company' union, though from several points of view the industrial union has had more in common with it than have the others. No industry in Britain has been exclusively served by one union, but to the extent that it has been, there are certain evident advantages.

Employers have tended to organise on an industrial basis, and it has not been difficult to appreciate, that if the representatives of one employers' association have met representatives of one trade union round the negotiating table, it has been convenient to both sides. The difficulties of the Ford Motor Company, obliged to negotiate with representatives of 20 trade unions, for most of the century can readily be appreciated. Moreover, it has been alleged, a more rational wage system, based on responsibility, skill, and other comparable criteria, could be worked out if both sides were concerned solely with the one industry, instead of the unions having to consider what effect decisions taken in one industry might have on their members in another. Thirdly, industrial unionism would lead to greater interest in union matters, since branches would be based on the work-shop, in which all would have a common concern, instead of on localities, where members might be in a variety of firms, with nothing but their skill or union membership to hold them together.

The popularity of industry as a basis for union organisation has been challenged by those who feared the instability of industry. The line between one industry and another has always been difficult to draw, and has become more so as technological changes have created new industries out of old. To change the organisation of the trade unions every time an industry changes its frontiers would be to encourage conflict, and embarrass both sides. Further, British trade unions have derived much of their strength from their historical loyalties and traditions. To break these might construct a tidy scheme at the expense of a work force unwilling to trust its own leaders. In spite of these warnings, a considerable body of opinion, both inside and outside the movement, has declared itself in favour of a growing alignment of the unions to industry.

Another method of classification (Turner, 241 *et seq.*) is the 'open' and 'closed' union. Since this notion has a good deal in common with professional associations (p. 206), it is worth examining here. The 'open' unions have imposed no restriction on entry into the occupations they have organised, but have been content to recruit such workers as the employers themselves engaged. Examples would be the general unions, or the Cardroom Amalgamation in the textile industry. Since they have been unable to exert pressure on the employers by controlling the supply of labour to a key stage in the production process, they have had to rely for their strength on a large membership. But as the members have tended to be heterogeneous, in the sense of having little occupational solidarity, they have compensated by employing a large full-time staff to keep up the recruitment, to exert pressure on the employers, and to promote political activity. The maintenance of staff has itself been costly, and could only be financed by stepping up the membership. The 'open' unions have been, therefore, the large unions—expansionist, politically active, and to some extent the dominators of the trade union movement (over half the T.U.C. total affiliated members have been found in no more than six unions).

'Closed' unions, such as those in the printing industry, on the other hand, have tried to regulate entry to union membership, and to restrict employment to members of the union. The strength of their policy has lain in the capacity of the members to withhold their labour, and thus to bring the process to a standstill. Where a few key workers have stood out for their demands, it has been a fairly inexpensive experience for the union, though a damaging one for production. Thus 'closed' unions have tended to be relatively small, and to maintain their restrictionism as a matter of policy.

Some unions have grown to be both 'open' and 'closed', in the sense that certain departments have carefully controlled entry to the 'qualified', but owing to the need to organise ancillary occupations, or even labourers, who service the craftsmen, the union has created other departments for them, and these have been open to all comers. The Amalgamated Society of Woodworkers might be an example of this.

Federations. The weakness inherent in the operation of hundreds of independent self-governing unions has not gone unnoticed in the movement itself. One answer has been the merging of unions,[1] a process deliberately encouraged during the 1960s by the T.U.C., which called meetings of kindred unions for the purpose. Another method has been the federation of individual unions for specific purposes. The advantages of this kind of combination are many. It has preserved the autonomy of each union, while encouraging a united front when necessary. It has made possible the participation of a single union in several federations, thus giving both strength and flexibility, yet preserving the organised solidarity of the members. A few small groups have feared this method, claiming that unless their interests were in the main stream of the federation's work they might be neglected, but on the whole, where it has been adopted, the advantages have been overwhelming.

About 40 federations have come into being, and three have been outstandingly important: the Confederation of Ship-building and Engineering unions (37 unions), the National Federation of Building Trade Operatives (about 12 unions), and the Printing and Kindred Trades Federation (16 unions.)

Trades Union Congress

When the public have envisaged the federative organs of the

---

[1] For example, in the decade 1954–64 the total number of unions fell from 711 to 591, and though some of the lost unions had died out, most had amalgamated.

movement, they have usually thought of the T.U.C., a national body, consulted by governments of every party, speaking for industrial democracy in Britain, and representing the workers' point of view on international occasions.

With an unbroken history since 1868, the T.U.C. has been the affiliate body of all the major unions in the country. The relationship has at no time been automatic, and seldom more than one in four of the unions have joined. The reason is complex. Sometimes it has been the T.U.C. itself which has refused the application; or the union has disliked T.U.C. policy, or felt too small or too localised. In spite of this, some 85 per cent of all trade union members have been in unions affiliated to the T.U.C., and the Congress has justly been able to claim that it represents the bulk of trade unionists in Britain.

The Congress has met each year, usually in September, and delegates from the affiliated unions have attended, in the proportion of one for each 5,000 members. Voting has been based on union membership, and majorities of several millions have therefore been common. One of the more important functions of Congress has been the annual election of the General Council of the T.U.C., to carry on the executive transactions throughout the year. The members have always been full-time officials of their own unions, but not of the T.U.C., which has had its own staff, of whom the General Secretary has been the chief.

Its authority has been quite distinct from its power. Created and financed by the unions, the T.U.C. has exercised only that amount of power the unions have delegated to it. Many have thought it should have the right to coerce the unions, to compel them to amalgamate, or to force them to adopt a 'regulation of incomes' policy. But the individual unions, like independent nations, have found it hard to give up their autonomy. Yet the way in which the General Council, or its full-time staff, have used the power they possess has profoundly affected trade unionism in Britain, and enlarged the status of the T.U.C. in the eyes of the world.

For instance, the disputes committee of the T.U.C., backed by the 1924 resolution on 'the principles of good trade union practice', and strengthened by the Bridlington Agreement in 1939, has been able to intervene in disputes between the unions about spheres of influence, transference of members, poaching and other sources of irritation, inevitable in human institutions. As an

The Trade Unions

arbitrator, its findings have usually been accepted, though more speedy decisions would be an advantage. (Evidence to the Royal Commission on Trade Unions by I.P.M. 1966.) A committee appointed in 1966 had great potential. Its duty was to sift trade union claims for increased pay, or changes in the conditions of employment. Many saw in this the best machinery for implementing the incomes side of a planned economy.

The T.U.C. has had wider duties than arbitration and advice, for it has been recognised by the government as the representative of the workers. In any question of policy, legislation or administration, likely to affect labour or labour relations, the matters have been discussed with the General Secretary or the Council before anything has been done. Similarly, when the government has required workers' representatives on international bodies (for example, the I.L.O.), it was to the T.U.C. it looked for advice on personnel.

In consequence of this personal relationship with the government, and its standing as a national institution, the T.U.C. has gained a status far greater than the actual power with which it has been provided. When one adds the fact that it has been fortunate in the high calibre of its top men and women, who themselves have had a profound experience and knowledge of unionism, it is not surprising the T.U.C. has become the spearhead of the movement, respected and generally supported by the rank and file of the unions.

Some have thought that the T.U.C. would need a radical reorganisation, if it is to lead the workers into the 21st century—especially if national planning becomes a reality. For, though planning has not been absent from the 'free economy', and the restrictions imposed by the plans have been intolerable to many, the workers have felt themselves too far from the seats of power to be personally involved in responsibility, and have organised themselves to withstand the frustrations as best they may. In the process, they have developed a 'free for all' among themselves, tacitly accepting that impersonal economic forces were as much a reality in pursuing their policy as in that of the economy as a whole. National planning would certainly alter this, as the workers would be involved both in responsibility for the plan itself, and in the acceptance of a curb to their own freedom to further their sectional interests independently. It would be hard to visualise an unreformed T.U.C., that is one without specific powers over the unions, and having to depend on persuasion and moral force, leading its members into involvement as radical as this.

The T.U.C. for England and Wales is both the oldest and the strongest of the federated bodies, though Northern Ireland and Scotland have developed T.U.C.s of their own. In 1940, the English one established regional advisory committees of full-time trade union officials to advise on industrial production. These have become increasingly important as the source of employee representation, first on the Regional Boards for Industry, and later on the Regional Economic Planning Councils. The C.B.I. (p. 204) has developed similar regional boards, and has regarded them as one of their most valuable activities.

Trades Councils

To some extent, the local counterpart of the T.U.C., the trades councils, have encouraged the affiliation of all local trade unions, even if they have not been connected to the T.U.C. itself. They first appeared about 1860, in the larger industrial centres, and were a local response to the trade union need for mutual support and fellowship on industrial matters. At first, they were political centres, but as local Labour Parties became organised in the 20th century, the industrial and political roles were separated, and few of them thereafter have held political meetings in the Trades Halls.

The organisation of the trades councils has remained autonomous, and most of them have interpreted their concern as being mainly educational and propagandist for the unions. In times of stress, such as a strike, they have provided a central rallying ground for the local organisation. But even this has declined since World War II, since so few strikes have been official, or involved more than one union. Most of the halls belonging to the trades councils have been centres for social gatherings which have played a normal and effective part in trade union life.

Behind the educational, social and industrial activity of the centre, the trades councils have interested themselves in the local community. Resolutions on housing, education, and other matters of public importance have been passed, and sent to the local authority, or whatever body has been appropriate. The councils have been designated, moreover, to select members to represent the employees' side on various public bodies, such as appeal tribunals, hospital boards and the like.

The trades councils have manifested a sizeable local coverage for the trade unions (in 1966 there were just over 500 trades councils in England and Wales, and 50 in Scotland), and cannot be ignored by the T.U.C. Yet between them has developed a love-hate relationship that might be difficult for some to understand; especially as the T.U.C. is said to have owed its inauguration to one of them, and up to 1895 received direct affiliation from them. But times have changed; collective bargaining, so much a national activity, has left them out in the cold, and they have declined in importance. With this has come a tendency, in some, to pursue policies contrary to those of the Labour Party, or the T.U.C., and this has resulted in several unions withdrawing their affiliation. Further, minority groups, sometimes communist, have occasionally moved in, causing additional estrangement from the T.U.C.

The Trade Union Congress would wish to think of the trades councils becoming more like local branches of itself. Since 1924, T.U.C. policy has been to accept registration, on condition that regular information would be received about membership; that the councils would distribute T.U.C. literature; help and advise the local unions if asked; seek to improve local social services; but under no circumstances initiate trade union policy. In return a joint consultative committee was set up, to which the General Council of the T.U.C. sent six members, and the trades councils six, elected from the 23 regional federations into which they had been organised. Summer schools and meetings for trades councils' officials have also been offered. But to all these gestures the response has been somewhat half-hearted, many trades councils preferring to remain independent.

Trade Union methods

It was customary, before 1940, to think of trade union methods revolving round three concepts: collective bargaining, political pressure, and the strike. These elements were to be seen after the war, but in the presence of vast economic changes bringing full employment, and balance of payments difficulties, with accompanying monetary pressures, the emphasis has changed radically. Political pressure has to some degree become political participation; the strike is a sanction to be used rarely as an official weapon, and collective bargaining, in its various forms, has dominated the scene.

Collective bargaining. The phrase 'collective bargaining' was coined by the Webbs, though others have preferred to call it 'joint regulation' (Flanders, p. 21). It has been thought of as a process beginning with a dispute, arising over a desire to alter the *status quo*, or the interpretation of an agreement, continuing to a final agreement by peaceful methods, mainly discussion. The phenomenon has been composed of certain principles, of which the chief would seem to be: mutual recognition, sincerity, a willingness to keep the rules, and the concept of job and worker status.

Thus, in the first part, both sides to the dispute—usually the employers and workers—must have recognised each other as the fit and proper representatives of accredited organisations, and as having sufficient authority to guarantee the effective honouring of any agreement reached.

Secondly, both sides must have genuinely sought a solution to the problem. There would be little point in discussing a way out of an impasse, if it were known beforehand that one or both sides had determined not to budge an inch. This has not meant that either side would expect the other to give up basic principles, but between these hard realities there has often been considerable scope for manoeuvre, to the satisfaction of both parties, and the avoidance of public conflict. They have in general believed that agreements voluntarily reached have been more enduring than those imposed from outside. They have continued to believe this, even where such agreements have implied certain evils, like injustices, such as overpaying some and underpaying others, or tolerating restrictive working practices, or deliberately curbing productivity.

Thirdly, during the long history of collective bargaining, each negotiating group has built up a series of procedural rules, such as the way in which each case should be presented, the time regarded as reasonable to reach agreement, the methods to be employed should anything go wrong, the willingness or otherwise to use conciliation or arbitration (p. 118) machinery. The net effect of this build-up of procedural rules has been to establish the status of the parties. For instance, the trade unions might be said to represent their members only, yet any agreement would apply to members and non-members alike. Similarly with employers, it would be expected that all would have to pay the new wage scale, whether they approved or not, and in certain cases, failure to do so could be challenged in the courts (p. 129). Thus the State itself has been brought into the status relationship, through the negotiating procedure.

Fourthly, the subject of discussion, and therefore the terms of the agreement, may have covered some or all matters affecting the job, or the persons engaged in it. For instance, if the agreement covered the remuneration for a particular type of job, the amount of work expected (for instance the 'stint' in mining), or the number of hours to be spent, then the job itself would achieve a certain status compared with other jobs; and the status so acquired would not necessarily depend so much on the merit of the job, as on the negotiating strength of the contending parties. Job coverage might, moreover, extend to job environment, like health and safety, and the social services would thus be directly affected by the nature of the collective bargaining, and the strength of the parties.

Or again, if the agreement has covered the personnel, it may have created an artificial hierarchy. For instance, settlements have frequently decided the relative positions of union and non-union labour, or craft and non-craft labour, in the employment policy of an industry. They have regulated the wages, holidays and conditions of 'senior' labour, and have defined seniority, whether it be by length of service, responsibility, authority, or simply by the age of the worker. Thus have agreements built up a set of rules affecting the status of workers. For instance, if the redundancy policy has been 'last in first out', then the latest recruit clearly has a status short of the next to the latest. Or if a worker has been granted an extra five days holiday a year, because he has worked for ten years in the industry, his status is superior to the one who has worked only nine years. The Redundancy Payments Act 1965 (p. 140) has underlined this point very well.

In all cases an agreement might have been reached on one of three levels. It might have been national in scope, covering every firm in the industry or service. It might have been for the district or region only; or it might merely have been to cover the situation in the individual plant. But whatever the geographical coverage, the general principles would apply.

Collective bargaining has shown itself to have had many advantages, from ending a dispute without recourse to force, to providing a discipline for both sides. It has taught the worker to use the recognised methods of change, when seeking to improve his standard of living, or to redress a grievance. It has limited the freedom of the employer to undercut his rival by underpaying his workers.

It has had its shadier side. For in essence it has been a 'free for all', and 'the devil take the hindmost'. Each side to the joint negotiation has thought of itself as a citadel protecting its own rights, and sallying forth to achieve something better when it saw the opportunity. To that extent, each has been completely self-regarding, aiming through reason, force, or whatever seemed the strongest weapon, to improve the lot of its members. In the clash, the strongest has won. Though this has been the essence of the situation, it would be untrue to conclude that agreements have been reached by the savage use of naked force. The statesmanship of all parties, the need to consider the public good, the desire to protect the consumer, and above all, the growing determination of every government, no matter what its colour, to plan a regulated economy, have had their effect; and in the latter half of the 20th century, neither side has pressed its advantage as far as it might. This has been as true of the unions as of anyone else. At the same time, free collective bargaining has resulted in an irrational wage structure, making the creation of a sound 'incomes policy' a labour of Hercules.

Political. The early history of trade unionism in Britain was mainly concerned with the struggle to be recognised by management. To attain political power was not the aim, since neither the Whigs nor the Tories showed much sympathy. If measures favouring the unions were introduced by either party, it was merely to gain a transient political advantage, and not to invite the enduring allegiance of the unions. The rise of the Labour Party put a different complexion on things, and when, in the last decade of the 19th century some Labour M.P.s were elected, the unions began to look more hopefully towards political action. Formal affiliation to the party was precipitated by a series of legal decisions, culminating in the Taff Vale decision, when the funds of a union were said to be at risk, through peaceful acts arising out of a strike. Adverse legal decisions have bedevilled the unions for a century, and though some relief was gained by Acts of Parliament, the complex legal tangle so achieved has had to be tackled by a Royal Commission in the late 1960s. It was such political action, reversing the Taff Vale decision in 1906, that brought the unions into an alliance with the Labour Party, an alliance that has remained unbroken, though with varying consequences, ever since. To the Labour Party it had been both a gain and a loss, a gain, because of the steady trade union loyalty and financial backing; a loss, because with heavy trade union representation on the party executive, political policy has been subjected to considerable union pressure, a pressure that has sometimes been resented as not being radical enough.

For the unions, the effect of the alliance has been similar. Clearly a movement concerned with protecting and furthering the interests of the employee group needed political power to influence the processes of change. Countries like the U.S.A., whose labour interests have no special political outlet, have found the truth of this, and their trade unions have sought to bring pressure on the government in other ways.

In Britain, those unions that have ballotted in favour of affiliation to the Labour Party, have used it as one method of ensuring a political voice, and a very effective one, because of the improvement in Labour Party fortunes after the Second World War. Another method has been the direct sponsoring of trade union candidates for membership of the House of Commons (and a few to the House of Lords). Such members have shown themselves loyal party supporters, but have not been allowed to forget their sponsors, or that the unions needed their services too. Thus, whether the Labour Party were H.M. Government or H.M. Opposition, the unions were assured of a direct say in Parliament itself. Moreover, such has been the growth in prestige and status of the unions, and their organisations, especially the T.U.C., that no government would by-pass them if changes likely to affect them were contemplated.

But the political nexus has not decreased trade union complexities. For, apart from their relationships with the State, and their difficulties during Labour Party government in maintaining loyalty to the party, and yet promoting the sectional interests of their members, they have been subject to legal pressures from without, and philosophical ones from within. In 1913, an uneasy legal truce was reached, when an Act set out the conditions under which unions could be allowed to partake in political action. This truce created anomalies from which the movement has suffered for the better part of this century. For instance, no union could affiliate at all, without a majority of its members declaring their assent through a ballot. Individual members were protected from paying the political levy, or supporting the party, if they declared themselves unwilling (contracting-out). The difficulties of a trade union branch chairman, who is not a political levy-payer, during a political and economic crisis can be imagined (Grunfeld 'Political independence in British Trade Unions' *British Journal of Industrial Relations*, Vol. 1 No. 1), since in the last resort the separation of industrial and political questions is an impossibility, especially as industrial planning grows.

In spite of the fact that more than a million members have contracted out each year, the general public has tended to view all trade union members as adherents of the Labour Party. And this, in many cases, has been a direct disincentive to union recruitment, raising once again the philosophical problem of the right of the individual to maintain his freedom, and to refuse to join a movement having affiliations with which he has no sympathy.

One aspect of the political side, that has long troubled the trade unions has been the alleged Communist influence in their affairs. Communists and 'fellow travellers' have been a dedicated, and well organised, body of politically active individuals, anxious to penetrate the corridors of power in the trade union movement. Sometimes financed from external sources, always prepared to go to endless trouble to obtain office, and surround themselves with sympathisers, the communists have undoubtedly gained control of some local branches, and in a few cases of the union itself. Their tactics of stirring up discontent among workers with genuine grievances, and the notorious apathy in administrative affairs common to union members, have helped the communists to entrench themselves, and gain a certain popularity, not for their political doctrines, but for their willingness to fight on the workers' behalf. Their influence should not be over-stressed, for in nearly every struggle between labour and management, and even between the unions themselves, a communist plot has been suspected, when the real trouble has been much more complex and deep-seated.

The Strike. 'Strikes are always regrettable, but not always reprehensible' (Flanders and Clegg) would seem a fair description of the modern attitude to the phenomenon. Perhaps, because of the growing understanding and tolerance of the official strike as the ultimate sanction, the British have not only tried to avoid them—they have also succeeded. Of the great industrial countries, excluding the U.S.S.R., time lost through strikes has been smaller in Britain than almost anywhere else. (*Ministry of Labour Gazette*, October 1965. Average yearly loss per 1,000 employed workers through strikes 1955–65: W. Germany, 52 days; U.K., 294 days; France, 336 days; Japan, 391 days; Canada, 597 days; U.S.A., 1,044 days.)

The strike, as a method, has not ceased to play an important role, even though it has latterly been so seldom invoked. A well-placed strike among a few key workers has been able to paralyse an industry, and affect every corner of the economy. Admittedly, it has brought a serious drain on the family resources of the participating workers, but it has meant loss of production and future contracts to the employers, and an interruption to the whole industrial progress of the community. Threat of such an upheaval has been a potent weapon to hold in reserve, and trade unions have been reluctant to let it go. At the same time, the burden has been unequally shared by the workers, as industrial unrest appears to have been mainly concentrated in only four industries: the mines, motor car manufacturing, the docks, and ship-building—together employing about seven per cent of the total working population. The rest have seldom needed to call a strike, as benefiting from the disruption caused by the few, the threat has been enough.

One other curious facet has been the growth, in the latter part of the century, of the 'unofficial strike', not recognised by the union, but where the local groups have withdrawn their labour. The reasons for this development, like the reasons for crime, have been complex, and largely unexplored. It would be presumptuous, therefore to do more than summarise the explanations that have been offered. Some, it is alleged, have arisen out of the frustration of the men on the bench, who have seen their claims for improved status disappear, months earlier, into the maw of the negotiating machinery, with no apparent results. Others have been the inevitable result of the lack of contact by the men on the shop floor, either with management, or with trade union officials, who have lacked the time to appreciate the workers' grievances. Failure in communication and consultation has in other cases resulted in workers repudiating agreements jointly reached over their heads. In some instances, the overweening power of the shop steward has been blamed, though it would be hard to justify such an argument over a long run, were there not some deeply-felt, unresolved, grievances that men had found intolerable.

The unofficial strike has not gone undefended. For instance, it has been said[1] to spur on union efficiency, and remind officials of the need to improve their service to their members. Others[2] have regarded them as the failure of the large organisation, where the individual has felt himself lost in the multiplicity of interests involved. One answer to this difficulty would be to form another union, but as this would be frowned upon, and thwarted by the rest of the movement, the only alternative has been the unofficial strike. Others have argued that they have often been a safety valve, letting off steam at points of tension, and thus avoiding bigger explosions.

Whatever the causes, unofficial strikes have rarely had a favourable press, and the gathering irritation they have engendered has led to demands for their legal suppression, subject to appeal. Thus the evidence to the Royal Commission on Trade Unions, 1965 onwards, was a mixture of arguments from the employers' side in favour of suppression, and from the workers' side against it. The Ministry of Labour pointed to the difficulty of implementing the idea, since mass punishment of large numbers of determined workers would not be possible, and would certainly be unlikely to improve industrial relations.

Problems

Only four of the great problems will be considered, but they are of such crucial importance to the future that no study of trade unions, however brief, could omit them. The 'closed shop' has

[1] A. Strang, 'The Virtue of Strikes', *New Statesman*, 12 November, 1965.
[2] S. W. Lerner, 'Breakaway Unions, and the Small Trade Union'.

long been a matter of controversy; but union officials, the relative importance of the local and the national bargain, and shop stewards have grown in importance, and would seem the key to the whole future of industrial relations in this country.

The closed shop

The phrase could have one of two meanings. It might include those firms, all of whose workers have joined a union, any union; or those firms which recognise only one union to which all must belong.

The one union closed shop has certain obvious advantages from the management viewpoint, since negotiation with one union would be more convenient, more speedy, and more likely to reach an agreement that would be honoured by all parties. From the trade union angle it might be thought that strength would lie in unity, and the democratic response from the members be more vital, if all were in the same union, bringing their day-to-day experience to bear on union activity. But the movement has, on the whole, been opposed to this, as a general policy. Unions have argued that they should have fundamental freedoms of their own, and that no unnecessary obstacle should stand in the way of their exercise. Furthermore, unions have offered different attractions to various categories of workers, as in the crafts, and it would be a retrograde step to make such workers join another union. The ever-present danger has been the creation of a closed shop by a 'breakaway' union—an absolute 'sin' to the trade union movement.

To meet the problem of the multiplicity of unions in the closed shop, the unions have experimented with several devices, such as the federation, or the 'recognised' union. The latter has been more popular in America than in Britain, and implies the right of each union to recruit appropriate members in any one firm, but to recognise only one union as having the right to negotiate. It is a method not unknown among professional associations, who have recognised the parallel rights of other associations to recruit, though negotiation has been limited to a selected few (for example, teachers).

Though the T.U.C. and the movement as a whole have not encouraged the one-union closed shop, there has long been active approval of the principle of the closed shop, in which all workers are union members. To achieve it has needed the co-operation of management, who have tacitly accepted the idea, without publicly promoting it by national agreement.[1] There are arguments to support it, for example: all workers ought to be members because all have benefited; differential benefits would be unthinkable both to workers whose standards of living would be threatened by cheap labour, and to employers whose costs of production would be menaced by unscrupulous rivals; trade unionists should have the right to refuse to work side-by-side with non-unionists. The opposite view has been taken by some moralists, who have claimed that every worker in a free society should have the right to refuse to join a voluntary organisation, and that this right should be manifestly seen to apply. Whatever the relevance of these arguments[2] there is no denying that circumstances themselves may vary. For instance, seamen, or musicians, who move from job to job, could not sustain a viable union without the closed shop; or where entry to a trade has been through a union ticket, as with the woodworkers, closure has been inevitable.

The closed shop has had its serious problems, particularly in the preservation of discipline. Sometimes this has involved restrictive practices, many of which were agreed, to protect the craftsmen against unfair competition from unqualified labour, and to maintain the quality of the job itself. Were an individual or group of workers to set aside these practices, on promise of favourable recognition in pay and status, but without union approval, suspension or even expulsion from the union might result. In a closed shop arrangement, this might be very serious for the individual, involving loss of job, and sometimes the loss of the right to continue working at the craft in any other job—a loss that has led to some of the more irritating legal decisions of recent years. It is a situation parallelled in the professional field, where a person expelled from a 'closed' profession, is unable to work in his profession at all (for example, doctors). The right of appeal therefore seems essential. Whether the court to hear such appeals should be independent, in contradistinction to the tribunals of the professions, would be another matter, though the general trend of opinion would favour it.

Whatever the morality of the closed shop policy, it has not

[1]Evidence to the Royal Commission on Trade Unions 1965 onwards; many Employers' Organisations advocated the recognition of the closed shop in return legal excommunication of unofficial strikes.
[2] A. Fox, 'The closed shop', *New Society*, 16 December, 1965.

ceased to gain ground. For by the late 1960s, half of all manual worker-members of trade unions were employed in full union shops.

One unexpected result has been the growing practice of employers of deducting, by agreement, the union subscription from the pay cheques. This could only be done by written request from the individuals, but it is a break in a tradition that management gives no active support to the union, and that the essence of union development lies in the principle of voluntaryism. The Coal Board was one of the first to accept the idea (some coal-owners had already operated it before nationalisation), but a number of private firms have done so too. The British Institute of Management (*New Society*, 19 August, 1965) surveying the 'check-off', found that many employers had accepted it as part of a bargain in which the unions safeguarded their finances and saved the time previously used for collection, and the employers in return were able to limit the time spent by shop stewards pursuing union business in working hours. Sometimes the bargain included payment of wages by cheque, or even the abandonment of the demand for a 'closed shop' policy on the part of the workers. The Survey indicated that few employers had regretted the 'check-off', and some even welcomed it as a means of knowing the exact strength of the union in the plant.

Union officials

Nothing has been said in this résumé about the organisation and control of the unions. Their methods have differed according to the needs of the members, and the particular theories uppermost at the time of constitution-making. The problem that has emerged from them all, and that is likely to have profound effects, both on the future of the movement and on the future of British industry, has been that of the full-time official.

As the unions have grown, and their work extended, the appointment of full-time officials has become a necessity, and any union hoping to play a significant role in the industrial scene, must increase their number. Therefore the method of appointment, the calibre of those chosen, and the adequacy of their number, has become crucial to the scope and quality of the work they do.

A small number of the unions has been content to appoint officials from outside the ranks of the membership, from people who have not necessarily grown up in the industry or the movement. But the majority have ruled that only those who have been members, and have experienced the life of the grass-root worker, could be eligible for a job in the union. The system has worked, because sufficient intelligent, active members have been prepared to give voluntary, enthusiastic service in the branch, or at district meetings, to provide a reservoir from which full-time officers could be chosen. But the Education Act 1944 was, in a sense, the beginning of a new era for trade unions. Free secondary education, with its process of creaming off the best of the late teenagers for university work, has meant a diminishing supply of suitable experienced trade unionists. The 21st century will be faced with a serious alternative—either to appoint full-time officials from university graduates, and thus to jeopardise the understanding between them and the rank and file—or to accept the unpalatable fact that the pool of suitable candidates for these posts will have seriously shrunk.

Some unions have used the democratic method of electing their officials, assuming that the most energetic and appropriate men will have shown their merits, first in the local scene, and later to wider audiences, and that members can be relied upon to distinguish between the gold and the dross in the officials they choose. Many excellent appointments have been made this way. Yet the dangers of the system seem all too apparent. There is not only the fear of demagogy, but more serious, the danger that members will not have realised the real changes that have come over the nature of the officials' work. The need for negotiating skill, for subtlety of mind, for quickness in taking a point, or appreciating a flaw in an argument, the ability to take a broad view, and to see the wood as well as the trees—these have become the basic essentials of a union official's equipment. He has had to know the intimate details of the industrial position, and to understand and sympathise with the workers' feelings; he has had to get along with people, and possess the ability to communicate with his members in acceptable terms; but without the mental and personal equipment of a negotiator, his work for the union could not be of the best. Whether these essentials have been, or could be understood by the rank and file, so that an election would choose the right man, is not always plain to see.

One might have thought that some analysis of trade union work

o   195

would have evolved a system of training for would-be officials. Training for industrial management has been recognised as a necessity. Training for trade union officials, apart from the in-service apprenticeship common in most unions, and the short courses that are continuously available, has not been systematically organised, because it depends on a much closer study of their function than has so far been attempted.

When once appointed, full-time officials have been ham-strung by two factors: by the change and growth in the work of the unions, and by the lack of staff. The change in union work has arisen out of the greater recognition of union significance. When it is seriously contended by all parties that the future of industrial relations lies in a partnership between management and workers, the whole scope of union work takes on a new look. Instead of being on the defensive, to safeguard the hard-won rights and status of the workers, or on the offensive to improve the workers' pay and conditions, the unions have begun to accept a new dimension, a share in the responsibility for the progress and welfare of the whole productive process. This has already happened in the nationalised industries (Acton Society Trust 'The Future of the Unions'), and it will increasingly permeate other industries, as joint consultation, participation in management, staff status for the rank and file, and actual financial involvement in the industry by the unions (as in the Fairfield Shipyard on the Clyde, which was partially financed by union moneys in 1965), gain momentum. All this will make new demands on the officials and require new skills and specialities.

It will also require more officials. At this point, the finances of the unions need an overhaul. The weekly subscription, still too low, will need to be raised, or the number of members paying it will have to be enlarged, or some other method of financing the organisation evolved. To expect a small number of full-time officials to attend the multiplicity of meetings; to get to know their own members personally; to appreciate the working conditions first hand; and to give enough thought to the complex problems that have to be solved, is asking too much. (Marsh 'Managers and Shop Stewards' in 1963 estimated the number of full-time officials as 2,500, or 1 to 3,800 union members.) Trade unionism, to be viable, must provide itself not only with suitable officials, but with enough of them.

National v. local bargaining

The need for more full-time, well trained officials, particularly locally, is underlined by the growing importance of the plant as the centre for agreements. Up to about the middle of the 20th century, the assumption had been cherished that national agreements had overriding advantages over local ones. They had been fought for by the trade unions for more than a century, because they were seen to be the only way to protect the individual against the employer, and had been supported by employers as a means of using most effectively the scarce resources (for both sides) in skilled and experienced negotiators. Employers in expanding industries had tended to favour them as a means of withstanding the demands of organised labour, in those local areas where labour was short; and many others had supported them, because they wanted to divorce their own firms from the unpleasant task of pay negotiation, involving as it must, comment on their own arrangements.

Since about 1950, a gradual change in the general approval of national agreements has been seen. Economists have argued that during full employment, if labour was to be encouraged to go to expanding industries, where efficiency and low costs would combine with high productivity to make a saleable article, or service, in a competitive market, the jobs must be attractive. But if wages have been nationally agreed, and paid equally in all branches of the industry, where would be the incentive to move? In practice, progressive firms have tended to offer wages higher than the national rates, to attract the needed labour, thus creating a 'wage drift'. These, in turn, have become stepping stones to new agreements for higher national minima, and the progressive firms have then been obliged to raise their offers still higher. Economists are therefore coming round to the view that national wage agreements are too prodigal, because they increase rewards to workers in efficient and inefficient firms alike. If wages are to be linked with productivity, local differentials would seem the logical way. But if this should occur, on any scale, the position of the local trade union official would be radically altered, and the need to improve both the number and the skill of such men would grow.

Another factor in the trend has been the nature of many of the nationally negotiated agreements in modern times. They have become so complex, have implied so many reciprocal responsibilities, that unless they have been properly discussed, explained and agreed by the rank and file, their chances of adequate implementation are remote. Indeed, many workers have been faced with promises made on their behalf that they have neither agreed to, nor understood. Such are the intricacies of incentive payment schemes, technological change, and other modifications, that without local negotiation about their practical implications the agreements have been a dead-letter, or worse still, the cause of friction. In the absence of enough union officials for this delicate process, shop stewards have often filled the vacuum, but such is their status with the unions, that they have themselves been a source of friction. A careful reappraisal of the unions' local functions, and their relations with the shop stewards, seems to be an urgent necessity.

Shop Stewards

Information about the origins and general development of the shop steward movement is not plentiful, but it seems that he has existed in some form since the beginnings of the factory system.[1] During the 19th century, the importance to working people of unity in the work-shops was everywhere understood, and the practice grew of appointing one of their fellows to represent the common interest to the management. He voiced their grievances, negotiated the price of a job, requested an increase in wages, or opposed a threatened decrease. He was the spontaneous answer to an obvious need, but as such, the original shop steward appears to have arisen independently of the unions. By the 20th century, some unions, particularly the A.E.U., and kindred ones (like the E.T.U.) had appreciated their importance, and found a place for them in the union organisation. But others, though insisting that they should be union members, have not integrated them into the organisation.

The unions' attitude, while varying from union to union, has tended to be ambivalent. They have expected the shop stewards to collect the membership dues, check that all have paid, and represent union policy in the work-shop, but have demanded that

[1] See W. E. J. McCarthy, 'The Role of Shop Stewards in British Industrial Relations'; A. Marsh, 'Managers and Shop Stewards'.

they refrain from independent local negotiations, unless with the express approval of the unions. Since local decisions have some-times required speed, which the union has not always been geared to provide, the stewards' position has been perplexing. Their strength has lain in their intimate knowledge of the plant, of the workers' reaction to the management's demands, to trade union responses, and the general industrial and political climate of the times. This knowledge has in most cases been far more accurate and detailed than that of the trade union officials, and whether it were a question of policy, the price for a job, or the threat of a dispute, stewards have been faced with the dilemma, either to feed the problem into the pipe-line of the trade union organisation, with the fear of delay and frustration, or to make an on-the-spot decision.

The position of the unions has not been easy either. Inadequately supplied with full-time officials, they have, as a rule, tried to work with the shop stewards, and have relied upon them for information and advice, as well as for their help in making known union policy, and putting it into practice. But sometimes, they have been faced with the inevitable dangers of workshop demagogy. There have been examples of stewards, chosen for their militancy, perhaps Communists or fellow-travellers, anxious only to keep the pot of conflict boiling. Where this has occurred, difficulties both for unions and management have multiplied. Such examples have been given wide publicity, though it is doubtful whether they have represented more than a tiny fraction of the estimated 150,000 shop stewards in the whole of British industry. Nevertheless, the problem of how to integrate the representatives of the local work group with the union has continued to pose insuperable difficulties. Further, complications have been added by the independent organisation of the stewards themselves. If a work-shop has con-tained members of several unions, each recognised by the employer for negotiating purposes, and each with its own shop steward, it has been common for them to co-ordinate policy by forming a shop stewards' committee, with the senior steward as chairman and spokesman. Each steward has thus been a member of, and responsible, to his own union, but neither the stewards' commit-tee, nor the senior steward, have been responsible to anyone. The employer has thus been placed in an impossible position; having made an agreement with the unions, he has found himself faced by a different organised body on the shop floor, to whom he must look for implementation of the agreement. But this body has had neither any part in making the agreement, nor any feeling of loyalty for putting it into practice—and what would appear on the surface to be repudiation of a properly negotiated agreement might well be the result.

Various suggestions for improving this state of affairs have been put forward (for example, I.P.M. evidence to the Royal Commission on Trade Unions 1965, or McCarthy, pp. 73–5). The most often made has been that there should be closer integration of the stewards in union activity, that they ought to have more responsibility when decisions are taken, and that their functions should be more clearly spelt out in the rules of the union.

The basic objection to this is that the unions cannot abrogate the duty to protect the long-term interests of the totality of their members, while the stewards, being essentially concerned with the primary unit of the organisation, have tended to respond to sectional interests only. Another idea has been to create 'bargaining units' at shop level, so that where a number of unions has operated, the one most acceptable to the workers could be chosen to represent them on all negotiating occasions. Whether the actual person operating the scheme be the shop steward, or the trade union official, would be a matter for decision. But whoever it was, he should be the fully accredited representative of the union, privy to its discussions, and trusted by it to do his best for the workers in the shop, without embarrassing his colleagues elsewhere.

Many have approved the extension of federated unions at the local level, as in the building trades. In their case, each union has been able to maintain its independence, but has federated with kindred unions for purposes of work-shop negotiation. Though this would not necessarily solve the problem of the shop steward, it would at least ease his burden, by recognising one union organisation to which he could look for guidance, and to whom he could feel loyalty and obligation.

The T.U.C. has so far developed no coherent policy towards shop stewards. apart from recognising them when they have been given a place within the structure of an affiliated union (as in the A.E.U.). It has given a warm reception to such training schemes as have so far appeared. But these are sporadic and haphazard.

Sometimes they have taken the form of adult education courses in social history or trade union organisation, sometimes of T.W.I. courses on 'supervision', or short courses run by the unions themselves, but there has nowhere been a coherent programme of training for 'primary negotiators', available and compulsory for all. Indeed a concerted effort to end the isolation of the stewards, and give them adequate preparation for their job, seems to be the next step.

Employers' Organisations

If trade unions have played an important part in the way the social services in industry have been organised and developed, employers' organisations have been equally powerful. They have represented that side of industry which has not generally been thought to benefit directly from the social services, and which in some cases has opposed their development. Yet, paradoxically, without their support, financial and moral, none of the schemes could have prospered.

Unfortunately, much less is known about them than of the trade unions, as they have preferred to work in private, and have seldom issued public statements or produced annual reports. Unlike the unions they have not registered with the Registrar of Friendly Societies, so the indirect information that might have been obtained from that source has been absent. In spite of this, it is generally known that few pieces of social legislation have been put before Parliament since the First World War without considerable discussion having taken place between the employers' organisations (or their representatives) and the government, or without them making very clear what their views have been.

The secrecy surrounding their size, structure, personnel, and working has hampered those who might have been encouraged to write about them, or to offer criticisms and suggestions for their future development.

Origins and present pattern

It is known that employers have joined together for various purposes over a long period, sometimes to reduce competition and avoid undercutting; at others, to obtain joint action in commercial, legal and other services; or, particularly since World War I, in response to government policy, such as the encouragement of 'rationalisation' in industry in the 1920s, or the attempt to regulate prices and incomes in the 1960s.

But of all the reasons for forming an employers' association, the need to present a united front against organised labour has probably been the most persistent. During the 19th century organisations of employers were formed as soon as their workers had united to press for change. For instance, the formation of the Amalgamated Society of Engineers in 1851 was followed almost immediately by the establishment of a central organisation of employers in the industry. And during the 20 years from about 1870, the number of local employers' organisations increased rapidly in those industries where the trade unions had become firmly established (Richardson, pp. 69–70). The speed increased during the last decade or so, and one cannot escape the conclusion that the growing strength and general recognition of the unions has had a lot to do with it. The tactics of the unions must have accelerated the process, as for instance in the 'strike in detail' device, in which a union arranges for its members to go on strike against one employer at a time, the strikers being supported by contributions from the wages of their fellows still at work in other firms (the bakers used this method in 1966). Such a method must have compelled many firms to unite, who might otherwise have hesitated. This is not to say that presenting a united front to the unions has been their sole concern, because, besides furthering their trading interests, many tried to give their members practical help and advice in developing positive employment policies, like the provision of advisory services on the recruitment and training of staff. Indeed, if some consistent research were to be undertaken into the practices of employers' organisations, it might be found that the multiplicity of their activities was a source of weakness, especially compared with the single-mindedness of the trade unions.

On the other hand, the employers' organisations have been favoured, because their finance and organisation have not presented undue difficulties. Compared with trade unions, the number of potential members has been small, and a well written letter, or a friendly approach, has brought most managements into an association, especially where influential firms have already joined. Refusals have usually occurred if the firm is employing non-union labour, or prefers its own approach. But most have realised that unity is strength, and have joined.

Combination has tended to be on an 'industrial' basis, particularly where the industry has been homogeneous, though in other cases, where the range has been more complex, each part has developed its own association, and has federated for collective bargaining purposes. (For example, the Engineering and Allied Employers Federation.) In this event, individual firms have not been members of the national federation, but have joined their local association (district or region), which in turn has joined similar associations to form a national body.

On the whole, the larger the organisation, the greater has been its strength. Small ones have been unable to appoint competent staff, and have suffered the inevitable consequences; or having obtained a seat at national collective bargaining tables, they have been an embarrassment to the employers' side by their sheer numbers. Their actual strength has always been difficult to estimate. The Central Office of Information thought there were about 1,500 associations in 1959, of which 80 were national federations; but Corina (p.21) using another method of calculation, thought there were as many as 2,000 to 3,000 in 1963, and that about 15 million workers were in the firms so covered. Whatever the truth may be, they outnumber trade unions by more than two to one. The big employers' organisations have become very large indeed, and about a dozen of them dominate the scene (such as those for engineering, building, ship-building, textiles, chemicals, printing, shipping and others).

Though small associations have not had sufficient financial strength, lack of money has not been a general source of weakness, the criteria of contribution varying from the annual fee paid equally by all to the levy according to size, output, or number of workers on the payroll. As for the final authority, a local or small national association has tended to use the quarterly or annual meeting, with managements of member firms having the right to attend; in the larger bodies, firms have not, as a rule, been directly represented at the national level, where the policy and executive functions have been exercised, but only indirectly through their membership of local associations.

Every union of any size has had to appoint full-time staff to negotiate on the workers' side. Employers have done this individually through personnel officers, if they were large enough, and have therefore found no necessity for skilled negotiators in their associations. Nevertheless, some of these bodies are beginning to make appointments of industrial relations officers and it is thought that the idea might be extended, especially for advisory work among the smaller firms.

The Confederation of British Industry (C.B.I.)

Most important of all the associations concerning employers is the supra-organisation, developed to represent this side of industry, on national and inter-national questions. Since this is likely to have a profound effect on the working of the social services in industry, it is valuable to look at its composition and policy.

Formed in July 1965, the Confederation of British Industries was an amalgam of three associations: the British Employers' Confederation (1919), the Federation of British Industries (1916), and the National Association of British Manufacturers (1915). Of these, the most powerful in labour matters was the B.E.C., which had represented the employers in negotiation with the government, at the I.L.O. and other international meetings. The F.B.I., had concerned itself with commercial matters, and tended to be the British shop window in international markets. The N.A.B.M. had protected the interests of manufacturers against domestic legislation, including social services, likely to interfere with business interests, and against foreign activities which might produce an unfair situation for British trade. It had been thought for a long time that the interests of these three were too close for them to remain separate, and accordingly in 1965 the Confederation of British Industries was born, a body of great influence and power, prepared to face the T.U.C. as the other vigorous organ of industry.

The C.B.I. was not all-embracing in membership, since it was mainly confined to productive and manufacturing firms. In 1966 there were 251 employers' organisations, and nearly 13,000 member firms. Local authorities were outside it, though nationalised industries have developed a special relationship (Industrial Associates). Full membership for government firms was thought to be undesirable, since some of the discussions might prove embarrassing, but the interests of private enterprise and nationalised industry were clearly too close for the latter not to be included in some way. As in most large organisations, it has used its standing committees to think out its policy and ideas, and has inaugurated regional councils to watch over the more local developments, and to co-operate with the regional economic planning councils, on which it has had representation.

It has not become an authoritative body, in the sense of being able to commit member firms to any particular policy, such as a social service. But its closer consultative relations with the government, and its role as an interpreter of employers' interests in national policy, have given it a stature unlike any other body (see *The Times*, 18 November, 1966), and this in itself has enhanced its authority with individual firms.

As the power and size of the C.B.I. and T.U.C. have grown, they have come to be recognised by the government and the nation as the natural complement to each other, when discussions arise on the many important and far-reaching proposals on the social services and man-power problems that the last few years have generated. If the initiative in this aspect of industry has seemed to emanate more from the T.U.C. than the C.B.I., this is perhaps understandable, since the T.U.C.'s priorities in the past have lain in that direction, while employers' organisations have been followers—sometimes unwilling ones. All the same, it is a category of industrial life in which the C.B.I. is likely to take, and will need to take, a more active role. Already a new spirit of joint endeavour has turned what used to be defensive and aggressive organisations, mostly at enmity with one another, into institutions ready to negotiate and co-operate in furthering the industry of the country, and the needs and aspirations of those who work in it.

X

THE PROFESSIONS

PROFESSIONS ARE IMPORTANT social institutions, whose members are often intimately concerned with the working of the social services. Without the doctors, lawyers, social workers, personnel officers, nurses, and others whose training and mode of working are generally understood as 'professional', the social services could not maintain their quality. It is appropriate, therefore, to analyse the chief characteristics of the professions, and to consider what is expected of the members and how acceptance of professional rules imposes loyalties separate from those governing the behaviour between employers and staff.

Professionalism is the application to a vocation of an intellectual technique, based on a body of theoretical knowledge. (Carr-Saunders and Wilson, 'The Professions', contains the most extensive analysis of the subject. See also G. Millerson, 'The Qualifying Associations.) The technique can only be acquired after a prolonged period of specialised training, and the practitioners must have undergone and passed tests of competence in both theory and practice. The difference between the professional and the tradesman, in industry, is not the length of the training, or the passing of examinations, but the fact that in the professions there has developed a large and growing accumulation of theory associated with the subject, and that no-one is admitted to professional practice without first having mastered the basic principles of the theory—a process that inevitably extends over years. The tradesman, on the other hand, though not without some theoretical background, spends most of his training in acquiring and perfecting practical skills.

The idea of professionalism, like that of a craft, has existed for many centuries in this country, and the characteristics of the older professions, such as the law and medicine, have tended to be the aspirations of the newer ones. Each profession has grown in its own way, and has therefore its own peculiarities, but certain fundamentals have become true of them all.

Analysis of the fundamental concepts. Comparison with Trade Unions

The first common factor has been the desire to limit practice to the qualified, so the meaning of 'qualification' has been of the utmost importance to the professions, and a standard of competence, everywhere recognised, has been the first necessity. The usual means of testing the standard has been by examination, and the problem of who shall set it, and how it shall be recognised, has been crucial. Various methods have been adopted. In some cases examining bodies, such as the universities, have been recognised for the purpose, as in the medical profession; in others, the profession has set up its own examining bodies, as have the barristers in their Inns of Court.

Once having accepted the qualification, a permanent record of those qualified has had to be established. The keeping of the 'register' has frequently been undertaken by the practitioners' own association, as in the case of the veterinary surgeons, though in others a statutory body, like the General Medical Council for the doctors, has undertaken the function.

As for the training that precedes qualification, this has been a much neglected aspect for many years. Some, like accountants, have learnt their theory through correspondence courses, while gaining practical experience by a system of pupilage. (Accountancy courses in universities are recognised by the profession.) For other professions, fully fledged university courses have been developed, where doctors, architects, and others, have had the advantage of full-time integrated theoretical and practical training. The movement to improve the selection and training of craftsmen (p. 28), while not preceding a similar trend in the professions, has been comparable to the growing interest, particularly by professionals themselves, in the kind of training provisions their potential colleagues should enjoy.

Round the development of 'qualification' has grown up an exclusiveness that is encouraged by the professions. This exclusiveness has had sound foundations, as its prime purpose was to limit recognition to the technically competent. Thus entrance has often meant the possession of certain preliminary qualifications, such as G.C.E. at Advanced Level, and the final test has been pitched at a standard that would eliminate all but the best. So long as this has been reasonable, it would seem a desirable protection of the profession, and of the public interest, though if exclusiveness has had other aims, like social prestige, or economic strength, it is another matter. Inevitably the long training, and the postponement of full earning power have provided their own restrictions; these were to some extent shared by the craftsmen who also had to forego early affluence in favour of training.

The next stage was the struggle to limit the practice of the skill to the qualified. In the process, many rights and privileges have grown up, some statutorily obtained, others achieved by custom and agreement. They were compared in many cases with the 'workshop practices' of the craftsmen, but instead of being modified and broken down, as in crafts, the professions have successfully fought for their extension, and the modern world has witnessed a race to achieve some kind of paper qualification that would guarantee a particular job, or function, for its owner, and a 'closed door' to the one without it. In this the professions have been far more prohibitive and self-regarding than the crafts, and though shortage of qualified practitioners has sometimes meant the use of 'ancillary' staff, as in medicine or teaching, the gulf between those who are 'in' and the rest has been profound. Anything like 'dilution of labour', an ever present menace to the qualified craftsman, has been withstood at all costs. Examples of these preserves have been the doctors' right to sign death certificates, the barristers' exclusive right to advocate in the High Court, the pharmacists' right to sell poisons, and the right to the title of 'dentist', which has been limited to those with the approved qualifications. A great variety of functions and titles have thus been reserved to the qualified, and where this has happened, the profession has been regarded as 'closed'. It has become the aim of most vocations to reach this position, by statute if possible. If the privilege has not included the reservation of certain posts, as the doctors' privileges did not, a concerted effort to achieve this has usually been made. In the 20th century, the medical profession has been highly successful in its aim, first by ensuring that none but the qualified should be recognised as 'panel' doctors, under the National Health Insurance Scheme of 1912, and then by insisting that only registered practitioners should man the National Health Service after 1948. Compared with success of this kind, the efforts of the craftsmen to obtain a 'closed shop', excluding all but those with a union card, have been relatively unavailing.

Privilege has always carried its responsibilities, and both unions and professions have found it necessary to exercise discipline over their members. In both cases, the conditions upon which penalties have been imposed have varied from organisation to organisation, and when exercised have ranged from the mild, involving a warning or minor fine, to the severe, including suspension, or the extreme penalty of actual dismissal from the profession and the withdrawal of a man's right to earn his living in the vocation for which he has been trained. The actual grounds for dismissal have varied. In a few cases, as with the colliery manager, the purpose of discipline has been to preserve competence, and if such a professional person acted incompetently he would expose himself to the ultimate penalty. But lack of competence has rarely been the reason for 'striking off' in the older and more established professions. The usual one has been 'infamous conduct in a professional respect'.

Code of Ethics

When challenged, 'infamous conduct' has been interpreted as 'something which would reasonably be regarded as disgraceful or dishonourable by his professional brethren of good repute and competency' (Carr-Saunders, p. 397). To help the members to an understanding of their professional responsibilities, most professions have developed their own Code of Ethics, agreed to, and accepted by all practitioners. The Codes have naturally varied, but most professions have included clauses concerning: professional secrecy; the obligation at all times to render their best service in the interests of the client; the prohibition on accepting indirect remuneration (such as a share in the damages, if a barrister has been successful in winning them, through the Court); prohibition on price-cutting; or advertisement (the rigours of the latter have been slightly modified, in recent years, in the medical profession, to meet the public demand for more education on health matters); or the 'covering' of unqualified practice by the professional. The Code of Ethics has in the main been strictly adhered to, and has been a powerful curb on those members who might be tempted to unprofessional conduct. The Codes have not been concerned with general law, though a professional person having fallen foul of the law in certain directions might find himself in difficulty with his profession as well. It has also been true that a professional person showing incompetence, particularly negligence of the kind likely to endanger the life and limb of others, might find himself facing charges, both in the court of law, and before the disciplinary committees of the profession. On the other hand, 'incompetence' as a single charge, has not in general been as dangerous to a man's standing in his profession as many would have thought. New ideas and new methods have often been called 'incompetence' by other members of the profession intent on a heresy hunt, and this is something the professions have always wished to avoid. The policy has therefore been to guarantee professional competence before the practitioner is registered, and thereafter to keep him up to the mark by watching his professional conduct.

Tribunals of discipline

The power of the profession to erase a practitioner's name from the roll of the qualified has involved the establishment of judicial machinery. In many cases this has taken the form of a tribunal, composed of members of the profession. The concept that judgement by one's peers is right has been sustained by the argument that it takes members of one's own profession to understand its climate and appreciate the details of the charge; and since the code of conduct has developed out of the standards and opinions of the profession, it is they who are best fitted to understand what is alleged, and to deal with it in the light of the needs of the profession. What has been notably lacking, particularly in some of the older professions, such as medicine, has been any system of appeal, though cases have often been re-opened by the same tribunal. Yet with few exceptions the system has worked. Newer professions, under Act of Parliament, have made provision for appeal; architects, dentists, and nurses, have had the machinery of appeal written into the legislation.

In some cases, the body responsible for setting up the disciplinary machinery has been outside the general control of the profession, for instance, the G.M.C., one of whose functions is to act as a judicial agency for misdoers in the profession. Though the tribunal in this case has been composed of medical men, it has not represented the profession as a whole. But in other cases, such as the veterinary surgeons, the professional association has selected its own committee for the purpose.

Professional associations

Professional associations have played a crucial part in the growth of each profession. They have usually been formed in the first instance as meeting points, where members could discuss the skills and techniques of their work. These associations have consequently tended to throw their resources into research and education. Research has been of paramount importance if the profession were not to stagnate. Though the cost of research has multiplied with the years, and reached proportions the associations could not hope to meet, yet in stimulating it wherever it occurred, and communicating to members through journals, meetings and other means, the professional associations have played an active part. Similarly in education, they have been eager to improve the standards of qualification, and to guarantee that the best possible people entered the profession. Veterinary surgeons, architects, accountants, nurses, are all examples of professions which have reorganised their system of qualification since the Second World War.

There is one development among professional people that has had far-reaching effects on the work of their associations. This has been the gradual change from payment by the client, to payment by an agency, whether it be the State, the local authority, or the firm. Some professionals, like the general practitioners, have found themselves in a half-way position, where their major payment has been from the Treasury, through the local Executive Councils, and yet who have been allowed to take private patients who pay a fee direct. Architects have been similarly placed, though in their case, men in private practice, and salaried government servants, or employees of firms, have usually been separate individuals. Nevertheless, whenever payment by an agency has become an important factor, the association has felt itself caught up in

P   211

negotiations about payment and conditions of service—the trade union function. In periods of inflation and a rising standard of living, this function has played an ever increasing role in the activity of the professional body—so much so, that some of them have seriously considered affiliating to the T.U.C. N.A.L.G.O. joined in the 1950s, and the N.U.T. did so in the 1960s. But without affiliation, many (like the B.M.A.) have exercised considerable pressure on the paying agencies to improve the material standards of their members.

Though professional associations have strengthened their protective functions, and though their pressure on paying bodies has been as persistent and unrelenting as any trade union's, they have not been bedevilled with inter-association rivalry and demarcation disputes in the way the unions have. The reasons are not altogether clear. Certainly, they have spent more time on developing and improving their expertise than the unions, and have therefore a more clear-cut notion of their limits than many craftsmen would have; and at a time when new professions are developing, one would have expected more quarrels over the function of each one, than have in fact occurred. The history of the professions has been by no means free from disputes of this kind, as the early battles between the barbers and the surgeons on demarcation would show, so the danger of future trouble cannot be ruled out.

So far the State has not seen fit to interfere in the craftsmen's problems, except to help them to reach a settlement of an immediate difficulty, but in the professions the picture is very different. Parliament has statutorily regulated certain professions, so that the qualified can be distinguished from the unqualified (through the Register), and has granted monopoly privileges to the registered (for example the issuing of legal certificates by the doctors and architects, a monopoly function to dentists, and to some extent to midwives). Why the State has regulated certain professions and not others has been partly a matter of expediency in the public interest, and partly the effect of a profession's own power to force parliament to act.

Carr-Saunders and Wilson (op. cit., p. 304–7) have distinguished five reasons for State regulation. Firstly, where the service rendered has been vital, as in the medical group: doctors, veterinary surgeons, pharmacists, nurses and midwives. In these cases anyone might need professional help at any time, and the public should be protected from the unqualified, in what might be situations involving life or death. Secondly, where the profession has been fiduciary, like barristers, solicitors and patent agents. Once again, anyone might need the services of these people, perhaps at a moment's notice, and the clientele might not be well-informed about where to turn, and should be protected from the amateur. Thirdly, some services have been intimately concerned with public safety, like the mine-managers or officers of the merchant navy, and State regulation to guarantee a recognised degree of initial competence has been thought necessary. Fourthly, if the State itself has become an employer of certain professionals, or has been concerned with grant-aid to their pay, it has stated what qualifications it will recognise either for employment, or for pay-scales, or both. Teachers, social workers, health visitors, engineers, have fallen within this class. Finally, a miscellaneous group, including architects, auctioneers, estate agents, accountants and others have also achieved State regulation and privilege. Their number will doubtless increase, as pressures from newer professions grow, and the extent of State employment enlarges.

Criticisms

As the importance of the professions has waxed, and their influence on every aspect of social and industrial life has grown, a critical look at their constitutions and functions has been made by several interested observers.[1] It has been alleged that they are a socially divisive, institutionalised élite, with members conscious of their superiority, yet anxious to preserve an aura of mystery about their calling, and tending to oppose the public will. Thus the members of the medical profession, it is said, have preferred to maintain secrecy about their craft, and in spite of a universal wish to inaugurate a general health service, have deliberately used delaying tactics to resist the enactment. Thereafter, by their propaganda, and their actions, they have persisted in their recalcitrance.

Another criticism of the privileged position of the professions has been in their use of restrictive practices, and their determination to avoid competition. Examples of this have been the practice, in

[1] See articles in *The Economist* during 1966. Also T. Raison 'In defence of the Professions'. *New Society*, 18 August, 1966.

the legal profession, of requiring a client to approach a barrister through his solicitor; the inability of a solicitor to plead in the High Court, and similar practices which have inevitably increased the expense of litigation. As for competition, nearly all professions have forbidden advertising, or price-undercutting, and have done so on the grounds that business practices of this sort would be unbecoming in a professional, and might reduce the quality of his professional service. Against this, Dr Lees[1] has declared that the professionals are there to perform a service for the public, and not to maintain their social status; and that the evidence that competition reduces quality has not been borne out in practice.

Another ground of attack is that professionals have tended to be conservative, in the political, though not necessarily in the party sense. The legal profession has provided examples of this; the reluctance of many doctors to accept the teachings of psychiatry has also been cited as evidence that new techniques in treating the 'whole person' have been resisted by them. Architects were for a long time precluded from serving on the boards of construction companies, and the bar has been lifted too late to avoid many architectural errors.

A further problem, increasingly evident within industry has been the dual role and the dual loyalty of the professionals. So long as the organisation of industry was simple, where the entrepreneur started the business, controlled it, extended it, provided the capital, made all the decisions, and was remunerated by profit, there was little scope for the professional. But the complexity of modern industry has meant the sub-division of the entrepreneur's functions, and the establishment of professionals at almost every stage. It is here that the duality arises. If the business is concerned with the making of profit, and it requires its lawyers, accountants, engineers and the rest to bend their energies and brains to that end, these professionals must inevitably find themselves in difficulties vis à vis their colleagues in the rest of the profession, and their duties to the standards of their profession. The same problem could well arise in the local government service, and in the national one. Architects, for instance, might find themselves required to erect a building they know would not be in the best taste, or the public interest. It might be said they could resign, and

[1] D. Lees, 'Economic Consequences of the Professions', Institute of Economic Affairs.

214

this has sometimes happened. But not everyone can take such an independent line. So professionalism has had to give ground in favour of more powerful interests. Conversely, the employer may have taken on a professional, only to find his profession had limited his functions. An example of this could be found in the hospitals, when medical social workers were pressed by their association to limit their duties to social case work, though other hospital workers expected them to fulfil a much wider variety of functions.

The professional associations have so grown in prestige and status that most of them have gained national and sometimes international recognition, but there has been no attempt to create a superstructure, such as the T.U.C., to be a spokesman for all professions. Considering the enormous power and authority of many of the professional organisations, there may be no visible need for such an affiliate body, though one would have thought there were arguments in favour of creating a united voice that would be able to speak for the British professions, just as there is one to speak for the British trade unions. Instead, one of the tendencies in the professions has been towards proliferation through the growth both of new professions, with their appropriate associations, and of secondary associations in existing professions. So far they have managed to live together fairly harmoniously, and it is not uncommon for one person to be a member of more than one profession, or a member of several associations within one profession. The variety of objectives, and the importance of knowledge and research have made this possible. It may happen in time, that these vissiparous trends will have a weakening effect, and the need to unite may become stronger. This has long been felt among social workers, who after many false starts, were at last able to form a single organisation in 1968. The engineers, too, have had their troubles, though there is little sign that the civil, mechanical, electrical and other specialist groups of engineers are any nearer combining for even the most basic common needs. The trade union movement has been similarly rent by separatist movements, and it has taken a deliberate effort by the T.U.C. to promote amalgamation and federation. So far there is little sign of such a development in the professions, though in 1966, the Government set up a committee to examine all the issues.

XI

EVALUATION. WHAT CRITERIA?

CRITERIA FOR EVALUATING the social services are not the easiest to make. One reason is that there can be so many of them.[1] For instance, when social services are introduced into industry, a perfectly understandable criterion could be, do they contribute to the success of the firm and its ultimate profitability? Or, do they undermine the absolute power of the employer, and protect or promote the freedom of the worker?

The general tenor of this book has been concern with public policy, and it is in this context that some basis for evaluation is being sought. In the last resort, social policy depends on the prevailing philosophy of the time, on political and social values, and on the general view of the relationship of the individual and the State, and between the individual and other individuals or groups. Though there may be a general opinion, implicit or expressed at any one time, the views of individuals can range from one extreme to another.

Thus, at one end, it can be held that a person's sole responsibility is for himself and his family, and for no-one else; that it is his duty to provide his own material, emotional and other requirements, independently of others; that he should not seek help from others, least of all from the State, and that only by each one pursuing self-fulfilment in this way can a sturdy self-reliant society be built. Even the Utilitarian philosophers, at their most extreme, would not deny the value of combined action, through the armed forces, for protection from enemies abroad, or the need for a well-developed police force to preserve peace and harmony

[1] See K. M. Slack, *Social Administration and the Citizen*, especially Chapters 3 and 4.

216

within society. There would therefore be a limit to what the most individualistic citizen might expect to provide for himself.

Having once accepted the idea that community action has the edge on the purely individual approach in certain spheres, it is not difficult to evolve a modification of the extreme theory, and admit that while a man has these expectations for himself or his friends, they are too idealistic for everyone. For instance some, through no fault of their own, such as mental subnormality, or physical disablement, may not be able to live independently; and others, through lack of opportunity, cannot do as well as they might. The fact of life's casualties, and the need to give help, are admitted by the most extreme individualists. Further, it is generally recognised that personal charity can go only so far, and in the last analysis, the best way of helping is through some organised service, which can bring help of the right kind, at the right time, to the right people. The corollary to this view has usually been that those who have had the chance to be independent, and have not taken it, and those who by their own misdeeds have fallen by the wayside, have not been deserving of help, either individual or communal. Help should be the prerogative of the 'deserving'.

Uncomplicated though this view may seem, it has never been wholly accepted by everyone. Some have preferred to avoid seeking the causes of poverty, sickness, degradation, unemployment, sloth, misery or squalor, and have come forward in pity to help, when they saw the need. Sometimes they have justified their sentimentality on religious grounds, or have pointed to the very practical fact that though an adult may have deserved all that has befallen him, his children surely are innocent, and should be protected. Whatever the grounds may have been for such action, the criterion usually presupposes two worlds, the givers and the receivers—the one paternalistically offering help, the other, in his need, accepting it, with or without gratitude—but in the unspoken assumption that neither changes place with the other.

One variant of this attitude is the theory that if only some way could be found to cure the problems that give rise to poverty and the rest, there would be no need for social services. In general, such an idea is founded on a materialist conception of social ill, that is, that if everyone had enough money or opportunity, all would be able to guard against the risks of life; should this happen, social services could be eliminated, since each would then provide for himself; and the best of all possible worlds would have arrived. Others are not so confident, either of the power of money, or the ability of some individuals to use it in the most rational way, and though improving material conditions should reduce the need for the services, there is considerable doubt whether they can be superseded altogether, even in an egalitarian and affluent society.

One other variant of the materialist concept is the view that it is the inequalities of our economy which are responsible for many social ills, and that re-distribution of income would go a long way towards a solution. Since expenditure on the social services might be expected to help towards this, there is no need to seek further for a justification of them. Whether the social services are, in fact, paid for more heavily by those who use them less, than by those who use them more, is not known. There is a strong suspicion that the poor, the sick, those with large families, the aged, and other sections who need community help, are contributing relatively as much or more to the cost of the social services, through direct contributions and indirect taxation, than those who have not so far needed to use the services. If this is so, the argument that payment for the social services is re-distributing income on a more equal basis does not hold water, and that particular justification for their development falls to the ground.

At the other extreme from the individualist theory lies the doctrine founded on the belief that the dangers of sickness and misery exist for each one of us; that no-one knows when he may be at risk, that we are all members one of another, dependent on each other directly, and to an even greater degree, indirectly; that we cannot exist in two worlds, but must create a society in which those who are well will help those who are ill. Life is in fact, like a see-saw, sometimes up, and sometimes down. This view is supported by the realities of modern industrial society, in which it is so difficult for a person to provide, alone, against the rainy day, or to have to depend solely on what help can be given by family and friends. A telling example of the failure of man's best endeavours has been found in modern monetary policy, where a man might save to provide himself with the means of living in old age, only to find that inflation has whittled away his capital to a fraction of its previous worth.

In the light of such experience, and as an alternative to the individualist solution, the idea of building up a web of community services has developed. In this way the productive power of a whole society is brought in to help each member in his hour of need, whoever he may be. This theory does not preclude the need for individual responsibility and effort. It demands something even greater. Each now has a responsibility for the progress of the community as a whole. His personal obligation is to work as hard as possible, so that society may be successful, and that the social services may be as good as human beings can make them. In such a community it becomes a duty for each so to conduct himself, that he makes as few demands on the available resources as possible, and that he behaves in such a way that the resources he does use are not wasted. Thus, if he is sick, it is incumbent on him to accept all the help there is, and return to health at the earliest moment. If he is unemployed, he should be willing to train for other work, if this is the best method of utilising his labour for the common good. There are many to carp at such sophisticated theorising, declaring that universal care all too often means universal careless-less; the more 'you' give, the more 'they' take, until the whole of society becomes demoralised. What is really interesting is that in many industrialised societies the 'community' view is implicitly accepted, and a high degree of public service and responsibility is being shown by large numbers of people, from every rank of society.

The economic aspect has also to be considered, since it is apparent that no country is in a position to afford as much as it would wish for the protection of the weak, and that responsibility extends beyond national boundaries, so that the wealthy nations are expected to help the developing ones.

No country has the social services it would wish, and a system of priorities is therefore a regrettable necessity. A struggle on principle emerges. For instance, the most serious social ill in the world, apart from war, is poverty, particularly if children are being deprived of the means of physical, mental and emotional well-being to ensure their reasonable growth and development. But if material wealth were to be used to end poverty, it might well be at the expense of many cherished principles. For instance, in some countries, one cause of poverty is a high birth-rate. This could be eased by family limitation. Yet ignorance, apathy or the very cultural pattern itself might defy all methods, short of dictatorial ones; and the dilemma has to be faced, that one dearly held objective, that is the path to social well-being, might be attained only at the expense of another dearly held ideal, the democratic principle. In the United Kingdom itself, one means of reducing poverty might be the expenditure of large sums of money in family allowances. But if this expenditure were to be kept within the resources of the country, it might involve the necessity for families to prove their need for help through a Means Test. Faced with the alternative of an adequate service for those in greatest need, and the abolition of the principle of universality, the dilemma is all too clear.

In what way do these criteria apply to social services in industry? We saw in the introduction that services appear at two points, firstly at the point of change, and secondly, to meet the need of those who could not otherwise protect themselves. Examples of the first are the services to provide training (as through the Y.E.S., the Industrial Training Act, the Ministry of Labour, the G.T.C.), or a job, or to ease the passage of those dismissed from their work through redundancy (the Redundancy Payments Scheme), or income maintenance during the emergencies of life (National Insurance). Examples of the second are the Factories Acts, Wages Councils Acts, and to some extent the machinery for industrial arbitration.

What separates these services from those not industrially focused is the traditional view of where responsibility should lie, what a man and his family could be expected to provide, and what could not be expected. Thus apprenticeship and vocational training have not been a family matter—they have always been the responsibility of the employer. The trainee has paid for the acquisition of skill by giving his services freely, or for a small wage. Similarly, the safeguarding of wage rates, the protection against adverse factory conditions or long hours of work, the provision of legal machinery to settle disputes—none of these have been personal matters, resting with the man himself. They have been group problems, in which the employer has taken a paramount part. Nevertheless, the philosophical dichotomy between belief in individual freedom and responsibility, and belief in community responsibility and control, operates in people's attitude to the social services in industry too.

If these services interfere with an employer's right to prosecute his business to the best of his ability, or the worker's freedom to take his services where he wants, then to the first school of thought they are anathema. And there can be no doubt at all that that is what they actually do. An employer's freedom to train is limited by the industrial training boards; his freedom to employ women and young people beyond certain hours is inhibited by the Factory Acts. Freedom on wage payment can be interrupted by wages councils. Freedom to dismiss can be governed by the Contracts of Employment Act, and the Redundancy Payments Act. These, and many more examples, have shackled the rights once enjoyed by employers of labour. As for labour itself, it too can be fettered by some of the services. The young may not work as long as they wish; lorry drivers must take rest; miners must observe safety regulations. Established workers may not leave their jobs without working out their notice. Experience has suggested that some wages councils have actually prevented the voluntary negotiation of better wages for certain classes of workers.

Against this, the defendants of the supremacy of 'community responsibility' would argue that all social services in industry are directed at improving the position of the workers, and the better their position, the better, in the long run, the position of industry as a whole, including the employers. Without the Factory Acts, the arbitration machinery, the vocational guidance, the training schemes, the special facilities for the disabled or the young, and the elaborate paraphernalia of income maintenance during periods of non-earning, there is less chance of using the best talents in production, of maintaining justice and dignity in individuals of every class, and of avoiding the demoralisation that can come through poverty, ignorance, and ill-health.

The real problem of the social services in industry is paternalism. Most of the services have been fought for, and won, by well-meaning people, who were appalled at the abuses they saw, and wanted to create measures that would alleviate them. Rarely have the schemes been initiated by the potential recipients themselves. Rarely has there been any conception of self-help, or democratic control. Admittedly, in a democratic society it could be alleged that ultimate control rests in the people, but this is a long way from the works manager's desk, and a great deal further from the man on the bench. The notion that social services in industry might be re-drawn, so that workers' control could become a reality, has not been absent from thinking on the subject. But a really workable scheme (apart from friendly societies that proved unfeasible in the first N.H.I.) has yet to be conceived.

This raises a further problem—the method of financing the services. The variety of schemes in operation is amazing. They range from Treasury payment, as in the Ministry of Labour services, or local rate payments, as in the shops' legislation, to tripartite contributions, as in National Insurance, or the employer alone paying, as in certain aspects of health and welfare, and in training. It was fashionable in the 1960s to deride the tripartite contributory method, and to advocate a greater concentration of payment for social services in the hands of the employers. For instance, it was thought, short term sickness and unemployment benefit, and most superannuation might become an occupational responsibility, the State confining itself to long-term sick and unemployment cases only. Were this accepted, it was argued, opportunities for democratic control would be enhanced, as each firm could develop its own scheme, with a joint worker-management committee to operate it. There was much that was attractive about such a proposal, but it suffered from all the drawbacks of occupational schemes (p. 167), and since some people would inevitably escape inclusion, a national scheme to pick up the strays would need to be available. Moreover, it has yet to be shown that the arguments surrounding the tripartite system of contribution (p. 148) are invalid. Clearly, what was achieved in 1912, with the commencement of the process of de-pauperisation, would not be overturned if the tripartite system were ended; but it might be thought a backward step if a number of separate schemes, based on occupation, were to replace one founded on a whole society; and to those in favour of the philosophy of communal provision, it would seem disastrous.

In the long run, then, the only criteria for evaluating social services in industry are moral ones, and revolve round the conception of the 'human good'. Whether this may best be achieved by each furthering his own interests, or by each working for the common weal, is a matter for individual decision.

Appendix

RÉSUMÉ OF THE CHIEF FORMS OF INCOME MAINTENANCE

THE SOCIAL INSURANCES

General principles

(a) Normally they are available during interruption of earnings, but occasionally at recognised periods of increased family expenditure.

(b) All are dependant on insurance eligibility, special arrangements being made for certain classes such as: Students and Apprentices (N.I.30, N.I.31); Families entering Great Britain (FAM 32); Nurses and Midwives (N.I.46); War Pensioners (N.I.50); recent members of H.M. Forces (N.I.53); Seafarers and Airmen (N.I.24); Widows and recently divorced women (N.I.13, N.I.51, N.I.95, N.I.10, N.I.15A). Men over 65, and Women over 60 (N.I.15); Married Women (N.I.1).

(c) Benefit consists of cash payment for the claimant and his relevant dependants (unless otherwise stated).

(d) Benefit is available according to the rules in each case.

(e) There is a general principle (with a few exceptions) that no two benefits may be obtained by the same person at the same time.

(f) If cash is received during loss of earnings (except retirement), weekly contribution credits are recorded, so that other benefits are not jeopardised through non-payment.

(g) *Appeal Tribunal.* Though the determination of a claim is made by the insurance officers at the local office of the Ministry of Social Security (the Ministry of Labour, or Youth Employment Officer in the case of unemployment benefit), they may review decisions if further evidence is submitted. If the applicant is dissatisfied, he may ask to have his case reviewed by the local appeal tribunal, a completely independent body composed of a chairman (usually a lawyer), a representative of workers' organisations, from a panel set up for the purpose (often on the advice of the local trades' council), and one other member appointed from a panel representing employers. These are appointed for three years, but can be re-appointed. The final appeal is to the National Insurance

Commissioners (all legally qualified). The High Court is still bound to hear appeals from the Commissioners on points of law, but nothing else.

(h) *Hospital Care* (leaflet N.I.9). In certain cases of stay beyond eight weeks in hospital, benefits are reduced in respect of the patient himself (whether he is the claimant or the dependant). The reason is that certain expenses, like food, are borne by the hospital, and as these are freely provided, a reduction of benefit is made to help to balance the cost. But for very long-stay claimants, resettlement benefit may be paid (N.I.9).

(i) In general the National Insurance scheme for Great Britain operates in Northern Ireland and the Isle of Man, and there are reciprocal schemes with a few others countries (leaflet N.I.38).

(j) What the payments are, and the conditions of eligibility at any particular time, may be found by reference to the appropriate Ministry of Social Security leaflet which is freely obtainable.

Unemployment Benefit (leaflet N.I.12, N.I.20, N.I.155, N.I.157)
This is reserved for Class I contributors, and is available to them after contributing a year or more to the fund. The cash benefit is smaller for youngsters under 18, and for married women living with their husbands, if he is the main financial provider in the home. It is closely linked to the employment exchange (or Y.E.O.), and can only be paid after registering for a new job. There is a maximum number of benefit days, and anyone wishing to re-qualify can do so after going back to work, and paying a minimum number of new contributions. No benefit is paid unless the applicant is capable of work, and 'available for work', or if he is already in gainful employment, on paid holiday, or being paid by the employer in lieu of notice. There are unpaid 'waiting days' to reduce short-term or frivolous claims. A man is automatically disqualified for not more than six weeks if he leaves his job 'voluntarily without good cause', or loses it 'through misconduct', or fails to take a 'suitable' job, or to carry out 'reasonable recommendations, given in writing by an officer of the employment exchange to help him find suitable employment', or refuses training approved by the Ministry of Labour. Disqualification also operates in the case of those on strike.

The benefit itself may be of two kinds: flat rate, and earnings-related supplement. The latter is paid, for a limited period only, to those in the higher income bands, and is not available to married women who have opted out of the flat rate contributions.

Redundancy payments (see p. 140 and leaflets R.P.L.1 or N.I.140A). A résumé of this scheme, as it affects workers, is included here. For though it does not involve benefit payable through the Ministry of

Appendix

Social Security, and there are no contributions required from workers, it is certainly a method of income maintenance during interruption of earnings. It was introduced as a lump sum payment for Class I workers who were dismissed as redundant. No one can receive payment until the age of twenty, and then only after at least two years employment with the same firm. The benefit depends on a worker's age, and weekly pay, for each completed year's service. Under 40 it rises to one week's pay for each year in the firm, and thereafter, up to pensionable age, a week and a half's pay for each year, but with a ceiling of twenty years, based on pay up to a maximum amount.

Sickness Benefit (leaflets N.I.9, N.I.16, N.I.20, N.I.41, N.I.144, N.I.155, N.I.157). Cash benefit, during *bona fide* illness, is obtainable by all Class I and II contributors, but not normally by Class III. In most cases full benefit is available after a year's contributions, but only for a limited period. Sick benefit is paid for the whole of an extended illness after three years' contributions have actually been paid (credits are not counted). There is a waiting period. Benefit is composed, as in unemployment, of flat rate, plus earnings-related supplement. The latter is not paid for the first few days of incapacity, or for more than a limited period.

No one can claim sickness benefit without submitting a medical certificate, which may be 'closed' or 'open'. The former is short-term, and the latter longer (showing the doctor's estimate of the length of the illness).

No income tax is levied on sickness benefit, though a prolonged stay in hospital of either the claimant or his dependants may attract a reduced benefit (leaflet N.I.9). Claimants are not eligible if gainfully employed, unless under doctor's orders as part of the treatment and at a nominal wage.

One of the rules states that no beneficiary who is sick should behave in a way 'that may delay recovery', and to do so may lead to complete disqualification from receiving benefit.

Maternity Benefit (leaflet N.I.17A). There are two types, one or both of which may be claimed on the mother's or the husband's contributions.

Of these, the oldest is the *Maternity Grant*, paid when a baby is born, even if it is a still birth, provided the pregnancy has lasted most of its time. A multiple grant is paid if there are multiple live births. The purpose of the grant is to provide for the extra expense a birth imposes on a home, and can be paid a few weeks before, or after, the actual arrival. There are contribution conditions, which are not onerous. The grant is not subject to income tax, and is available to all classes of subscribers.

Appendix

The *Maternity Allowance* is available on the mother's contributions alone, and is limited to Class I or II subscribers (some Class III contributions may help to make up the number of contributions). To obtain the full allowance, the mother should have been a contributor for a period longer than gestation, though she may get a reduced allowance by starting to contribute after pregnancy has begun. The object is to release an expectant mother from her job well before the baby is born, and to maintain her for several weeks afterwards. She can, in certain circumstances, claim dependants' allowances, including payments for other children, and for a dependant adult, such as a person to look after the children. Where a woman is eligible for the allowance, she is automatically eligible for the grant too. Payments are available to both married and unmarried.

N.I. Retirement Pension (leaflets N.I.15, N.I.15A). Provided a contributor complies with the rules, retirement pension is available to Classes I, II, and III. But the rules are fairly stringent, as they demand not only a minimum number of paid-up contributions (not credits), but also a yearly average (including credits). If these conditions are met, a man at 70 (or woman at 65) may receive the pension without further ado, and can continue working if he wishes. Between 65 and 70 (60 and 65) the earnings rule operates, and a contributor, in effect, must retire from full-time employment before being able to claim the full pension. Though retirement is crucial for those between 65 and 70 (60 to 65), to obtain the pension, contributors may cancel the retirement for a time, and continue with, or return to, their jobs. Even if retirement has taken place, the earnings rule is reasonably generous, and a certain level can be earned without affecting the pension.

The pension may be composed of one or more of four parts:

(a) The *flat rate* resulting from basic contributions.

(b) The *extra pension* if a person remains in, or returns to, full-time employment after 65 (60), and pays basic contributions. This results in a small weekly increase of the pension, for every three months worked up to age 70 (65), and was introduced as a means of encouraging older workers to continue at their jobs.

(c) The *graduated pension*, paid on the basis of actual contributions, each 'unit' of which represents a small weekly addition to the pension.

(d) *Additions for dependants*, including children and spouse. Where the wife is non-earning, is living with her husband, and is not herself insured, 'extra pension' may also be available for her, if the husband has earned it, and if she is over pensionable age.

Retirement pension is liable to income tax.

Appendix

Death Grant (leaflet N.I.49). A grant payable in respect of all classes of contributors; there are stringent rules about eligibility. Contributors must have paid after 5 July, 1948, and though a reduced amount is available for those who have not paid sufficient, the full amount requires a minimum number of payments. A husband or wife may claim in respect of the spouse's contributions, and in certain cases, divorced couples may use each other's eligibility. As for the children, death grant may be paid in respect of one's own. If someone else's child who has become part of one's family should die, a grant may be available for him out of one's own contributions. The amount of the grant varies according to whether the person to be buried is a child, or an adult. In no case is the death grant subject to estate duty.

Widows (leaflets N.I.13, N.I.15A, N.I.51, N.I.155). One of the changes initiated by Beveridge was the division of widows into several groups. But whatever the category, the widow can claim benefit in respect of her husband's contributions alone, and this applies whether he was Class I, II or III. He must have had both a minimum number of paid (not credit) contributions, and an average annual contribution record (including credits). Nor can she claim in respect of any man other than whoever was her lawful husband at the time of his death. So long as she receives widow's benefit, no 'earnings rule' operates, and she may therefore take a full-time job without forfeiting any of her pay. On the other hand it is subject to income tax.

There are five kinds of benefit for which a widow may seek eligibility:

Widow's Allowance paid at a higher rate to every widow for the first few months after her husband's death, to give her time to adjust to the altered circumstances. In addition, she may receive a 'Supplementary Allowance', based on her late husband's eligibility for earnings-related benefit, provided he had not retired on pension. Dependants' benefits are additional to these.

Widowed Mother's Allowance is specifically intended for the mother of young children, and the allowance, plus dependants' benefits, is supposed to provide a total sum sufficient to live on without the mother having to go out to work. In the early years of the scheme, and to the end of the 1960s, there were no additions by way of earnings-related benefit, except if she were herself a contributor and became sick or unemployed; and in general, the level of the payments was low.

Widow's pension is for the older widow below retirement age, or whose children have grown up. She must be over 50, and have been married for three years at least.

Appendix

Widow's Basic Pension is a small benefit paid to a widow not eligible under any of the above categories, but who had been married before 1948 to a man insured under the Contributory Pensions' Acts. If working, and under sixty, she can claim unemployment and sickness benefit, though the basic pension must be deducted in such a case. At sixty she can retire and take the retirement pension, but retain the title to the widow's basic pension until 65, in case she decides to return to work.

Retirement Pension. A widow having a widow's pension may keep it until she is 65, when it will be replaced by a retirement pension. She may also benefit from her husband's graduated contributions. She is thus in a more advantageous position than an unmarried woman whose income has been below the graduated contribution level, but who has contributed all her working life to her basic retirement pension, since, in her case, the earnings rule operates between 60 and 65.

The Widow who Works. As there are no earnings rules in widows' benefits, she can take a full-time job, and keep her full benefit. She has to face the problem like all gainfully employed married women, of whether or not to opt out of the flat-rate contributory scheme. Like them, she must, in any case, pay industrial injuries and graduated contributions, if she is within the income band. Women on Widow's Basic Pension are not allowed to opt out of the flat rate scheme, and those on Widow's Allowance are automatically excused during the period of the allowance. Whatever the widow herself does, her employer is obliged to pay his share to the scheme.

Should she be eligible for such benefit as unemployment and sickness pay, she would normally be excluded from taking both widows' and another benefit, but she would receive earnings-related benefit if she had contributed. At retirement age, she would have several choices before her: to claim retirement pension, to keep the widow's pension and go on working, or to give up the widow's pension, continue working, pay full flat-rate contributions, and ultimately draw the extra flat-rate pension.

Some widows are not eligible for a widowed mother's allowance or a widow's pension, and if they take a job, they are obliged to pay flat-rate contributions, like single women. On the other hand, they are allowed some concessions, and in certain cases can claim retirement pension on the husband's contribution record. Moreover, if they are sick, or unable to get a job at the husband's death, they will normally be eligible for sickness or unemployment benefit once the widow's allowance ends, without having the contribution record a single woman would need.

Appendix

Guardian's Allowance (leaflet N.I.14). This is, in some ways, like a family allowance for an orphan, though what constitutes an 'orphan' or his 'family' is complex. It is only payable if one or both of his parents have been *bona-fide* contributors to the N.I. He must be under the age limit, and the claimant must have included him as part of the family. The amount of the benefit is substantially higher than a family allowance, and no child dependant's claim can be made in respect of him on any of the N.I. benefits.

Married Women in Employment (leaflet N.I.1). A married woman who takes a job is obliged to pay contributions under the industrial injuries scheme, and, provided she is within the income band, to the earnings-related part of the N.I. But she is given the choice whether to pay the flat-rate insurance, or to rely on her husband's contributions for benefit. If her husband dies while she is working, she is given special concessions, but if she loses her husband through divorce, she is normally obliged to revert to the position of a single woman, and pay her contributions. In any case her employer (if she is in Class I) must pay contributions. Should she be self-employed, or employed by her husband, she may pay Class II contributions, or none at all.

If she decides to pay the full contributions in any class, she is eligible for all the benefits of that class, except the widow's benefit; but sickness and unemployment pay would be at a lower rate than if she were a single woman. The reason for this disparity is that her husband would have met the standing charges of the home, and it is assumed there is no need for her benefit to include them. It is a curious anomaly, especially as her benefit may be raised to the standard rate without further contributions, if she can prove her husband is incapable of earning his living. At her own retirement she is eligible for the standard rate. As for graduated payments, she can claim these, if she has contributed, and 'extra' pension, if she works beyond the minimum age of retirement.

Where a married woman opts out of paying the basic contributions, she has to depend for benefit, for the most part, on her husband's eligibility. When she retires, though she will not receive a flat-rate pension in her own right, she can claim graduated pension if she has contributed. Her position on graduated contributions elsewhere is not so favourable. Though she is obliged to contribute, she cannot receive earnings-related benefit in unemployment or sickness, since it is a condition that this must accompany flat-rate payment.

Family Allowances (leaflet FAM 1). Strictly, these should not be included in a chapter on income maintenance, since they are not intended as part of a man's wage, nor does he contribute directly to their payment, and the scheme is in no way industrially orientated. Nevertheless, a summary of the chief characteristics would seem appropriate, especially as the scheme is operated through the Ministry of Social Security. The plan came about as a result of the Family Allowances Act 1945, and was a payment by the Exchequer to the family, without a Means or other test, except nationality and domicile until 1968. It was paid in respect of the second child in the family, below the age limit (usually school leaving age, or 18 years if the child were in full-time education), and to all subsequent children. Special arrangements have been made for children not living at home, or where the parents are not living together. Legally, the allowance belongs to the mother, though in certain cases the right may be transferred to the father. Should there be additional children in the family, like step children, illegitimate or adopted ones, or simply children who have become part of the family, it is usual to regard them, for this purpose, as eligible. As with so many of the social security payments, the encashment is through the Post Office. Family allowances were from the beginning subject to income tax.

The Industrial Injuries Scheme (leaflets N.I.2, N.I.4, N.I.5, N.I.6, N.I.7, N.I.8, N.I.9, N.I.10, N.I.155, N.I.157). Right to benefit is in the main limited to Class I contributors, and is not dependent on the number of contributions paid. All paid workers in Class I are obliged to contribute to industrial injury insurance, even married women, or widows, who opt out of the general scheme. Since the rate of basic benefit is higher than that for sickness, and the alternatives more varied, it is advantageous, when incapacitated through accident or disease, to qualify for this benefit rather than sickness insurance. None of the benefits under the Act are subject to income tax. The types of claims available are:

Injury Benefit (leaflet N.I.5). This implies that a person is unable to work through an accident arising out of, and in the course of, his employment. Payment is made after a few waiting days, but is refunded if incapacity lasts more than a minimum period. This benefit is limited in duration to the time when the person is totally incapacitated, or for six months, whichever is the shorter, and it carries dependants' allowances as well. As with sickness benefit, it is available on production of a medical certificate, and carries the responsibility to accept suitable medical treatment, and to behave in no way likely to prejudice recovery. Earnings-related supplement is also paid, but only if the claimant would otherwise have been entitled to basic sickness benefit (thus excluding married women who opt out), and has contributed to the earnings-related scheme.

Appendix

Disablement Benefit (leaflet N.I.6). This can be claimed at the time of the accident, if no injury benefit has been paid, or during the period of absence from work when injury benefit has ceased, or from the onset of the disease in such occupational hazards as pneumoconiosis. It is in no way dependent on a man's capacity to earn a living, but is paid according to the degree of disablement suffered. Loss of two hands, for instance, would attract 100 per cent disablement pension, and lesser injury, a fraction of this. The period of the assessment may be provisional, when it would be reviewed; or final, when it appears the condition is not likely to change much. The final assessment may be for life, or for a limited period after which no further appreciable disability is to be expected. There is always the possibility of reviewing even a final assessment, if the situation changes. Medical appeal tribunals have been constituted to hear cases of dissatisfaction about medical assessments, and are an addition to the local appeal tribunals which hear objections about the cash determination, decided by the insurance officers.

Should the medical assessment of disablement be less than 20 per cent, a *gratuity* (or lump sum) is normally paid instead of a weekly benefit. Otherwise the *pension* is paid weekly according to the scale, and is quite independent of a man's earnings. Should he claim social security supplement (p. 162) and be subjected to a means test his disability pension is wholly or partly ignored. On the other hand, a disablement pension does not, of itself, entitle a person to dependants' benefit, since it is paid in compensation for proved loss of capacity, and not because of interruption of earnings. But should a pensioner become eligible for any other N.I. benefit, like sickness, unemployment, or retirement, he will receive it in the ordinary way. This is one example of two types of benefit being paid at the same time to the same person. Receipt of a disability pension, with any of its additions, does not affect a person's liability to pay contributions when he is earning. Earnings-related benefit is not extended to this part of the scheme.

Additional Benefit. Anyone who is eligible for a disablement allowance, pension, or gratuity can apply for one or more of the additional benefits:

(a) *Special Hardship Allowance* (leaflet N.I.8) is the most widely used, and is intended for those whose assessment of incapacity does not reach 100 per cent, but whose earnings are seriously affected by the disablement. In this case, an addition may be given, though not to bring the disablement allowance to more than 100 per cent. As soon as it can be shown that earnings are not being seriously affected, the allowance is stopped, and in practice the majority continue for little more than a year.

233

(b) *Unemployability Supplement* (leaflet N.I.7) is paid if a person on disablement pension is incapable of work, because of his injury or disease, and is likely to remain so permanently. Dependants' benefits are also payable in these circumstances. The claimant is allowed to earn small weekly sums, but no one on this supplement can receive special hardship allowance (which implies full-time work), or the other benefits associated with interrupted earnings, such as sickness, unemployment or retirement benefits. On the other hand he is not prevented from undertaking training through a Ministry of Labour scheme, though his training allowance would be reduced by the amount of the unemployability supplement. Contributions to N.I. are normally credited during the payment of the supplement.

(c) *Constant Attendance Allowance* (leaflet N.I.7) is available if the person is so handicapped by his injury that he needs someone to help him attend to his personal needs—for instance, if he is bedridden. It is not a way of financing a housekeeper, though a wife or relative would be eligible, if personal help, every day, and for a prolonged period, was required. It can be paid only where the assessment of disablement is the equivalent of 100 per cent; may be varied from time to time according to the amount of the attendance needed; and is usually assessed by the medical board responsible for deciding the degree of disablement. It may be paid even if a person is gainfully employed, and contributing in the ordinary way (as for instance if he is blind), and it continues to be paid even if he becomes eligible for other N.I. benefits.

(d) *Exceptionally Severe Disablement Allowance* (leaflet N.I.7) may be paid to those who are completely, or nearly, helpless, and where considerable attendance is required night and day. It can be paid to the person in hospital, or at home, who is entitled to the constant attendance allowance at the maximum rate. Thus a person may be eligible at the same time for full disablement pension, unemployability supplement, constant attendance allowance, and severe disablement allowance. If he were to forego unemployability supplement from the above list (and with it, dependants' benefit) he might become gainfully employed, as a Class I contributor, and receive, when eligible, sickness, unemployment or retirement pension as well, since these particular allowances can be drawn at the same time as other N.I. or industrial injuries benefits.

(e) *Hospital Treatment Allowance* (leaflet N.I.4). Where a disablement assessment has been made at less than 100 per cent, and the handicapped person has to become an in-patient, in hospital, through the industrial injury, he can claim this allowance, which will bring him up to the equivalent of a weekly disablement pension at 100 per cent, but no more. He will also be able to claim for his dependants.

Widow's and other dependants' benefit (leaflets N.I.10, N.I.13, N.I.155). The one exception to non-liability for income tax, under the industrial injuries scheme, is the pension for widows and other dependants. Those who may claim the benefit include the widow of the man killed in an industrial accident, or who died from a prescribed disease; and the widower who has been relying for more than half his maintenance on his contributing wife; parents similarly dependent on the son or daughter (Class I only); or more distant relatives. Children of the dead man or woman are also eligible. So long as the industrial death has come within the meaning of the Act, and the dead person has been a Class I contributor, no further conditions of eligibility are necessary. This benefit is subject to tax.

In effect, industrial widows are separated into categories, receiving widows' allowances, widowed mothers' allowances, widows' pension or retirement pensions like widows under the ordinary N.I. scheme (p. 229), and the widows' supplementary allowance, based on the late husband's earnings will be added to the widow's allowances. Exceptions to the above are: that the rules under the Industrial Injuries Act relating to the widowed mother's allowance are more generous; that a widowed mother can claim the widow's pension at forty; that no stipulation about the length of marriage affects the issue; that she can claim the full pension at any age, if she is permanently unable to support herself at her husband's death. Further, the normal rate is higher for the industrial widow, and is never extinguished altogether, unless she remarries.

As for children, the allowance is usually higher than in ordinary N.I. cases, except where the widowed mother remarries. Other relatives may claim death benefit on the basis of their dependence on the deceased. If it was maximum dependence, a weekly pension (much lower than for the widow) may be paid, otherwise the benefit may take the form of a gratuity.

Selected Bibliography

Abel-Smith, B. *The Reform of Social Security*, Fabian Research Series, 161, 1953
—— and Townsend, P. *The Poor and the Poorest*, Social Administration Occasional Papers, 17, 1965
Acton Society Trust. *The Miners' Pension*, Nationalised Industry Series, 5, 1951
—— *The Future of the Union*, 1951
Amulree, B. W. *Industrial Arbitration in Great Britain*, Oxford University Press, 1929
Bayliss, F. J. *British Wages Councils*, Blackwell, 1962
Beer, S. H. *Modern British Politics*, Faber, 1965
Bruce, M. *The Coming of the Welfare State*, Batsford, 1961
Carr-Saunders, A. M. and Wilson, P. A. *The Professions*, Oxford University Press, 1933
Clark, F. le G. *New Jobs for Old Workers*, Nuffield Foundation, 1955
—— *Bus Workers in their Later Lives*, Nuffield Foundation, 1957
—— and Dunne, A. C. *Ageing in Industry*, Nuffield Foundation, 1955
Clegg, H. A., Killick, A. J. and Adams, R. *Trade Union Officers*, Blackwell, 1961
Cole, D. and Utting, J. *The Economic Circumstances of Old People*, Social Administration Occasional Papers, 4, 1962
Cole, G. D. H. *Payment of Wages*, Allen and Unwin, 1928
Corina, J. *The Labour Market*, Institute of Personnel Management, 1966
Cormack, U. *The Welfare State*, Family Welfare Association, 1953
Ferguson, T., Macphail, A. N. and McVean, Margaret I. *Employment Problems of Disabled Youth in Glasgow*, Medical Research Council Memorandum, 28, 1952
Finer, S. E. *Anonymous Empire*, Pall Mall Press, 1966
Flanders, A. *Industrial Relations. What is Wrong with the System?* Faber, 1965

Flanders, A. *Trade Unions*, Hutchinson, 1952
—— and Clegg, H. A. *The System of Industrial Relations in Great Britain*, Blackwell, 1964
Florence, P. Sargent. *Industry and the State*, Hutchinson, 1957
Fox, A. *The Milton Plan*, Institute of Personnel Management, 1965
—— 'The Closed Shop', *New Society*, 16 December, 1965
Genders, J. E. and Urwin, N. R. *Wages and Salaries*, Institute of Personnel Management, 1962
Gilbert, B. B. *The Evolution of National Insurance in Great Britain*, Michael Joseph, 1967
Gilling-Smith, G. D. *The Complete Guide to Pensions and Superannuation*, Pelican (Special), 1967
Glennerster, H. *National Assistance. Service or Charity?* Young Fabian Pamphlet, 1962
Goldstein. *Government of British Trade Unions. A Study of Apathy and the Democratic Process in the T.G.W.U.*
Grove, T. W. *Government and Industry*, Longmans, 1962
Grunfeld, C. 'Political Independence in British Trade Unions', *British Journal of Industrial Relations*, Vol. I, No. 1
Guillebaud, C. W. *The Wages Council System in Great Britain*, Nisbett, 1958
Hall, M. P. *The Social Services of Modern England*, 6th Ed., Routledge and Kegan Paul, 1963
Heginbotham, H. *Youth Employment Service*, Methuen, 1951
Hilton, G. W. *The Truck System*, Heffer, 1960
Hunter, D. *Health in Industry*, Pelican, 1959
Hutchins, E. L. and Harrison, A. *History of Factory Legislation*, King, 1926
Hutchinson, J. S. and Wansborough, N. *Redundancy, a Survey of Problems and Practices*, Acton Society Trust, 1958
Ince, G. *The Ministry of Labour and National Service*, Allen and Unwin, 1960
Jacques, E. *Changing Culture in a Factory*, Tavistock, 1951
Jephcott, P., Seear, N. and Smith, J. H. *Married Women Working*, Allen and Unwin, 1962
Jewkes, J. and Winterbottom, A. *Juvenile Unemployment*, London, 1933
Klein, V. *Women Workers' Working Hours and Services*, Organisation for Economic Co-operation and Development, 1965
L.C.C. *From School to Work. Work of Youth Employment Service in London*, 1958–61, 1962
Lerner, S. W. *Breakaway Unions and the Small Trade Union*, Allen and Unwin, 1961
Lewis, R. and Maude, A. *Professional People*, Phoenix House, 1953

Selected Bibliography

Lockwood, D. *Blackcoated Worker*, Allen and Unwin, 1958

Lupton, T. *On the Shop Floor. Two Studies of Workshop Organisation and Output*, Pergamon, 1963

Lynes, T. *National Assistance and National Prosperity*, Social Administration Occasional Papers, 5, 1963

Macdonald, D. F. *The State and the Trade Unions*, Macmillan, 1960

Macleod, I. and Powell, J. E. *The Social Services, Needs and Means*, Conservative Political Centre, 1951

Marsh, A. *Industrial Relations in the Engineering Industry*, Pergamon, 1965

Marsh, A. I. *Managers and Shop Stewards*, Institute of Personnel Management, 1963

Marsh, D. C. *The Future of the Welfare State*, Penguin, 1964

Marshall, T. H. *Sociology at the Crossroads*, Heinemann, 1963

National O.P.W. Council. *Employment and Workshops for the Elderly*, National Council of Social Service, 604, 1962

Nicholson, J. H. *Help for the Handicapped*, National Council of Social Service, 1958

Nuffield Provincial Hospitals Trust. *Casualty Services and their Setting*, Oxford University Press, 1960

Polter, A. *Organised Groups*

Pribicevic, B. *Shop Steward Movement*, 1959

Rackham, C. *Factory Law*, Nelson, 1944

Raynes, H. E. *Social Security in Britain*, Pitman, 1960

Reader, W. J. *Professional Men*, Weidenfeld and Nicholson, 1966

Reid, G. L. and Robertson, D. J. *Fringe Benefits, Labour Costs and Social Security*, Allen and Unwin, 1965

Rhodes, G. *Public Sector Pensions*, Allen and Unwin, 1965

Richardson, J. H. *Economic and Financial Aspects of Social Security*, Allen and Unwin, 1960

—— *An Introduction to the Study of Industrial Relations in Great Britain*, Allen and Unwin, 1954

Roberts, B. C. *Industrial Relations, Contemporary Problems and Perspectives*, Methuen, 1962

Robson, W. A. *Social Security*, Allen and Unwin, 3rd Ed., 1948

Ross, N. *Workshop Bargaining. A New Approach*, Fabian Tract, 1966

Saxena, S. K. *Nationalisation and Industrial Conflict*, Martius Nijhoff, 1955

Seldon, A. *Pensions in a Free Society*, Institute of Economic Affairs

Sheldon, J. H. *The Social Medicine of Old Age*, Oxford University Press, 1948

Shenfield, B. E. *Social Policies for Old Age*, Routledge and Kegan Paul, 1957

Sprott, W. J. H. *Human Groups*, Penguin, 1958

—— *Sociology at the Seven Dials*, Athlone Press, 1962

Stewart, J. D. *British Pressure Groups*, Clarendon, 1958

Thomas, E. and Ferguson, T. *The Handicapped School Leaver*, Tavistock, 1961

Tillyard, F. *Worker and the State*, Routledge and Kegan Paul, 3rd Ed., 1948

Titmuss, R. M. *Essays on the Welfare State*, Allen and Unwin, 1963

—— *Choice and the Welfare State*, Fabian Tract, 1967

—— *Income Distribution and Social Change*, Allen and Unwin, 1962

Tracey, H. *Trade Unionism, its Origins, Growth and Role in Modern Society*, Labour Educational Series, 1952

Turner, H. A. *Trade Union Growth, Structure and Policy*, Allen and Unwin, 1962

Vernon, H. M. *Hours of Work and their Influence on Health*, British Association for Labour Relations, 1943

Webb, B. *The Case for the Factory Acts*, Grant Richards, 1901

Wedderburn, D. *White Collar Redundancy. A Case Study*, Cambridge University Press, 1964

Wedderburn, K. W. *Trade Union Structure and Closer Unity*, Trades Union Congress

—— *The Worker and the Law*, Pelican, 1965

Williams, G. *Recruitment to Skilled Trades*, Routledge and Kegan Paul, 1957

Wootton, G. *Workers Unions and the State*, Routledge and Kegan Paul, 1966

Young, A. F. *Industrial Injuries Insurance*, Routledge and Kegan Paul, 1964

GOVERNMENT PUBLICATIONS
ANNUAL REPORTS. PERIODICALS. ETC.

1909 Cmd. 4499, xxxvii. *Poor Laws and Relief of Distress.* Royal Commission Report

1908 Cmd. 4442, lix. *Truck Acts.* Departmental Committee (Shaw, Ch.). Vol. I. Report

1917–18 Cmd. 8606, xviii. *Relations between Employers and Employed.* Reconstruction Committee (Whitley, Ch.). Interim Report. Joint Standing Industrial Councils

1942–3 Cmd. 6404, vi. *Social Insurance and Allied Services.* Inter-departmental Committee (Beveridge, Ch.). Report

1942–3 Cmd. 6414 vi. *Rehabilitation, and Resettlement of Disabled Persons.* Inter-departmental Committee (Tomlinson, Ch.). Report

1945 Non-Parliamentary, Ministry of Labour. *Juvenile Employment Service*. Committee. (Ince, Ch.). Report

1946, 1949, 1958 Non-Parliamentary, Ministry of Labour. *Rehabilitation and Resettlement of Disabled Persons*. Standing Committee Reports

1952 Non-Parliamentary, Ministry of Labour. *The Worker in Industry*

1952–3 Cmd. 8963, xi. *Employment of Older Men and Women*. National Advisory Committee (Watkinson, Ch.). 1st Report

1955–6 Cmd. 9628, xvii. *Employment of Older Men and Women*. National Advisory Committee (Watkinson, Ch.). 2nd Report

1954–5 Cmd. 9333, vi. *Economic and Financial Problems of the Provision for Old Age*. Committee (Phillips, Ch.). Report

1955–6 Cmd. 9791, xxii. Ministry of Labour and National Service. Report for the Year 1955, Chapter 9: Resettlement of Disabled Persons

1955–6 Cmd. 9883, xiv. *Rehabilitation, Training, and Resettlement of Disabled Persons*. Committee (Piercy, Ch.). Report

1956 Non-Parliamentary, Ministry of Labour. *Industrial Accident Prevention*. National Joint Advisory Council, Industrial Safety Sub-Committee. Report

1958 Non-Parliamentary, Ministry of Labour. *Training for Skill*. National Joint Advisory Council Sub-Committee (Carr, Ch.). Report

1960 Non-Parliamentary, D.S.I.R. *The Older Worker and His Job*, by H. M. Clay. Problems of Progress in Industry, No. 7

1961 Non-Parliamentary, Ministry of Labour. *Industrial Relations Handbook*. Rev. Ed.

1962 Non-Parliamentary, Ministry of Labour. *Services for the Disabled*. 2nd Ed.

1962 Non-Parliamentary, Ministry of Labour. *Short Guide to the Factories Act, 1961*

1962–3 Cmd. 1892, xxxi. *Industrial Training*. Government Proposals

1962 Non-Parliamentary, Ministry of Education. *Forward from School. The Link between School and Further Education*

1963 Non-Parliamentary, Ministry of Education. *Half our Future*. Central Advisory Council for Education (Newsom, Ch.). Report

Eliz. 2, 1963, c.41. *Offices, Shops and Railways Premises Act*

Eliz. 2, 1964, c.16. *Industrial Training Act*

1964 Non-Parliamentary, Ministry of Labour. *Duties of Local Authorities under the Factories Acts*. 2nd Ed.

1964 Non-Parliamentary, Department of Education and Science. *Day Release*. Committee (Henniker-Heaton, Ch.). Report

1964 Non-Parliamentary, Ministry of Labour. *Occupational Sick Pay Schemes*. National Joint Advisory Council Sub-Committee Report

1964 Non-Parliamentary, Ministry of Pensions and National Insurance.

*Incidence of Incapacity for Work. Scope and Characteristics of Employers'
Sick Pay Schemes.* Enquiry Report. Part I
1964 Ministry of Labour. Wages Council Act 1959. Committee of
Inquiry Report
1964–5 Cmd. 2548. Proposed Action by H.M. Government on a Convention Adopted at the 47th Session of the I.L.O.
1965 Non-Parliamentary, Ministry of Labour. *Future Development of the
Youth Employment Service.* National Youth Employment Council
Working Party (Albemarle, Ch.). Report
1965 Non-Parliamentary, Home Office. *Retail Trading Hours.* Suggested
Provisions for Amending the Shops Act, 1950
1965–6 Cmd. 2847. *Assessment of Disablement.* Committee (McCorquodale,
Ch.). Report
1966 Non-Parliamentary. *Trade Unions and Employers Associations.* Royal
Commission. Research Paper I. *The Role of Shop Stewards in British
Industrial Relations* by W. E. J. McCarthy
1966 Non-Parliamentary, Ministry of Labour. *Appointed Factory Doctor
Service.* Industrial Health Advisory Service. Sub-Committee. Report
1966 Non-Parliamentary, Ministry of Labour. *Preservation of Pension
Rights.* National Joint Advisory Council Committee. Report
1966 Non-Parliamentary, Treasury. *Occupational Pension Schemes.* Survey
by the Government Actuary
1965 Non-Parliamentary, Central Office of Information. Reference
Pamphlet 31. *Labour Relations and Working Conditions in Britain.* 4th Ed.
1966 Non-Parliamentary, Central Office of Information. Reference
Pamphlet 3. *Social Services in Britain.* 7th Ed.
1967 Non-Parliamentary. *Trade Unions and Employers' Associations.* Royal
Commission. Research Paper 6. *Trade Union Growth and Recognition,* by
G. S. Bain
Ministry of Labour. *First Aid in Factories.* Safety, Health and Welfare
Booklets
—— *Health at Work.* Safety, Health and Welfare Booklets
—— *Organisation of Industrial Health Services.* Safety, Health and Welfare
Booklets
—— *Fire Fighting in Factories.* Safety, Health and Welfare Booklets
—— *Industrial Relations Handbook.* Safety, Health, and Welfare Booklets

Annual Reports
Chief Inspector of Factories
Chief Inspector of Factories on Industrial Health
Ministry of Pensions and National Insurance
Ministry of Social Security
National Assistance Board
National Youth Employment Council

NON–GOVERNMENT PUBLICATIONS
ANNUAL REPORTS PERIODICALS ETC.

British Council for Rehabilitation. Working Party 1960.
(Thomas. Ch.)
British Journal of Industrial Relations
The Economist
Industrial Welfare and Personnel Management Journal
Lloyds' Bank Review
New Society
New Statesman
Personnel Management Journal
Progress—Unilever Quarterly
The Times
Confederation of British Industry. Annual Reports
Trades Union Congress. Annual Reports

LEAFLETS OBTAINABLE AT
THE MINISTRY OF SOCIAL SECURITY

R.1	Contracting out
N.I.1	Married Women
N.I.2	Prescribed Industrial Diseases
N.I.3	Pneumoconiosis and Byssinosis
N.I.4	Hospital Treatment Allowance
N.I.5	Injury Benefit for Accidents at Work
N.I.6	Disablement Benefit for Accidents at work
N.I.7	Unemployability Supplement, Constant Attendance Allowance, Exceptionally Severe Disablement Allowance
N.I.8	Special Hardship Allowance
N.I.9	Hospital Patients
N.I.10	Industrial Death Benefit for Widows and Dependants
N.I.12	Unemployment Benefit
N.I.13	Widow's Benefit under N.I.
N.I.14	Guardian's Allowance
N.I.15	Retirement Pensions
N.I.15A	Retirement Pensions for Widows
N.I.16	Sickness Benefit
N.I.17A	Maternity Benefits
N.I.20	Employers' Guide to Flat Rate N.I. Contributions
N.I.24	Seafarers and Airmen
N.I.27	Persons with Small Incomes

N.I.29   N.I. for Young People
N.I.30   Students
N.I.31   Apprentices
N.I.38   N.I. for People Abroad
N.I.39   Contract of Service
N.I.41   Self-employed Persons
N.I.42   Non-employed Persons
N.I.46   Nurses and Midwives
N.I.48   Late Paid, or Unpaid Contributions (Effect on Benefit)
N.I.49   Death Grant, and other N.I. Matters arising on Death
N.I.50   War Pensioners in N.I.
N.I.51   N.I. Guide for Widows
N.I.53   Information for Men and Women Leaving H.M. Forces
N.I.92   Cancelling Retirement
N.I.93   Child's Special Allowance
N.I.95   Women whose Marriage is ended by Divorce or Annulment
N.I.114   Employers' Guide. Contracted out Payments
N.I.116   Employers' Guide to Graduated N.I. Contributions
N.I.125   Training for Further Employment
N.I.132   Guidance to Employers of Persons Abroad
N.I.138   Higher N.I. Benefits
N.I.140A   Redundancy Pay Scheme. Employers' Contributions
N.I.144   Medical Certificates
N.I.155   Guide to Earnings-related Short-term Benefits
N.I.157   New Graduated Contribution Rates
N.I.158   The Ministry of Social Security
S.1   Supplementary Allowances for People under Pension Age
S.L.3   Supplementary Allowances for Handicapped People
S.L.5   Supplementary Allowances for Women with Dependant Children
S.L.8   Supplementary Allowances for Unemployed Persons
S.L.9   New Supplementary Benefits Scheme
FAM 1   Guide to Family Allowances
FAM 32(A)   Families Leaving Britain or Entering Britain
FAM 33   Children Absent from their Families
FAM 34   Children over the Age of 15
S.P.1   Supplementary Pensions for People over Pension Age
P.N.1   Disablement and Death Benefits for Uncompensated Cases
W.S.1   Supplements to Workmen's Compensation

S.A. series on reciprocal agreements with other countries are obtainable from the Overseas Group of the Ministry of Social Security, Newcastle upon Tyne.

LEAFLETS OBTAINABLE
AT THE MINISTRY OF LABOUR (E. & P.)

I.R.L.1	This is a True Story. Joint Consultation
I.R.L.3	Selecting the Man for the Job
N.L.06	Nursing
N.L.07	Local Authority Nursing Services
P.L.322	Persons Undergoing Training in Workshops for the Blind. Allowances
P.L.354	Youth Employment Service
P.L.362	Employment in certain European countries
P.L.366	Y.E.S. Training Allowance Scheme for Youths when Training away from Home
P.L.379	Six points about Jobs for Handicapped Young Persons
P.L.380	First Year Apprenticeship Training in G.T.C.
P.L.392	Supervisory Training Pays. T.W.I.
P.L.393	Weekly Rates of Industrial Rehabilitation Allowance
P.L.394	Weekly Rates of Training Allowance. All Workers
P.L.400	At your Service. Main Services offered by Ministry of Labour
P.L.401	Professional and Executive Register
P.L.403	Weekly Rates of Training Allowances in Sheltered Workshops
P.L.406	A Second Chance to Learn a Trade. Training Opportunities
P.L.407	Additional Training Service for ex Members of H.M. Forces
P.L.408	Additional Training Service for Disabled people
P.L.410	Personnel Problems. The Service of the Industrial Relations Officer
P.L.412	Patient has an Employment Problem. Services Available through Medical Social Worker and D.R.O.
P.L.413	The Commercial Register. For Employers Seeking Office, Shop or Catering Staff
R.H.L.1(E)	Industrial Rehabilitation. Description of Scheme
E.D.L.123	Grants and Allowances to Transferred Workers
E.D.L.124	Grants and Allowances to Workers accepting Work away from Home
E.D.L.125	Commonwealth Immigrants Act 1962. Notice to Prospective Employers
E.D.L.127	Commonwealth Immigrants Act 1962. Industrial Training
D.P.L.1	The Disabled Persons' Register

D.P.L.2	The Disabled Person (Employment) Act 1944. The Quota, and Designated Employment Schemes
D.P.L.5	The Disabled Persons (Employment) Act 1944. Employment of Epileptics
D.P.L.6	The Disabled Persons (Employment) Act 1944. Ex-Miners Affected by Pneumoconiosis, and Silicosis
D.P.L.7	The Disabled Persons (Employment) Act 1944. Employment of the Deaf and Dumb
D.P.L.8	Employment Services for the Blind
D.P.L.11	Employment in Sheltered Workshops—Grants and Allowances to Voluntary Agencies
D.P.L.12	Training for Sheltered Employment. Conditions re Payment of Allowances
I.T.L.1 and 2	Redundancy Payments Act 1965. Appeals and References
I.T.L.3	Contracts of Employment Act 1963. Appeals and References
R.P.L.1	Offsetting Pensions against Redundancy Payments
R.S.6	Civilian Employment. A guide for the Regular Officer. Training and Settlement
Race Relations Board	Racial Discrimination in Public Places
P.L.427	Industrial Training in Britain for Officially Sponsored Trainees from Developing Countries

List of abbreviations used in text

A.E.F.	Amal. Engineering and Foundry Workers Union
A.E.U.	Amalgamated Engineering Union
A.F.D.	Appointed Factory Doctor
B.E.C.	British Employers' Confederation
B.M.A.	British Medical Association
C.B.C.	County Borough Council
C.B.I.	Confederation of British Industry
C.C.	County Council
D.R.O.	Disablement Resettlement Officer
E.E.C.	European Economic Community
E.O.	Employers' Organisation
E.T.U.	Electrical Trades' Union
F.B.I.	Federation of British Industries
F.W.A.	Family Welfare Association
G.B.	Great Britain
G.C.E.	General Certificate of Education (O) Ordinary level; (A) Advanced level
G.M.C.	General Medical Council
G.M.W.U.	General and Municipal Workers' Union
G.P.O.	General Post Office
G.T.C.	Government Training Centre
I.L.O.	International Labour Organisation
I.P.M.	Institute of Personnel Management
I.R.U.	Industrial Rehabilitation Unit
I.TO.	Industrial Therapy Organisation
L.A.	Local Authority
L.E.A.	Local Education Authority
M.P.N.I.	Ministry of Pensions and National Insurance
M.R.C.	Medical Research Council
M.S.S.	Ministry of Social Security
N.A.B.	National Assistance Board

Abbreviations

N.A.B.M.	National Association of British Manufacturers
N.A.L.G.O.	National and Local Government Officers Organisation
N.C.B.	National Coal Board
N.H.I.	National Health Insurance
N.I.	National Insurance
N.U.M.	National Union of Mineworkers
N.U.R.	National Union of Railwaymen
N.U.T.	National Union of Teachers
O.E.C.D.	Organisation for Economic Co-operation and Development
P.A.C.	Public Assistance Committee
P.A.Y.E.	Pay-as-you-earn
S.S.A.F.A.	Soldiers, Sailors, and Airmen's Families Association
T.G.W.U.	Transport and General Workers Union
T.U.C.	Trades Union Congress
T.W.I.	Training Within Industry
U.N.E.S.C.O.	United Nations Educational, Scientific and Cultural Organisation
U.P.W.	Union of Post Office Workers
U.S.D.A.W.	Union of Shop, Distributive and Allied Workers
Y.E.B.	Youth Employment Bureau
Y.E.O.	Youth Employment Officer
Y.E.S.	Youth Employment Service

Index

248

Index

Index

Bridlington Agreement 1939, 181
British Aluminium Co. Ltd., 138–9
British Council, 18
British Employers' Confederation,
  30, 110, 140, 204 *see also*
  Confederation of British Industry
British Institute of Management, 194
British Medical Association, 212
British Safety Council, 86

careers *see* vocational guidance;
  youth employment
Carr Report, 31
Carr-Saunders, A.M., & P. A.
  Wilson, 206, 209, 212–13
Cave Committee, 103
Central Committee of Study Groups, 35
Central Training Council, 34, 35–6,
  38, 86
Central Youth Employment
  Executive, 46
charity, as a source of income, 146–7
children:
  employment of, 73, 74, 79–80
  hours of work, 75, 76, 79–80
  see also young persons
Church of England, 'Holidays with a
  purpose' scheme, 49
City and Guilds of London Institute,
  32, 37, 38
Clark, F. Le Gros, 166*n*.
Clay, H. M., 165*n*.
Clynes, J. R., 119
Cobbett, William, 80
Coleman, J. C., 39
collective bargaining, xii, 81, 116,
  184, 185–7, 197–8
Colleges of Advanced Technology,
  34, 40
coloured workers, 116
  employment exchange policy for,
  13, 16–18
  see also immigrants
Common Market *see* European
  Economic Community
Communist Party, 184, 189–90, 199
community action, need for, 217,
  218–19, 221, 222

Confederation of British Industry,
  183, 204–5
Confederation of Shipbuilding and
  Engineering Unions, 124, 180
Conservative Party, 161
Corina, J., 203
County Agricultural Wages Committees, 105–6
courts:
  wages payment and, 109, 186
  workmen's compensation and, 171
  see also industrial courts; labour
  courts
Courts of Inquiry, 121–3
crafts:
  boundaries between, 29, 177
  problems of, 34–9, 61
craft unions, 176–7

day-release schemes, 31, 37–8, 47, 49
deaf persons, 53
Defence, Ministry of, 15
dependants, in national insurance
  schemes, 151, 154, 157, 170–1,
  228–35 *passim*
development areas (districts), 4, 7,
  10, 11, 12
disabled persons, x, 9, 51–70
  advisory committees for, 54, 56
  augmentation of wages, 66, 69
  definition of, 51–2
  designated employment for, 64
  employment exchange services for,
  13, 43, 56
  grants for business ventures, 70
  homeworking schemes, 69
  Piercy Report, 43, 51, 55, 57, 63–4,
  66, 68
  quota system, 54, 56, 62–4
  registration of, 53–4, 56
  rehabilitation, xiii, 43, 51–3,
  57–60
  resettlement, 52, 54–6
  sheltered workshops for, 44, 52,
  56, 62, 64–9
  social security provisions, 51
  Tomlinson Report, 51–3, 57, 64
  training of, 52, 60–2, 157

disabled persons—cont.
  voluntary organisations and, 44,
    56, 64–5, 69
  Youth Employment Officer and,
    43–5, 58
  see also industrial injuries insurance
Disabled Persons' Employment
  Corporation, 67
Disablement Resettlement Officer,
  functions of, 54–6, 58
diseases, industrial, 89, 90–2, 169–70
dismissal of employees, 134–5 *see
  also* Acts of Parliament:
  Contracts of Employment 1963;
  Redundancy Payments, 1965
Dismissal Procedures, Cttee., 132
disputes, industrial, 117–32, 177
  definition of, 130

earnings-related benefits, xii, 59, 144,
  147, 152, 161–2, 163, 168, 172,
  226, 227, 232
Economic Affairs, Dept. of, 6*n.*, 35
economic planning:
  employment exchanges and, 6–7
  T.U.C. and, 182–3
Economic Planning Councils, 183, 205
Edinburgh Gazette, 108
Education, Board of, 21
Education, Ministry of, 15, 23, 34,
  40, 46
Electrical Trades Union, 198
employers:
  attitude to older workers, 165–6
  collection of union subscriptions
    by, 194
  compulsory arbitration and, 128–9
  courts of inquiry and, 121
  dismissal rights of, 134–6, 137
  industrial courts and, 118, 119
  industrial health and, 89, 93–4
  joint consultation and, 125–6
  national insurance and, 148
  organisations of, 201–5
  prosecution of, 98–9, 109
  recognition of trade unions by,
    122, 187, 192
  redundancy payments and, 141–4

restrictions on freedom of, 220–1
safety and, 84*n.*
transfer grants and, 11, 12
Wages Councils and, 109–10, 111,
  115, 116
workmen's compensation and,
  170–1
see also collective bargaining;
  truck system
employment, loss of, 133–44
Employment and Productivity,
  Dept. of *see* Labour, Ministry of
employment exchanges, 3–19
  early development, 3–7
  economic planning and, 6–7
  juvenile departments, 21
  mobility of labour and, 9–13
  occupational guidance, 18–19
  placement services, xiii, 5, 7–8, 18
  public image of, 4–5, 18, 19
  registers for special occupations, 8–9
  services for special categories of
    workers, 13–18, 56
  wartime functions of, 5–6
  see also youth employment
Employment of Older Men and Women,
  Cttee., 165–6
Engineering and Allied Employers'
  National Federation, 124, 203
English Electric Aviation Ltd, 138–9
Esso Petroleum Co. Ltd, redundancy
  scheme, 138–40
European Economic Community,
  8, 144
ex-prisoners, employment exchange
  services for, 13–15
ex-service personnel:
  employment exchange services for,
    9, 13, 15–16, 18
  industrial training of, 16, 60–1
  King's National Roll, 51, 62–3

factories:
  first-aid provisions, 92
  medical departments, 93
  safety in, 74–5, 82–7, 99, 100
  welfare facilities, 75, 94–5
factory doctor, 89–90, 98

factory inspectors, 74, 84*n*., 95, 96, 97–9, 100
Fair Wages Resolutions, 123
family allowances, 162, 231–2
Federation of British Industries, 204
Ferguson, T., 54
finance:
  industrial rehabilitation, 59, 70
  industrial training, x, 10, 32, 33, 34, 39–40, 62
  labour transfer schemes, 11–13
  national insurance schemes, 148–9, 153–4, 172
  redundancy payments, x, 141, 142–3
  sheltered workshops, 65–6 *see also* Remploy Ltd
  social services generally, 218, 222
  superannuation schemes, 168–9
  training of coloured workers, 17
  workmen's compensation, 170, 171
  Youth Employment Service, 45–6
fire precautions, 84–5, 99–100
First-aid in Factories Order 1960, 92
first-aid provisions, 89, 92
five-day week, 76, 78
Flanders, A., 185, 190
Food Hygiene (General) Regulations 1960, 88
Ford Motor Co., 178
Fox, A., 138, 193*n*.
friendly societies, 147, 148, 149, 150–1, 176
fringe benefits, x, 95, 160, 167–9
Future Development of the Youth Employment Service (Albemarle), 24, 44, 50

General and Municipal Workers Union, 111, 177
General Medical Council, 207, 211
Gilbert, B., 150
government training centres, xiii, 10, 16, 29, 60–2, 220
group apprenticeship schemes, 30
Grunfeld, C., 189

handicapped persons *see* disabled persons

health, industrial, x, 74–5, 87–94, 99–100
Health, Ministry of, 56
health insurance *see* national health insurance
Heginbotham, H., 20, 23
holidays, 77, 103, 105, 108
Home Office, 14, 34
home-workers, 69, 95
hospitals, accident services, 94
hours of work, 74, 75–82
  adult males, 75, 80–2
  children, 75, 76
  research on, 82
  shops, 77–9, 100
  trade unions and, 75, 81 *see also* collective bargaining
  women, 75, 76–7, 78, 81
  young persons, 75, 76–7, *see also* shops *above*
Hutchins, E. L. and A. Harrison, 76

immigrants:
  work permits, 8, 17 *see also* coloured workers
Ince, Sir Godfrey H., 3–4, 6, 18, 124 *see also* Ince Report
Ince Report, 22–3, 40–1, 45
income:
  maintenance of, xi, 145–72, 220, 225–35
    Beveridge proposals, 149, 155-62
    early history, 145–55
    occupational schemes, 159–60, 167–9, 222
  redistribution of, 218
incomes policy, 113–14, 118, 130, 181, 182, 187, 202
Industrial Accident Prevention, 86
industrial courts, x, xiii, 118–20, 122, 123, 130
Industrial Development Certificates, 6, 12
industrial diseases *see* diseases, industrial
Industrial Disputes Orders, 128–9
Industrial Disputes Tribunal, 128–9
industrial health *see* health, industrial

lock-outs, 117–18, 128
London Gazette, 108
Lord Chancellor, 33
Lord Roberts Memorial Workshops, 65

McCarthy, W. E. J., 123*n.*, 198*n.*, 200
machinery, safety of, 74, 84, 85
Macleod, I. N. and J. E. Powell, 153
Macphail, A. N., 54
McVean, M. I., 54
Mann, P. M. and Mitchell, S., 26–7
Manpower Research Unit, 32
Marsh, A., 196, 198*n.*
means test, 4–5, 153, 154–5, 160,
    162, 220, 232, 233
Members of Parliament, sponsorship
    by trade unions, 188
Millerson, G., 206
Miners' Federation, 151
mines and quarries, 74, 75*n.*, 77, 83,
    100, 125, 135
mobility of labour, 9–13, 35

National Advisory Council for
    Juvenile Employment, 22
National and Local Government
    Officers' Association, 129, 212
National Arbitration Tribunal, 128–9
national assistance *see* national
    insurance, supplementation of
    benefits
National Assistance Board, 154, 158,
    162
    tribunals, 33*n.*
    see also Supplementary Benefits
    Commission
National Association of British
    Manufacturers, 204
National Coal Board, 194
National Economic Development
    Council, 6*n.*
National Federation of Building
    Trade Operatives, 180
national health insurance, 147,
    150–2 *see also* national insurance
national health service, 90, 156, 209,
    211

national insurance, xi, xii
    administration, 150–2, 172
    benefits, 227–32
    Beveridge Report, 149, 155–62,
        166–7, 172, 229
    compulsory, 150
    contribution rate, 149, 161
    dependants' allowances, 151, 154,
        157, 170–1, 228–35 *passim*
    early history, 147–55
    earnings-related benefits, xii, 59,
        144, 147, 152, 161–2, 163, 168,
        172, 226, 227, 232
    membership of early schemes,
        149–50, 158
    supplementation of benefits, 45,
        152–3, 155, 160, 162–3, 229, 233
    tribunals, 33*n.*, 131, 172, 225–6,
        233
    widows' benefits, 229–30, 235
    see also industrial injuries insurance;
        national health insurance;
        pensions; unemployment
        insurance
National Joint Advisory Council, 132,
    140
National Joint Industrial Council, 126
National Union of Mineworkers, 178
National Union of Railwaymen, 178
National Union of Teachers, 212
National Youth Employment
    Council, 46–7, 49
needs test, 162–3 *see also* means test
Nuffield Foundation, 93, 166

occupational guidance, *see* vocational
    guidance
Occupational Guidance Units,
    18–19
Occupational Hygiene Units, 84*n.*
occupational schemes, income
    maintenance, 159–60, 167–9, 222
occupiers *see* employers
offices:
    inspection of, 100
    working conditions, 75, 88
old age pensions *see* pensions
old people, employment, 13, 163–7

Index

trade unions—cont.
industrial unions, 178–9
membership of, 176, 179
Members of Parliament sponsored
by, 188
officials of, 194–6, 199, 200
'open' unions, 179
political parties and, 184–5, 187–90
problems of, 191–201
recognition of, 122, 187, 192
recognition of semi-skilled status
by, 30
shop stewards, 194, 198-201
strikes and, 190–1
wages councils and, 109–10, 111, 114
'work experience' scheme and, 25
*Trade Unions and Employers'
Associations,* R.Com., 115, 182,
188, 191, 193*n.*, 200
training, industrial *see* government
training centres; industrial
training
Training Allowance Scheme, 39–40
Training for Skill, 31
Training of Young People in Industry, 35
Training within Industry, 10–11, 34*n.*,
86, 201
transfer grants, 11–13
Transport, Ministry of, 83
Transport and General Workers
Union, 111, 177–8
tribunals, 184
contracts of employment, 131, 135,
136, 143
industrial disputes, 128, 129
Industrial Training Act, 33, 131,
136, 143
National Assistance Act, 131
National Insurance Acts, 33*n.*,
131, 172, 225–6, 233
professions, 210–11
redundancy payments, 131, 135,
136, 143
truck system, 95–7
Turner, H. A., 179

unemployment:
concentration of, 4, 5, 6–7

disabled persons, 70
income maintenance during,
145–72, 225–35
young workers and, 48–9
see also redundancy
unemployment insurance, 4
benefit payments, 18, 19, 45, 152,
226
early history, 147–54 *see also*
national insurance
local education authorities'
scheme, 21–2
see also Beveridge Report
Unemployment Review Officers, 162
Union of Post Office Workers, 178
Union of Shop, Distributive and
Allied Workers, 79*n.*, 111, 114,
177
universities:
professions and, 207
safety research and, 84*n.*
training in vocational guidance, 26

Vauxhall Motors, 60
Vernon, H. M., 82*n.*
vocational guidance, xi
parental participation, 26–7
role of employment exchanges,
18–19
role of teachers, 27
university course in, 26
see also youth employment
vocational training, 16, 220 *see also*
industrial training
voluntary agreements, industrial
relations, 116, 117, 118
voluntary effort, industrial health
and, 92, 93-4
voluntary organisations, disabled
persons and, 44, 56, 64–5, 69

wage drift, 197
wage freeze, 113–14 *see also* incomes
policy
wage-related benefits *see* earnings-
related benefits
wages:
agreements *see* collective bargaining

International Library of Sociology

Edited by
John Rex
University of Warwick

Founded by
Karl Mannheim

as The International Library of Sociology
and Social Reconstruction

*This Catalogue also contains other Social Science
series published by Routledge*

Routledge & Kegan Paul   London and Boston

68-74 Carter Lane London EC4V 5EL
9 Park Street Boston Mass 02108

Contents

● *Books so marked are available in paperback*
All books are in Metric Demy 8vo format (216 × 138mm approx.)

GENERAL SOCIOLOGY

Belshaw, Cyril. The Conditions of Social Performance. *An Exploratory Theory. 144 pp.*

Brown, Robert. Explanation in Social Science. *208 pp.*

Cain, Maureen E. Society and the Policeman's Role. *About 300 pp.*

Gibson, Quentin. The Logic of Social Enquiry. *240 pp.*

Homans, George C. Sentiments and Activities: *Essays in Social Science. 336 pp.*

Isajiw, Wsevold W. Causation and Functionalism in Sociology. *165 pp.*

Johnson, Harry M. Sociology: *a Systematic Introduction. Foreword by Robert K. Merton. 710 pp.*

Mannheim, Karl. Essays on Sociology and Social Psychology. *Edited by Paul Keckskemeti. With Editorial Note by Adolph Lowe. 344 pp.*
Systematic Sociology: *An Introduction to the Study of Society. Edited by J. S. Erös and Professor W. A. C. Stewart. 220 pp.*

Martindale, Don. The Nature and Types of Sociological Theory. *292 pp.*

● **Maus, Heinz.** A Short History of Sociology. *234 pp.*

Mey, Harald. Field-Theory. *A Study of its Application in the Social Sciences. 352 pp.*

Myrdal, Gunnar. Value in Social Theory: *A Collection of Essays on Methodology. Edited by Paul Streeten. 332 pp.*

Ogburn, William F., and **Nimkoff, Meyer F.** A Handbook of Sociology. *Preface by Karl Mannheim. 656 pp. 46 figures. 35 tables.*

Parsons, Talcott, and **Smelser, Neil J.** Economy and Society: *A Study in the Integration of Economic and Social Theory. 362 pp.*

● **Rex, John.** Key Problems of Sociological Theory. *220 pp.*

Stark, Werner. The Fundamental Forms of Social Thought. *280 pp.*

FOREIGN CLASSICS OF SOCIOLOGY

● **Durkheim, Emile.** Suicide. *A Study in Sociology. Edited and with an Introduction by George Simpson. 404 pp.*
Professional Ethics and Civic Morals. *Translated by Cornelia Brookfield. 288 pp.*

● **Gerth, H. H.,** and **Mills, C. Wright.** From Max Weber: *Essays in Sociology. 502 pp.*

Tönnies, Ferdinand. Community and Association. *(Gemeinschaft und Gesellschaft.) Translated and Supplemented by Charles P. Loomis. Foreword by Pitirim A. Sorokin. 334 pp.*

SOCIAL STRUCTURE

Andreski, Stanislav. Military Organization and Society. *Foreword by Professor A. R. Radcliffe-Brown. 226 pp. 1 folder.*

● **Cole, G. D. H.** Studies in Class Structure. *220 p.*

Coontz, Sydney H. Population Theories and the Economic Interpretation. *202 pp.*

Coser, Lewis. The Functions of Social Conflict. *204 pp.*

Dickie-Clark, H. F. Marginal Situation: *A Sociological Study of a Coloured Group. 240 pp. 11 tables.*

Glass, D. V. (Ed.). Social Mobility in Britain. *Contributions by J. Berent, T. Bottomore, R. C. Chambers, J. Floud, D. V. Glass, J. R. Hall, H. T. Himmelweit, R. K. Kelsall, F. M. Martin, C. A. Moser, R. Mukherjee, and W. Ziegel. 420 pp.*

Glaser, Barney, and **Strauss, Anselm L.** Status Passage. *A Formal Theory. 208 pp.*

Jones, Garth N. Planned Organizational Change: *An Exploratory Study Using an Empirical Approach. 268 pp.*

Kelsall, R. K. Higher Civil Servants in Britain: *From 1870 to the Present Day. 268 pp. 31 tables.*

König, René. The Community. *232 pp. Illustrated.*

● **Lawton, Denis.** Social Class, Language and Education. *192 pp.*

McLeish, John. The Theory of Social Change: *Four Views Considered. 128 pp.*

Marsh, David C. The Changing Social Structure in England and Wales, 1871-1961. *272 pp.*

Mouzelis, Nicos. Organization and Bureaucracy. *An Analysis of Modern Theories. 240 pp.*

Mulkay, M. J. Functionalism, Exchange and Theoretical Strategy. *272 pp.*

Ossowski, Stanislaw. Class Structure in the Social Consciousness. *210 pp.*

SOCIOLOGY AND POLITICS

Crick, Bernard. The American Science of Politics: *Its Origins and Conditions. 284 pp.*

Hertz, Frederick. Nationality in History and Politics: *A Psychology and Sociology of National Sentiment and Nationalism. 432 pp.*

Kornhauser, William. The Politics of Mass Society. *272 pp. 20 tables.*

Laidler, Harry W. History of Socialism. *Social-Economic Movements: An Historical and Comparative Survey of Socialism, Communism, Co-operation, Utopianism; and other Systems of Reform and Reconstruction. 992 pp.*

Mannheim, Karl. Freedom, Power and Democratic Planning. *Edited by Hans Gerth and Ernest K. Bramstedt. 424 pp.*

Mansur, Fatma. Process of Independence. *Foreword by A. H. Hanson. 208 pp.*

Martin, David A. Pacificism: *an Historical and Sociological Study. 262 pp.*

Myrdal, Gunnar. The Political Element in the Development of Economic Theory. *Translated from the German by Paul Streeten. 282 pp.*

Verney, Douglas V. The Analysis of Political Systems. *264 pp.*

Wootton, Graham. Workers, Unions and the State. *188 pp.*

FOREIGN AFFAIRS: THEIR SOCIAL, POLITICAL AND ECONOMIC FOUNDATIONS

Bonné, Alfred. State and Economics in the Middle East: *A Society in Transition. 482 pp.*
Studies in Economic Development: *with special reference to Conditions in the Under-developed Areas of Western Asia and India. 322 pp. 84 tables.*
Mayer, J. P. Political Thought in France from the Revolution to the Fifth Republic. *164 pp.*

CRIMINOLOGY

Ancel, Marc. Social Defence: *A Modern Approach to Criminal Problems. Foreword by Leon Radzinowicz. 240 pp.*
Cloward, Richard A., and **Ohlin, Lloyd E.** Delinquency and Opportunity: *A Theory of Delinquent Gangs. 248 pp.*
Downes, David M. The Delinquent Solution. *A Study in Subcultural Theory. 296 pp.*
Dunlop, A. B., and **McCabe, S.** Young Men in Detention Centres. *192 pp.*
Friedlander, Kate. The Psycho-Analytical Approach to Juvenile Delinquency: *Theory, Case Studies, Treatment. 320 pp.*
Glueck, Sheldon, and **Eleanor.** Family Environment and Delinquency. *With the statistical assistance of Rose W. Kneznek. 340 pp.*
Lopez-Rey, Manuel. Crime. *An Analytical Appraisal. 288 pp.*
Mannheim, Hermann. Comparative Criminology: *a Text Book. Two volumes. 442 pp. and 380 pp.*
Morris, Terence. The Criminal Area: *A Study in Social Ecology. Foreword by Hermann Mannheim. 232 pp. 25 tables. 4 maps.*
Trasler, Gordon. The Explanation of Criminality. *144 pp.*

SOCIAL PSYCHOLOGY

Bagley, Christopher. The Social Psychology of the Child with Epilepsy. *320 pp.*
Barbu, Zevedei. Problems of Historical Psychology. *248 pp.*
Blackburn, Julian. Psychology and the Social Pattern. *184 pp.*
● **Fleming, C. M.** Adolescence: *Its Social Psychology: With an Introduction to recent findings from the fields of Anthropology, Physiology, Medicine, Psychometrics and Sociometry. 288 pp.*
● The Social Psychology of Education: *An Introduction and Guide to Its Study. 136 pp.*
Homans, George C. The Human Group. *Foreword by Bernard DeVoto. Introduction by Robert K. Merton. 526 pp.*
Social Behaviour: *its Elementary Forms. 416 pp.*

Klein, Josephine. The Study of Groups. *226 pp. 31 figures. 5 tables.*
Linton, Ralph. The Cultural Background of Personality. *132 pp.*
Mayo, Elton. The Social Problems of an Industrial Civilization. *With an appendix on the Political Problem. 180 pp.*
Ottaway, A. K. C. Learning Through Group Experience. *176 pp.*
Ridder, J. C. de. The Personality of the Urban African in South Africa. *A Thematic Apperception Test Study. 196 pp. 12 plates.*
● **Rose, Arnold M.** (Ed.). Human Behaviour and Social Processes: *an Interactionist Approach. Contributions by Arnold M. Rose, Ralph H. Turner, Anselm Strauss, Everett C. Hughes, E. Franklin Frazier, Howard S. Becker, et al. 696 pp.*
Smelser, Neil J. Theory of Collective Behaviour. *448 pp.*
Stephenson, Geoffrey M. The Development of Conscience. *128 pp.*
Young, Kimball. Handbook of Social Psychology. *658 pp. 16 figures. 10 tables.*

SOCIOLOGY OF THE FAMILY

Banks, J. A. Prosperity and Parenthood: *A Study of Family Planning among The Victorian Middle Classes. 262 pp.*
Bell, Colin R. Middle Class Families: *Social and Geographical Mobility. 224 pp.*
Burton, Lindy. Vulnerable Children. *272 pp.*
Gavron, Hannah. The Captive Wife: *Conflicts of Household Mothers. 190 pp.*
George, Victor, and **Wilding, Paul.** Motherless Families. *220 pp.*
Klein, Josephine. Samples from English Cultures.
  1. Three Preliminary Studies and Aspects of Adult Life in England. *447 pp.*
  2. Child-Rearing Practices and Index. *247 pp.*
Klein, Viola. Britain's Married Women Workers. *180 pp.*
  The Feminine Character. *History of an Ideology. 244 pp.*
McWhinnie, Alexina M. Adopted Children. *How They Grow Up. 304 pp.*
Myrdal, Alva, and **Klein, Viola.** Women's Two Roles: *Home and Work. 238 pp. 27 tables.*
Parsons, Talcott, and **Bales, Robert F.** Family: *Socialization and Interaction Process. In collaboration with James Olds, Morris Zelditch and Philip E. Slater. 456 pp. 50 figures and tables.*

SOCIAL SERVICES

Bastide, Roger. The Sociology of Mental Disorder. *Translated from the French by Jean McNeil. 264 pp.*
Carlebach, Julius. Caring For Children in Trouble. *266 pp.*
Forder, R. A. (Ed.). Penelope Hall's Social Services of Modern England. *352 pp.*
George, Victor. Foster Care. *Theory and Practice. 234 pp.*
  Social Security: *Beveridge and After. 258 pp.*

● **Goetschius, George W.** Working with Community Groups. *256 pp.*
Goetschius, George W., and **Tash, Joan.** Working with Unattached Youth. *416 pp.*
Hall, M. P., and **Howes, I. V.** The Church in Social Work. *A Study of Moral Welfare Work undertaken by the Church of England. 320 pp.*
Heywood, Jean S. Children in Care: *the Development of the Service for the Deprived Child. 264 pp.*
Hoenig, J., and **Hamilton, Marian W.** The De-Segration of the Mentally Ill. *284 pp.*
Jones, Kathleen. Lunacy, Law and Conscience, *1744-1845: the Social History of the Care of the Insane. 268 pp.*
Mental Health and Social Policy, 1845-1959. *264 pp.*
King, Roy D., Raynes, Norma V., and **Tizard, Jack.** Patterns of Residential Care. *356 pp.*
Leigh, John. Young People and Leisure. *256 pp.*
Morris, Pauline. Put Away: *A Sociological Study of Institutions for the Mentally Retarded. 364 pp.*
Nokes, P. L. The Professional Task in Welfare Practice. *152 pp.*
Timms, Noel. Psychiatric Social Work in Great Britain (1939-1962). *280 pp.*
● Social Casework: *Principles and Practice. 256 pp.*
Trasler, Gordon. In Place of Parents: *A Study in Foster Care. 272 pp.*
Young, A. F., and **Ashton, E. T.** British Social Work in the Nineteenth Century. *288 pp.*
Young, A. F. Social Services in British Industry. *272 pp.*

SOCIOLOGY OF EDUCATION

Banks, Olive. Parity and Prestige in English Secondary Education: a Study in Educational Sociology. *272 pp.*
Bentwich, Joseph. Education in Israel. *224 pp. 8 pp. plates.*
● **Blyth, W. A. L.** English Primary Education. *A Sociological Description.*
1. Schools. *232 pp.*
2. Background. *168 pp.*
Collier, K. G. The Social Purposes of Education: *Personal and Social Values in Education. 268 pp.*
Dale, R. R., and **Griffith, S.** Down Stream: *Failure in the Grammar School. 108 pp.*
Dore, R. P. Education in Tokugawa Japan. *356 pp. 9 pp. plates*
Evans, K. M. Sociometry and Education. *158 pp.*
Foster, P. J. Education and Social Change in Ghana. *336 pp. 3 maps.*
Fraser, W. R. Education and Society in Modern France. *150 pp.*
Grace, Gerald R. Role Conflict and the Teacher. *About 200 pp.*
Hans, Nicholas. New Trends in Education in the Eighteenth Century. *278 pp. 19 tables.*
● Comparative Education: *A Study of Educational Factors and Traditions. 360 pp.*

7

Hargreaves, David. Interpersonal Relations and Education. *432 pp.*
● Social Relations in a Secondary School. *240 pp.*
Holmes, Brian. Problems in Education. *A Comparative Approach. 336 pp.*
King, Ronald. Values and Involvement in a Grammar School. *164 pp.*
● **Mannheim, Karl,** and **Stewart, W. A. C.** An Introduction to the Sociology of Education. *206 pp.*
Morris, Raymond N. The Sixth Form and College Entrance. *231 pp.*
● **Musgrove, F.** Youth and the Social Order. *176 pp.*
● **Ottaway, A. K. C.** Education and Society: *An Introduction to the Sociology of Education. With an Introduction by W. O. Lester Smith. 212 pp.*
Peers, Robert. Adult Education: *A Comparative Study. 398 pp.*
Pritchard, D. G. Education and the Handicapped: *1760 to 1960. 258 pp.*
Richardson, Helen. Adolescent Girls in Approved Schools. *308 pp.*
Simon, Brian, and **Joan** (Eds.). Educational Psychology in the U.S.S.R. *Introduction by Brian and Joan Simon. Translation by Joan Simon. Papers by D. N. Bogoiavlenski and N. A. Menchinskaia, D. B. Elkonin, E. A. Fleshner, Z. I. Kalmykova, G. S. Kostiuk, V. A. Krutetski, A. N. Leontiev, A. R. Luria, E. A. Milerian, R. G. Natadze, B. M. Teplov, L. S. Vygotski, L. V. Zankov. 296 pp.*
Stratta, Erica. The Education of Borstal Boys. *A Study of their Educational Experiences prior to, and during Borstal Training. 256 pp.*

SOCIOLOGY OF CULTURE

Eppel, E. M., and **M.** Adolescents and Morality: *A Study of some Moral Values and Dilemmas of Working Adolescents in the Context of a changing Climate of Opinion. Foreword by W. J. H. Sprott. 268 pp. 39 tables.*
● **Fromm, Erich.** The Fear of Freedom. *286 pp.*
The Sane Society. *400 pp.*
● **Mannheim, Karl.** Diagnosis of Our Time: *Wartime Essays of a Sociologist. 208 pp.*
Essays on the Sociology of Culture. *Edited by Ernst Mannheim in co-operation with Paul Kecskemeti. Editorial Note by Adolph Lowe. 280 pp.*
Weber, Alfred. Farewell to European History: *or The Conquest of Nihilism. Translated from the German by R. F. C. Hull. 224 pp.*

SOCIOLOGY OF RELIGION

Argyle, Michael. Religious Behaviour. *224 pp. 8 figures. 41 tables.*
Nelson, G. K. Spiritualism and Society. *313 pp.*

Stark, Werner. The Sociology of Religion. *A Study of Christendom.*
  Volume I. *Established Religion. 248 pp.*
  Volume II. *Sectarian Religion. 368 pp.*
  Volume III. *The Universal Church. 464 pp.*
  Volume IV. *Types of Religious Man. 352 pp.*
  Volume V. *Types of Religious Culture. 464 pp.*
Watt, W. Montgomery. Islam and the Integration of Society. *320 pp.*

SOCIOLOGY OF ART AND LITERATURE

Beljame, Alexandre. Men of Letters and the English Public in the Eighteenth
  Century: *1660-1744, Dryden, Addison, Pope. Edited with an Introduction
  and Notes by Bonamy Dobrée. Translated by E. O. Lorimer. 532 pp.*
Jarvie, Ian C. Towards a Sociology of the Cinema. *A Comparative Essay
  on the Structure and Functioning of a Major Entertainment Industry.
  405 pp.*
Rust, Frances S. Dance in Society. *An Analysis of the Relationships between
  the Social Dance and Society in England from the Middle Ages to the
  Present Day. 256 pp. 8 pp. of plates.*
Schücking, L. L. The Sociology of Literary Taste. *112 pp.*
Silbermann, Alphons. The Sociology of Music. *Translated from the German
  by Corbet Stewart. 222 pp.*

SOCIOLOGY OF KNOWLEDGE

Mannheim, Karl. Essays on the Sociology of Knowledge. *Edited by Paul
  Kecskemeti. Editorial note by Adolph Lowe. 353 pp.*
Stark, Werner. The Sociology of Knowledge: *An Essay in Aid of a Deeper
  Understanding of the History of Ideas. 384 pp.*

URBAN SOCIOLOGY

Ashworth, William. The Genesis of Modern British Town Planning: *A Study
  in Economic and Social History of the Nineteenth and Twentieth Centuries.
  288 pp.*
Cullingworth, J. B. Housing Needs and Planning Policy: *A Restatement of
  the Problems of Housing Need and 'Overspill' in England and Wales.
  232 pp. 44 tables. 8 maps.*
Dickinson, Robert E. City and Region: *A Geographical Interpretation.
  608 pp. 125 figures.*
  The West European City: *A Geographical Interpretation. 600 pp. 129 maps.
  29 plates.*
● The City Region in Western Europe. *320 pp. Maps.*

Humphreys, Alexander J. New Dubliners: *Urbanization and the Irish Family. Foreword by George C. Homans. 304 pp.*

Jackson, Brian. Working Class Community: *Some General Notions raised by a Series of Studies in Northern England. 192 pp.*

Jennings, Hilda. Societies in the Making: *a Study of Development and Redevelopment within a County Borough. Foreword by D. A. Clark. 286 pp.*

Kerr, Madeline. The People of Ship Street. *240 pp.*

● **Mann, P. H.** An Approach to Urban Sociology. *240 pp.*

Morris, R. N., and **Mogey, J.** The Sociology of Housing. *Studies at Berinsfield. 232 pp. 4 pp. plates.*

Rosser, C., and **Harris, C.** The Family and Social Change. *A Study of Family and Kinship in a South Wales Town. 352 pp. 8 maps.*

RURAL SOCIOLOGY

Chambers, R. J. H. Settlement Schemes in Africa: *A Selective Study. 268 pp.*

Haswell, M. R. The Economics of Development in Village India. *120 pp.*

Littlejohn, James. Westrigg: *the Sociology of a Cheviot Parish. 172 pp. 5 figures.*

Williams, W. M. The Country Craftsman: *A Study of Some Rural Crafts and the Rural Industries Organization in England. 248 pp. 9 figures. (Dartington Hall Studies in Rural Sociology.)*
The Sociology of an English Village: *Gosforth. 272 pp. 12 figures. 13 tables.*

SOCIOLOGY OF INDUSTRY AND DISTRIBUTION

Anderson, Nels. Work and Leisure. *280 pp.*

● **Blau, Peter M.,** and **Scott, W. Richard.** Formal Organizations: *a Comparative approach. Introduction and Additional Bibliography by J. H. Smith. 326 pp.*

Eldridge, J. E. T. Industrial Disputes. *Essays in the Sociology of Industrial Relations. 288 pp.*

Hetzler, Stanley. Technological Growth and Social Change. *Achieving Modernization. 269 pp.*

Hollowell, Peter G. The Lorry Driver. *272 pp.*

Jefferys, Margot, *with the assistance of Winifred Moss.* Mobility in the Labour Market: *Employment Changes in Battersea and Dagenham. Preface by Barbara Wootton. 186 pp. 51 tables.*

Millerson, Geoffrey. The Qualifying Associations: *a Study in Professionalization. 320 pp.*

Smelser, Neil J. Social Change in the Industrial Revolution: *An Application of Theory to the Lancashire Cotton Industry, 1770-1840. 468 pp. 12 figures. 14 tables.*

Williams, Gertrude. Recruitment to Skilled Trades. *240 pp.*

Young, A. F. Industrial Injuries Insurance: *an Examination of British Policy. 192 pp.*

ANTHROPOLOGY

Ammar, Hamed. Growing up in an Egyptian Village: *Silwa, Province of Aswan. 336 pp.*

Brandel-Syrier, Mia. Reeftown Elite. *A Study of Social Mobility in a Modern African Community on the Reef. 376 pp.*

Crook, David, and **Isabel.** Revolution in a Chinese Village: *Ten Mile Inn. 230 pp. 8 plates. 1 map.*
The First Years of Yangyi Commune. *302 pp. 12 plates.*

Dickie-Clark, H. F. The Marginal Situation. *A Sociological Study of a Coloured Group. 236 pp.*

Dube, S. C. Indian Village. *Foreword by Morris Edward Opler. 276 pp. 4 plates.*
India's Changing Villages: *Human Factors in Community Development. 260 pp. 8 plates. 1 map.*

Firth, Raymond. Malay Fishermen. *Their Peasant Economy. 420 pp. 17 pp. plates.*

Gulliver, P. H. Social Control in an African Society: a Study of the Arusha, Agricultural Masai of Northern Tanganyika. *320 pp. 8 plates. 10 figures.*

Ishwaran, K. Shivapur. *A South Indian Village. 216 pp.*
Tradition and Economy in Village India: *An Interactionist Approach. Foreword by Conrad Arensburg. 176 pp.*

Jarvie, Ian C. The Revolution in Anthropology. *268 pp.*

Jarvie, Ian C., and **Agassi, Joseph.** Hong Kong. *A Society in Transition. 396 pp. Illustrated with plates and maps.*

Little, Kenneth L. Mende of Sierra Leone. *308 pp. and folder.*
Negroes in Britain. *With a New Introduction and Contemporary Study by Leonard Bloom. 320 pp.*

Lowie, Robert H. Social Organization. *494 pp.*

Mayer, Adrian C. Caste and Kinship in Central India: *A Village and its Region. 328 pp. 16 plates. 15 figures. 16 tables.*

Smith, Raymond T. The Negro Family in British Guiana: *Family Structure and Social Status in the Villages. With a Foreword by Meyer Fortes. 314 pp. 8 plates. 1 figure. 4 maps.*

DOCUMENTARY

Meek, Dorothea L. (Ed.). Soviet Youth: *Some Achievements and Problems. Excerpts from the Soviet Press, translated by the editor. 280 pp.*

Schlesinger, Rudolf (Ed.). Changing Attitudes in Soviet Russia.
2. *The Nationalities Problem and Soviet Administration. Selected Readings on the Development of Soviet Nationalities Policies. Introduced by the editor. Translated by W. W. Gottlieb. 324 pp.*

SOCIOLOGY AND PHILOSOPHY

Barnsley, John H. The Social Reality of Ethics. *A Comparative Analysis of Moral Codes. 448 pp.*

Douglas, Jack D. (Ed.). Understanding Everyday Life. *Toward the Reconstruction of Sociological Knowledge. Contributions by Alan F. Blum. Aaron W. Cicourel, Norman K. Denzin, Jack D. Douglas, John Heeren, Peter McHugh, Peter K. Manning, Melvin Power, Matthew Speier, Roy Turner, D. Lawrence Wieder, Thomas P. Wilson and Don H. Zimmerman. 358 pp.*

Jarvie, Ian C. Concepts and Society. *216 pp.*

Roche, Maurice. Phenomenology, Language and the Social Sciences. *About 400 pp.*

Sklair, Leslie. The Sociology of Progress. *320 pp.*

International Library of Social Policy

General Editor Kathleen Janes

Jones, Kathleen. Mental Health Services. *A history, 1744-1971. About 500 pp.*

Thomas, J. E. The English Prison Officer since 1850: *A Study in Conflict. 258 pp.*

Primary Socialization, Language and Education

General Editor Basil Bernstein

Bernstein, Basil. Class, Codes and Control. *2 volumes.*
1. *Theoretical Studies Towards a Sociology of Language. 254 pp.*
2. *Applied Studies Towards a Sociology of Language. About 400 pp.*

Brandis, Walter, and **Henderson, Dorothy.** Social Class, Language and Communication. *288 pp.*

Cook, Jenny. Socialization and Social Control. *About 300 pp.*

Gahagan, D. M., and **G. A.** Talk Reform. *Exploration in Language for Infant School Children. 160 pp.*

Robinson, W. P., and **Rackstraw, Susan, D. A.** A Question of Answers. *2 volumes. 192 pp. and 180 pp.*

Turner, Geoffrey, J., and **Mohan, Bernard, A.** A Linguistic Description and Computer Programme for Children's Speech. *208 pp.*

Reports of the Institute of Community Studies and the Institute of Social Studies in Medical Care

Cartwright, Ann. Human Relations and Hospital Care. *272 pp.*
Parents and Family Planning Services. *306 pp.*
Patients and their Doctors. *A Study of General Practice. 304 pp.*
Dunnell, Karen, and **Cartwright, Ann.** Medicine Takers, Prescribers and Hoarders. *About 140 pp.*
● **Jackson, Brian.** Streaming: *an Education System in Miniature. 168 pp.*
Jackson, Brian, and **Marsden, Dennis.** Education and the Working Class: *Some General Themes raised by a Study of 88 Working-class Children in a Northern Industrial City. 268 pp. 2 folders.*
Marris, Peter. Widows and their Families. *Foreword by Dr. John Bowlby. 184 pp. 18 tables. Statistical Summary.*
Family and Social Change in an African City. *A Study of Rehousing in Lagos. 196 pp. 1 map. 4 plates. 53 tables.*
The Experience of Higher Education. *232 pp. 27 tables.*
Marris, Peter, and **Rein, Martin.** Dilemmas of Social Reform. *Poverty and Community Action in the United States. 256 pp.*
Marris, Peter, and **Somerset, Anthony.** African Businessmen. *A Study of Entrepreneurship and Development in Kenya. 256 pp.*
Runciman, W. G. Relative Deprivation and Social Justice. *A Study of Attitudes to Social Inequality in Twentieth Century England. 352 pp.*
Townsend, Peter. The Family Life of Old People: *An Inquiry in East London. Foreword by J. H. Sheldon. 300 pp. 3 figures. 63 tables.*
Willmott, Peter. Adolescent Boys in East London. *230 pp.*
The Evolution of a Community: *a study of Dagenham after forty years. 168 pp. 2 maps.*
Willmott, Peter, and **Young, Michael.** Family and Class in a London Suburb. *202 pp. 47 tables.*
Young, Michael. Innovation and Research in Education. *192 pp.*
● **Young, Michael,** and **McGeeney, Patrick.** Learning Begins at Home. *A Study of a Junior School and its Parents. 128 pp.*
Young, Michael, and **Willmott, Peter.** Family and Kinship in East London. *Foreword by Richard M. Titmuss. 252 pp. 39 tables.*

Medicine, Illness and Society
General Editor W. M. Williams

Robinson, David. The Process of Becoming Ill.
Stacey, Margaret. *et al.* Hospitals, Children and Their Families. *The Report of a Pilot Study. 202 pp.*

Routledge Social Science Journals

The British Journal of Sociology. *Edited by Terence P. Morris. Vol. 1, No. 1, March 1950 and Quarterly. Roy. 8vo. Back numbers available. An international journal with articles on all aspects of sociology.*
Economy and Society. *Vol. 1, No. 1. February 1972 and Quarterly. Metric Roy. 8vo. A journal for all social scientists covering sociology, philosophy, anthropology, economics and history.*

Printed in Great Britain by Lewis Reprints Limited
Brown Knight & Truscott Group, London and Tonbridge   21972